PETER BURTON
AND JOHN LANE

New Directions

Ways of advance for the Amateur Theatre

with an introduction by John Arden

METHUEN & CO LTD
11 NEW FETTER LANE, LONDON EC4P 4EE

First published 1970 by MacGibbon and Kee Ltd

© John Lane and Peter Burton 1970

First published by Methuen & Co Ltd
as a University Paperback in 1972

SBN 416 18510 x

Printed in Great Britain by
Latimer Trend Ltd
Whitstable Kent

To those who risk adventure
and dare to be vulnerable

Acknowledgements

We are indebted to all those who have kindly helped to make this book by making suggestions, verifying statements and reading the manuscript. In particular we wish to thank Valerie Beer for her chapter on Stage-management, John Fox for the section on Happenings and the account of the development of his own work which is printed as an Appendix; and Harland Walshaw for reading the typescript and making innumerable suggestions. We are also indebted to Alfred Bradley, John Butt, Bill Dufton, John Faulkner, Enid Foster, the late Stephen Joseph, Annette Kok, Ewan MacColl, Roland Miller, Charles Parker and Alan Plater for their invaluable assistance.

We are grateful to the following for permission to reproduce copyright material: Methuen & Co. Ltd for extracts from *Brechton Theatre* translated by John Willet; *Theatre at Work* edited by Charles Marowitz and Simon Trussler; *The Royal Pardon* by John Arden and Margaretta D'Arcy and *Close the Coalhouse Door* by Alan Plater and Alex Glasgow. The Bodley Head for an extract from *My Autobiography* by Charles Chaplin; Her Majesty's Stationery Office for an extract from *Education Survey No. 2 – Drama*; the Argo Record Company Ltd for an extract from the booklet written by Charles Parker and issued with the long-playing record *The Ballad of John Axon*; Barrie and Rockcliff for an extract from Stephen Joseph's *Theatre in the Round*; Sir Isaac Pitman and Sons Ltd for an extract from Stephen Joseph's *Scene Painting and Design*; the Society for Education in Film and Television for an extract from D. M. W. Barker's article *Strike Action* and the *Drama Review* for the Peter S. Schuman interview first published in the *Drama Review*, volume 12, No. 2 (T. 38, Winter 1968. All Rights Reserved.

Acknowledgements

We would also like to acknowledge our gratitude to the Committee of the British Children's Theatre Association for their kindness in allowing us to use their *Bibliography of Plays recommended for performance to Child Audiences* as a basis for our own list of plays under this heading.

Contents

Contents

Contents

List of Plates

Foreword

I have been, for the last eleven years, a full-time professional playwright. Before that, for about another ten years, I was an amateur – both writer and actor. The difference, as far as my own personal attitude goes, is nil – save that as a professional, I rely upon my theatrical work to feed myself and my family, whereas as an amateur I was living, first upon my parents and one or two convenient government educational grants, and then upon the salary I earned as an architectural assistant. The word 'amateur' means that one does what one does because one loves to do it. It therefore applies, in a general sense, to the work of the majority of people in the theatre, whether actors, authors, directors, or stage-staff. It may be assumed that those who also follow such employment 'professionally' – i.e. as a full-time paid activity – have the advantage of greater experience, and perhaps a regular training, over those who occupy their leisure hours in the theatre: but this does not necessarily mean that their finished product is of greater 'artistic' value. And it certainly does not mean that it is of greater 'social' value.

The theatre is a medium of communication; the communication is achieved by persons on a stage pretending to be someone else and so conveying the playwright's story to the audience. It is therefore inevitably a social activity, comparable to running a bus-service, a Darby-and-Joan club, or a clinic, far more than it is a solitary artistic mode of expression like writing novels or painting landscapes. A complete play, written, rehearsed and dressed, is only complete when it is presented to its audience. Whether the audience is seated in a West End theatre, in a village hall, or upon the flight-deck of an aircraft carrier, and whether the actors are members of the National Theatre Company or are drawn from the inmates of an old-folk's home, should not affect the basic nature of the activity. The play is a statement, which, at the time of stating (the two or three hours, or whatever, during which the actors are pretending to be someone else) is the most important thing in the lives of all concerned. The actors and author make the statement, the audience receives it and reacts accordingly; and the result should be a slightly different approach to the world in which we live – on the part of everybody present.

It is therefore important that the right to make and receive such statements should not be confined to those who pay and are paid on a commercial (or crypto-commercial – I am thinking here of subsidised civic theatres and the like) scale. Any group of people living together can experience theatre. The only difficulty is that if they have not received a professional training they may not know how to set about it. It has been said – indeed, I have said it myself – that anybody can act, or write a play, *if they really want to*. The urgent desire in itself is half the battle. The finished product may not be 'high art' but it will, if it is presented with sufficient sense of its inherent importance be of some social value. Naturally, this value will be increased if there is an elementary competence in the way in which the play is put on; and also in the way in which the play is chosen. There are few, if any, dramatists whose work is really 'for all time'. A play is written for a particular audience or a particular type of theatre, and it does not necessarily work if transplanted into a different environment.

There is a need for guidance in the amateur theatre today. I will not put it more strongly than that. A guide is a person who is supposed to know the road. He may be wrong, and he may be ignored. Those who ignore him do it at their own risk, of course, but they may easily be right, because the guide's presumed experience can be nullified by some recent change in conditions – a landslide, perhaps, or the presence of bandits, of which the persons whom he guides may have become cognisant without his prior knowledge. The authors of this book seem to me to be dependable guides, because they restrict themselves to pointing out where the road lies, and how the traveller may surmount such hazards as lie upon it. They also indicate that there is more than one road, and more than one available destination, and they make clear their own preference. But they do not dictate and they do not try to involve themselves personally in the choice of the traveller. This is not exactly a 'How-to-do-it' book. It asks a question as well as giving an answer: the question is 'How to do what?'

The reader must first answer this one himself: when he has done so, the book will then help him. While we are on the subject of guides, there is, in the Roman History of Livy, a remarkable use of the ablative absolute. Hannibal was led, by a native of Italy, into a morass which threatened to engulf his army. The chronicler writes: 'Duce cruciato, perrexit Hannibal' ('The guide having been crucified, Hannibal proceeded'). The point is that after this near-catastrophe the Carthaginian general went on to ravage Italy for years and years and the Romans were powerless to prevent him. He never took the city: but he came closer to doing so than any enemy of Rome for the next six centuries. He was also not particularly well supported by his government in Africa. He led his soldiers and his elephants over the mountains because he had devoted himself since childhood to this task; and he kept at it, one way or the other, until he died.

John Arden

Introduction

This is a book about some of the ways that amateurs can develop their work.

Some of it is concerned with the way that existing work could be improved, most of it is about the various ways in which amateurs could widen and enrich the whole scope of their activities. We look, for example, at the possibilities of work with puppetry, film-making and play-writing as well as documentaries, street-theatre and sound ballads. We discuss the role of improvisation and new forms of staging. We question the use of make-up. We ask: What is a play? What is an actor? What is a spectator? What is the relation between them? And there is always the question: What is an amateur?

The word itself is unfortunate, and has become almost pejorative. We do not intend to use it in this sense; comparison between amateur and professional is irrelevant and misleading as far as we are concerned. There is good theatre and bad theatre – and where it comes from matters very little – we have seen both sorts produced by 'amateurs' and 'professionals' alike, for sophisticated work by professionals has its own ways of being bad.

This book, then, is concerned with the kind of work amateurs could produce for themselves. We are not advocating any one particular method or approach which will depend on circumstances, talent, resources, aims: what we suggest is that there are a variety of structures from which a group can select, according to its own needs.

Nor are we advocating that plays should no longer be produced, far from it; but that public performances are merely the end-point of many months of research, discussion, experiment and practical work which might include aspects of drama which are now ignored.

These aspects might include a good deal of improvised drama as well as a more varied programme of plays, both well known and little performed. They might also include many of the developments outlined in Chapter 3 which need not always be presented as a 'performance', for they grow out of the needs of a particular group at a particular time, and find expression in forms that are uniquely personal.

The strength of such work lies in its sincerity: its uncomplicated honesty and freshness of approach, its directness and vigour. These qualities are obscured when a spurious faith in 'professionalism' encourages a concern for externals (imitation of the box-set, the proscenium stage and so on) at the expense of an endeavour to create real drama out of the very things that amateurs are best at. The way back to a more vigorous, less dependent amateur theatre lies through a rediscovery of such essentials.

We believe that, whatever form this drama takes, amateurs can (and should) build it for themselves. Maybe theirs will be only a modest home, even poky compared with the great mansion of professional theatre, but it need be no less exciting and meaningful in a different way. The materials are to hand, the design need be no imitation. Now it needs building – and though there will be difficulties, mistakes, whole sections which need reconstruction, it can be built if it is really wanted. We can take heart from those who have already begun.

Paul McCartney of the *Beatles* describing his first efforts to make a film said, 'We didn't worry about the fact that we didn't know anything about making films and had never made one before. We realised years ago you don't need knowledge in this world to do anything. All you need is sense, whatever that is.' His thoughts echo an idea of Malesherbes, which is, in effect, the theme of this book: '*Much more could be done if people believed less was impossible.*'

1 Explorations

To watch an amateur company take an embarrassed curtain call, awk-wardly bowing and shuffling round the footlights as the curtains jerkily open and close, is to clearly experience the difference between the amateur and the professional. In such moments one realises that there are different aims involved.

The professional actor is dedicated to the play and to his audience. The amateur is working for his own pleasure, satisfaction and release. He is a privileged individual, for whom the hard exigencies of box-office returns are only incidentals. Where no reputation is at stake, where finance does not dominate, the amateur group has a freedom to experiment and invent, to dwell upon the business of creating, so that everybody involved can get as much from the preparation as from the actual performance. This is not to say that either the performance or the audience are unimportant. They ignite the drama, but it is not for them that the flame is lit, it is for those involved. And if, when we take part in this activity, we do not feel a liberation, an increase in our lives, it is time to ask why.

In fact these are the values by which we should measure our 'success'. Enthusiastic audiences, critical acclaim and a good box-office are certainly welcome but fundamentally unimportant; they are not aims in themselves. For while the professional is answerable to outside interests – his career, the community he serves, the box-office, the Arts Council or his backer – the amateur can please himself. He 'does' drama because he enjoys it, because it regenerates; for him the aims, the methods and achievements of the professional theatre may be as irrelevant as Beethoven to a folk singer in a remote village.

All the more pity, then, that amateurs who have such opportunities to develop their own drama should jettison these opportunities by determinedly imitating the professional theatre; by producing the box-office success they do not need; by reproducing the elaborate set they have no means to achieve; and by their tendency to produce a play in order to put on a production rather than to learn from the actual struggle to create.

Such dependence is understandable – there is hardly an alternative; and amateurs are naturally anxious to learn about 'real theatre' in order to make it for themselves. But a policy of dependence and imitation is both inhibiting and mistaken. Inhibiting because the second-rate play can be very entertaining in the right context when played by trained actors; in a box-set in the church hall it provides nothing but the restrictions of its own narrow convention which, for amateurs who lack the professional skills of a Houdini, is a cramping and inescapable straitjacket. And mistaken because 'theatre', like painting, where an Alfred Wallis has worked entirely independently of the aims and methods of the professional painter, can be approached in a thousand different, even contradictory, ways.

For there is more than one kind of 'theatre'. As John Arden writes: 'The idea of a building with a fixed number of seats all facing a fixed stage, where a fixed number of people will watch a fixed performance for a fixed period of time, and then leave all together with fixed expressions (of pleasure or of boredom) on their faces, is not necessarily the only possibility. There is no reason why an entertainment should not include a variety of forms, music, plays, films, readings, recitations, dancing, etc., in front of an audience which may feel itself at liberty to go or come at any time it wishes. There is nothing particularly new about this, it has always happened in music halls or singing pubs or at pierrot shows or punch-and-judy on the beach: but it is perhaps less usually associated with "serious theatre". If it comes to that, there is no particular reason why "serious theatre" should be serious anyway.'

There are, too, or have been innumerable other forms: the mumming play, the Mediaeval mystery, the itinerant travelling troupe, the Commedia dell'Arte, the Sanskrit theatre of India, the Chinese puppet theatre, the Noh theatre of Japan of which Benjamin Britten has written 'I was lucky enough in my brief stay there to see two different performances of the same play – *Sumidagawa*. The whole occasion made a tremendous impression on me; the simple, touching story, the economy of style, the intense slowness of the action, the marvellous skill and control of the performers, the beautiful costumes, the mixture of chanting speech and singing which, with the three instruments, made up the strange music – it all offered a totally new operatic experience . . . The memory of this play has seldom left my mind in the years since. Was there not something – many things – to be learnt from it?'

His question is relevant; for though Britten saw the Noh play in terms of our own mediaeval drama others might have found in the absence of naturalism (the all-male cast and the non-theatrical lighting), the use of mime and dance and masks, not only a source of ideas for their own work but a challenge to their thinking about the widely held but limited concept of what 'theatre' should be. The three-Act farce from French's on a Pros. Arch stage is not all.

In order to throw off the paralysis of professional imitation, two alternatives are open to the amateur. Either he can aspire to the condition of true professionalism, as certain amateur societies (like the Questors) do, by training himself to the pitch of perfection expected from an orchestral player or student actor, so that mere imitation and solidified technique – the polished mannerisms and routine gestures which are the stock-in-trade of the 'established' actor – are replaced by true understanding. Or else, more humbly, he can create something of his own conceived in terms of his own needs and talents, and give this the simplest and most direct expression he can achieve. The former, which is not the immediate concern of this book, brings one into close contact with the really great minds – the minds like Shakespeare's or Chekhov's – and with drama at its most concentrated; the latter gives us a chance to contribute ourselves, our experience and talent in a way which can be relevant to the group in which we are working, or to the community as a whole. These approaches are complementary.

But whatever a group should decide to do must stem from conviction rather than fashion or aimless experiment. Once the aims of the work are clear – and these can only be worked out by a process of trial and error – whatever form the drama takes should be a precise expression of those aims.

How this can be achieved is the subject of the next chapter.

2 Improvisation

Trial and error, the confidence to take risks, and freedom from any rule-of-thumb methods are a necessary prelude to lively activity.

Two illuminating passages from Charles Chaplin's *Autobiography*[1] in which he describes his early association with Mack Sennett, and how the first films were made, are a good introduction to this free-wheeling approach in practice.

'Now I had confidence in my ideas, and I can thank Sennett for that, for although unlettered like myself, he had belief in his own taste, and such belief he instilled in me. His manner of working had given me confidence; it seemed right. His remark that first day at the studio: "We have no scenario. We get an idea, then follow the natural sequence of events" had stimulated my imagination.

'Creating this way made films exciting. In the theatre I had been confined to a rigid, non-deviating routine of repeating the same thing night after night; once stage business had been tried out and set, one rarely attempted to invent new business. The only motivating thing in the theatre was a good performance or a bad one. But films were freer. They gave me a sense of adventure. "What do you think of this for an idea?" Sennett would say, or "There's a flood down town on Main Street". Such remarks launched a Keystone Comedy. It was this charming alfresco spirit that was a delight – a challenge to one's creativeness. It was so free and easy – no literature, no writers, we just had a notion around which we built gags, then made up the story as we went along.

'For instance, in *His Prehistoric Past* I started with one gag, which was my first entrance. I appeared dressed as a prehistoric man wearing a bearskin, and, as I scanned the landscape, I began pulling the hair from

[1] *Charles Chaplin – An Autobiography* (The Bodley Head).

my bearskin to fill my pipe. This was enough of an idea to stimulate a prehistoric story, introducing love, rivalry, combat and chase. This was the method by which we all worked at Keystone. . . .'

'Under Sennett's direction I felt comfortable, because everything was spontaneously worked out on the set. As no-one was positive or sure of himself (not even the director), I concluded that I knew as much as the other fellow. This gave me confidence; I began to offer suggestions which Sennett readily accepted. Thus grew a belief in myself that I was creative and that I could write my own stories . . .'

Such an approach is not as difficult as it sounds, for once actors and directors believe in their capacity to cope with a more fluid situation than that provided by the set script, they discover an ability – and an appetite – to invent, to offer suggestions, to create for themselves. Watch children, for example, playing with glove puppets, inventing their own dialogue for a vaguely agreed story worked out on the spot with an immediate performance in mind. Each child gives his own puppet a certain character and makes him speak, quite spontaneously, from this viewpoint. The plot develops as the puppets react to one another in character, feeding off each other's inventions with all the cut and thrust of excited conversation in real life. Children do not call this 'improvisation'. They are involved in making a story. The same thing happens with team-games where there is a similar freedom to play, to invent, to improvise in a constantly changing but unpredictable situation, within the framework, not of a story, but of the rules of the game. No one needs to be 'rehearsed', to know the moves, to give a performance according to the rigid outlines of a set script, for 'everything' as Chaplin says of a different context is 'spontaneously worked out on the set'.

Such freedom need not be limited to children's glove-puppet plays and team-games. The same free, untrammelled attitude when making films, plays (see page 82), anthology-programmes or such work as Charles Parker's and Ewan MacColl's sound ballad *Romeo and Juliet* (see pages 93–100) can produce unexpected and vigorous results. In fact it is basic to the development of the kind of activity with which this book – and the next chapter in particular – are largely concerned. No set script: a story or scenario which can be developed as the work proceeds. No 'rehearsals', but a shaping process in which everyone is involved; for each work, far from being the reproduction of something which already exists, is a unique synthesis of the talents, the enthusiasm and the resources of the actual people involved. And at the end of it a performance where the work is shared with an audience.

There is no rule-of-thumb technique for doing all this; it is, as we have suggested, a matter of an attitude of mind, a determination to work without an author's script, to improvise for oneself. Sometimes it is best to work out a 'script' as one goes along, sometimes a 'script' can be written first and adapted as work proceeds (see pages 85–6). But in every case one is free to respond to the immediate challenge to make something new. There are no 'rules' for producing drama or making works of art, there are no 'rules' for judging them. The only criteria we have, for creating and appreciating, exist in our own unique sensibility. The whole point about the approach recommended in this book is that this is given rein.

Improvisation is also basic to the two elements – impersonation and interpretation – which are at the root of the actor's art. In fact what we work upon when we improvise is basic acting technique: the actor alive in a living situation. 'I had no idea what make-up to put on,' writes Charles Chaplin in another passage from his *Autobiography*, 'however, on the way to the wardrobe I thought I would dress in baggy pants, big shoes, a cane and a derby hat. I wanted everything a contradiction: the pants baggy, the coat tight, the hat small, the shoes large. I was un-decided whether to look old or young, but remembering Sennett had expected me to be a much older man, I added a small moustache, which, I reasoned, would add age without hiding my expression. I had no idea of the character. But the moment I was dressed, the clothes and the make-up made me feel the person he was. I began to know him, and by the time I walked on to the stage he was fully born. When I confronted Sennett I assumed the character and shuffled about, swinging my cane and parading before him. Gags and comedy ideas went racing through my mind.'

Chaplin's method was simply to sink himself into the imagined charac-ter and live this to the full. How this can be developed in a more complex situation can be seen from another example, in which a member of Joan Littlewood's Theatre Workshop[1] describes how a group of actors worked

[1] Quoted in *Theatre of Work*. Edited by Charles Marowitz and Simon Trussler (Methuen).

on Brendan Behan's *The Quare Fellow*, playing each part spontaneously, as Chaplin did, from their own imaginations:

'For the first week of rehearsals of *The Quare Fellow* we had no scripts. None of us had even read the play. We knew it was about prison life in Dublin, and that was enough for Joan. None of us had ever been in prison, and although we could all half-imagine what it was like, Joan set out to tell us more – the narrow world of steel and stone, high windows and clanging doors, the love-hate between warder and prisoner, the gossip, the jealousy, and the tragedy – all the things that make up the fascination of dreariness. She took us up on the roof of the Theatre Royal. All the grimy slate and stone made it easy to believe we were in a prison yard. We formed up in a circle, and imagined we were prisoners out on exercise. Round and round we trudged for what seemed like hours – breaking now and then for a quick smoke and furtive conversation. Although it was just a kind of game, the boredom and meanness of it all was brought home. Next, the "game" was extended – the whole dreary routine of washing out your cell, standing to attention, sucking up to the screws, trading tobacco, was improvised and developed. It began to seem less and less like a game, and more like real. By degrees the plot and the script were introduced, although some of us never knew which parts we were playing until half-way through the rehearsals. The interesting thing was that when she gave us the scripts we found that many of the situations we had improvised actually occurred in the play. All we had to do was to learn the author's words.'

Obviously the starting point for this kind of development need not be a prison – it can be almost anything – an incident, a story, an object, a phrase, a suggestion which all those who have the courage to involve themselves can explore and develop for themselves. Here is another example, this time from *Drama Education Survey 2*,[1] which describes how a group of children set about this: 'A class of pupils of 12 and 13 spoke a dialect thick with glottal stops, flattened vowels, and missing aspirates, as incomprehensible as anything heard elsewhere in the country. The period of warming-up had made little sense. But all at once the boys embarked on a play of their own contriving. Three of them found a one pound note. They hid it from the police and took it to the Queen who offered them £2

[1] *Drama. Education Survey 2*. Department of Education and Science (H.M.S.O.).

reward. This seemed to them a poor return for honesty so they made their apologies to the Queen, left the palace, and saw a notice offering £75,000 reward. What a curious way a young mind works! Then the girls took over and, stimulated by some "pop" music, they created a street market. The whole class became stallholders, shopkeepers, and the public. Some of the girls left the hall and came back wearing funny hats, scarves, oddments of jewellery, and carrying baskets, bags and a large assortment of "properties". As they became increasingly absorbed in what they were doing, the presence of the teacher was forgotten. They had made a small section of the environment their own. Our final memory is of a hairdresser spraying a client's hair with Airwick.'

Such work is valuable not only as a training method but because improvisation is still one of the best ways to explore a script. As a training method it is especially relevant to the amateur's most urgent needs, for performances, no matter how well rehearsed, are often untheatrical. And what, after all, can be expected? The amateur lives a busy life, his time and energy largely devoted to work unconnected with the theatre; his very existence as doctor, teacher, shop assistant or electrician's mate often depending on his being able to hide his strongest feelings behind a more or less impersonal mask. Improvisation helps us to rediscover and release these feelings.

For the actor's complete understanding of a character or situation with his whole being, it is not sufficient to learn the lines and be told how to react by somebody else. He must understand *why* those words were spoken and *how* the situation arose. He must understand *what* he is doing and why. For the actor, unlike every other artist, ultimately creates from himself and expresses himself through his own voice, his own gestures, his own person. The painter has his materials, the musician an instrument; the actor is his own instrument and material; he learns to act through living alone. He must find out for himself through personal experience. He needs all the experience of acting he can get.

Finally, of course, improvisation is one of the best ways to explore the script of a play that the actors are seeking to interpret. After all, the written text is the crystallisation of an emotional situation that the author has wanted to express. And until the actor has gone through the same stages of understanding as the playwright, he cannot hope to bring the script to life, to recreate its meaning. This is sometimes done by improvising the whole play without a text, or maybe one particular scene, having first decided what the key themes are. In one sense it does not matter how much the actors botch it, as long as they understand the character they are playing (and the playwright's skill) all the more when they return to the script. If, for example, two actors were asked to improvise the scene in *Othello* where Iago persuades Othello that Desdemona has been unfaithful, we can be sure that it would be done without much subtlety, and that the actors themselves would not be convinced by their first attempt. But as soon as they return to the script, they would see much more clearly how Shakespeare, in a short time, suggests the whole essence and drama of the psychological battle that is being fought. What's more, they would have a greater understanding of the whole structure, and therefore of the meaning in dramatic terms of each particular speech; how Iago's assumed reluctance reveals just enough to feed Othello's imagination; how he chooses the vital moment to bring his accusations into the open; how Othello's choked-back staccato speeches, his first controlled expressions of jealousy, burst into a bitterly impassioned tirade, as his early doubts are swept aside by the passion that consumes him. For an actor who has attempted this scene from his own resources, the opportunities that Shakespeare offers will seem all the richer.

In the same way improvisation can explore a situation analogous to the written text, as when Joan Littlewood, during rehearsals of *Macbeth*, got the actors to improvise a scene which Shakespeare never wrote, when Macbeth meets the murderers for the first time – in a pub. This kind of approach can enrich the background to a scene, and fill in the character for the actor who has to live the part.

'The artist, painter, writer or composer always starts with an experience that is a kind of discovery,' writes Joyce Cary.[1] Improvised work in drama can be the genesis of this discovery in the theatre. But in order to explore and give this shape, some form of expression, dictated by the nature of the original experience, will have to be devised. There are many ways of doing this: some are described in the next chapter.

[1] *Art and Reality*. Joyce Cary (O.U.P.).

Improvisation. John Hodgson and Ernest Richard (Methuen)
This book is immensely practical and full of general advice. Perhaps the best
general introduction to the subject; it discusses not only general points about
making a start, some possible preliminary sessions, building characterisation
and how improvisation can illuminate the text of a play but also the whole
theory of improvisation.

Building a Character. Constantin Stanislavski (Methuen)
An Actor Prepares. Constantin Stanislavski (Penguin)
Creating a Role. Constantin Stanislavski (Penguin)
Building a Character. Constantin Stanislavski (Penguin)
In these works the formulator of the 'method' deals with the physical realisation
of a character on the stage – his expressions, movement and speech.

3 New Directions

Is improvisation a form of dramatic expression in its own right? Is it a protracted preliminary to the acting of plays? The answer is surely that it is neither. We have seen that improvisation can not only lead to a deeper understanding of a written text; it can be the basis of aspects of dramatic work which it is difficult to characterise. In this chapter we describe these aspects, and show how they can be developed by groups looking for new forms of dramatic expression.

Few of the 'ideas' are new; some are older than the theatre as we understand it. Many belong to another tradition than the art-drama of the theatre, a tradition based on oral speech, on loosely extemporised developments within a framework, of collaboration rather than 'casting'. This tradition is the basis of the kind of work we are suggesting. If it helps amateurs to find release from forms which have grown old, it can do nothing but good.

ANTHOLOGIES

Anthology programmes can develop from discussion, improvisations or simply the recognition of a good idea, a consuming interest (for a more detailed description see page 66). They take many forms: John Barton's *Age of Kings* which chronicles the Kings and Queens of England comes from sources as varied as diaries, eye-witness accounts, histories and autobiographies. Charles Lewsen's *How Pleasant to Know Mr Lear* uses Lear's diaries, nonsense rhymes and stories, as well as the many watercolours he produced on his journeys which are projected on a screen.

One of the most moving we have seen was developed by seven sixth-formers. It was called, simply, *Dad*. This investigation of Dad's problems included poetry, prose extracts and songs (with guitar accompaniment) as

31

well as fairly sizeable chunks of Ionesco's *The Bald Prima Donna*, Edward Albee's *Who's Afraid of Virginia Woolf* and A. A. Milne's *Winnie the Pooh*. Dad, as a child, in love, married, with children, struggling to face personal tragedy, worried about religion, war and moral standards was seen to be as confused as the worst of us, and as much in need of love and understanding as the children whom he fathers. With seven chairs, a guitar, and the simplest props the group presented a programme that was at once entertaining and moving, modest yet rich in meaning.

Programmes of this kind are neither literature 'read aloud' nor fully developed productions. But they nevertheless need unobtrusive direction and a great deal of hard reading and research. Invariably presented without décor they could be staged as, for example, a complete reconstruction of an *Edwardian Soirée* which we once saw, in which the setting and costumes played as great a part as the actual 'performance' of recited ballads, pianoforte solos and accompanied songs.

BALLAD OPERAS AND MUSIC

The whole vogue of the Ballad opera began when John Gay's *The Beggar's Opera* was first performed in London in 1728, with a record run of sixty-three performances. Much of its popularity at the time was due to elements of political satire but its music, which was based on popular airs of the time, was irresistibly attractive. The main action was carried on in ordinary speech, interspersed with songs which were already old favourites.

Many groups now develop their own musicals or ballad-type operas using every available source of material as theme. The famous melodrama *Sweeney Todd* was developed as a musical by members of the People's Theatre in Newcastle. How this happened is described in their own words: 'William Scott had long been known to members as a witty writer who could turn out an apt verse to suit any occasion. He took an old script of the famous melodrama, *Sweeney Todd – the Demon Barber of Fleet Street* and by the addition of songs and lyrics, some of them written by fellow-members Ken Appleby and Alan Collis, he created the "book" for a musical. This he handed to Peter Stattersfield – pianist to the People's Theatre – who revealed a talent, hitherto unsuspected, for composing tunes which matched the wit and liveliness of the words and conveyed exactly the flavour of Victorian melodrama. The actors – singers and dancers now – performed with a zest and infectious enjoyment which evoked an immediate response from the other side of the footlights. Never was there such audience participation! They hissed and booed the villains, cheered the heroes and joined in the chorus until the roof timbers of that ancient ex-church in Rye Hill quivered and shook.'

Other forms, however, are possible. In recent years children have been encouraged to explore the raw materials of sound, and to make their own music, using not only their voices but a multiplicity of pitch percussion instruments. Much of this work has been outstandingly successful and there is no reason why adults using vocal sounds and effects, choral speaking of various kinds, singing and instrumental accompaniment should not develop an 'opera' or 'musical' on the same lines. Marc Wilkinson, the National Theatre's Director of Music now working on the National's first musical, explains what this might be like. 'What I want to do is to have the action broken up into many different levels – acting on the usual level, or dialogue and background mime, or dancing while singing, or dialogue with dancing and singing. By doing this there shouldn't be the customary differentiation between singing and talking, which is something that is apt to give the musical its pitiful air of total unreality.'

Future developments lie, it seems, in the no-man's-land between drama and music which actors and musicians must explore together. The local drama and opera societies as well as folk singers, bands and pop groups could collaborate to develop a ballad-opera, a musical, or cantata written by a local musician, and performed by the combined groups. This might include narration, choral speaking and singing, recorded voices and sounds, instrumental passages and solos for voices and instruments as well as a dramatised story. Things of this kind have already been developed on a small scale, notably by Steve Davies at Torrington Secondary School where staff and students have produced a series of cantatas with linked passages of narrative and choral singing. A full-scale opera is the next move. For the use of music in documentaries, sound-ballads, etc. see pages 92 and 269.

Opera in your School. Terence Dwyer (O.U.P.)
Let's do a Musical. Peter Spencer (Studio Vista)

COMMEDIA DELL'ARTE

Although the Commedia dell'Arte as such had its greatest vogue in the sixteenth and seventeenth centuries and died out in the mid-eighteenth its presence still haunts the theatre.

As a form its dialogue depended primarily upon the actor; and this from a simple exchange between two comedians to a full-scale play involving a number of actors, was entirely improvised, within the framework of a skeleton plot, which kept the players within bounds. By tradition the zanni, the comic servants whose antics made up the greater and most popular part of the entertainment, could take the basic situation of the play in performance as far from its prescribed path as they liked, provided they brought it back to a point where the plot could be picked up again. That called for an astonishing skill in improvised performance and a quick wit. But everything suggests that the actors in a Commedia dell' Arte troupe were unequalled performers, as dancers, acrobats, mime-artists, pantomimists and singers. As the comic actors wore masks they also developed a stunning command of gesture and shape.

The pre-arranged synopses involved a group of familiar characters – Arlecchino, Columbine, Pantaloon, Pierrot etc., and a series of stock situations in which the young lovers provide the mainspring of the comedy in their efforts to meet and marry. The heroine usually had a maidservant called Rosetta or Colombina (*Columbine*), her father, husband or guardian who tried always to prevent her escape, was called Pantalone (*Pantaloon*), while both he and his elderly friend, Graziano, had comic menservants or shrewish housekeepers. Once the plot was established the comic servants kept it going; among them were the best known of all the stock types: Arlecchino (*Harlequin*), Pulcinella (*Punch*), Pedrolino (*Pierrot*) Scapino etc. These names give some idea of the incalculable influence of the Commedia dell'Arte on the theatre of Europe – the English Punch and Judy, the Pierrot Show on the sands, Molière's Scapin, Watteau's Pierrot, and the circus clown though altered out of recognition, can all be traced back to their originals.

No good can come of direct revival, but the 'idea', the structure remains. Many modern dramatists are consciously or not drawing on this source: the vast Punch figure of Père Ubu in Jarry's *Ubu Roi*, John Arden's direct use of masks in *The Happy Haven*, Joan Littlewood's concert party

Pierrots in *Oh What a Lovely War* have hardly exhausted the potential which is being explored by a number of experimental American groups such as the Bread and Puppet Theatre (see page 101).

The World of Harlequin. A. Nicholl (Cambridge)
Italian Popular Comedy. K. M. Lea (Oxford)
The Commedia dell'Arte. Giacomo Oreglia (Methuen)
The Italian Comedy. Pierre Louis Duchartre (Dover)
Pierrot. Kay Dick (Hutchinson)

COMMUNITY DRAMA[1]

A great deal has been written about and very little achieved in the way of community drama. One of the troubles, as John Arden has said in an interview published in *Theatre at Work* (Methuen), 'is that a community, even a small one like Kirbymoorside, does not speak with anything approaching a single voice. I don't know that it ever did, but I take it that everyone in Athens used to go and see Aristophanes' Plays . . . We have too large a population, divided by too many disparities of class, income, occupation and culture, to revert to simple dramaturgy or simple democracy. Any sort of community drama can at present only work, if at all, on the most modest scale . . . for anything larger I have had to make use of the professional theatre with all its remoteness, its irrelevance, and its inability to attract a "popular" audience.'

The theatre's remoteness and irrelevance has troubled a great many people who have tried every possible means of involving or attracting a 'popular' audience. But the needs of a particular community can and have found expression in such productions as John Arden's own *The Business of Good Government* which was written for and first performed by the villagers of Brent Knoll, near Bristol; but these efforts have met with a very varying degree of success. Amongst others Joan Littlewood's work at Stratford, Peter Cheeseman's in Stoke-on-Trent, and Ed Berman's in London are striking examples of the various ways in which talented people have tried either to evolve a satisfactory dramatic form which has its roots in the life of the community in which they are working or to make the arts, especially drama, relevant to local community life. Another example, less well known perhaps but no less important on that account, was when Roland Miller was asked by the Warden of Hoxton Hall, a

[1] Please see page 101: Street-Theatre.

Quaker community in London, if he could present a view of War as it affected the whole community, whose age range varied from three to ninety. The problem was to resolve the conflict between the generations, to use the war experience of the older people, and the articulate protest of the younger, in the same 'entertainment'. Roland Miller describes how he set about this:

'The problem seemed to me to be resolved fairly well if one was prepared to create a framework, based on actual evidence of personal experience and conviction, and then let the performance(s) take place spontaneously within the framework. I began by picking a potential technical framework for the whole thing.'

His technical framework consisted of Hoxton Hall itself, of which he used a number of rooms, through which the audience was invited to circulate: tapes of reminiscences, songs, documents, posters, placards, souvenirs, projected slides; and spontaneous performances – this was the framework for the activity to take place.

'Although no rigid plan was laid down for the preparation of the production, what would actually happen on the dates set aside had to be determined. We aimed to open the Hall at 4.00 p.m. on a Sunday (28th May) and invite people to come and see and listen and have tea, and possibly watch some performances. (The vagueness of this invitation didn't seem to worry anyone; curiosity is a very powerful instinct.) We would let everyone wander through the two 'exhibition' rooms (the coffee room and the gym), watching slides and listening to the recordings, for about 30–45 minutes. Then tea would be served in the music hall, and when the mood was right there would be whatever performances the various groups in the community had decided they wanted to put on – on the stage and on the floor of the hall.'

The material he collected consisted of old people reminiscing about the first World War Zeppelin raids, a different generation talking about the blitz, young people singing protest songs, and a big community sing-song of first and second World War songs. The relevant slides included pictures of the Vietnam War. All this was prepared beforehand.

'The only part of the production that I left almost completely to determine itself was the performance. Three possibilities became apparent very early on. One of the older girls in the children's group (about 13 or

14) wanted to do a play with the kids – including the three-year-olds – about the evacuee children. She heard stories about evacuees from the parents, and of course some of these I had on tape, so that it was possible to feed the right information in again where required. A group of three or four teenagers wanted to do a dance drama about War and Peace (a symbolic killing and betrayal, etc., choreographed by themselves to a tape of Berg). And one youngster wanted to read out passages from a letter sent to him by a young American who used to work at Hoxton but is now doing Voluntary Service in Vietnam. The letter has some harrowing descriptions of American soldiers killing and maiming the Vietnamese.

'It was then a question of putting everything together for the "performance". Out of all these elements we did get a very successful performance, or "EVENT". The three actual performances were seen to be spontaneous, and the relaxed, continuous nature of the taped and photographed material – much of it identified by the people who contributed it – gave the whole thing a free, untheatrical feeling. I am not sure how far I succeeded in reconciling the young C.N.D. element and the Senior Citizens, but they certainly enjoyed each other's work, and it was definitely possible to feel a community of feeling between those who had experienced a war in their own homes and those who had only read about one thousands of miles away.

'One of the most important things in this production was the provision of a café at the end of the circulation pattern. It is difficult to relax the normal convention of performance starting times, curtain or light signals for the beginning, etc., unless you have something positive to replace them.

'I think that the technical framework is really the key to this sort of environment/community drama. Once that is fixed, the performances, events, happenings, etc., take shape organically. Of course there have to be certain moments of inducement, feedback of information, confrontation of one element with another; so that nothing is completely spontaneous, but this is all part of the framework. The modern children in my production were tremendously helped in re-creating the evacuee kids of the 1940s by my playing tape recordings for them; and the spectators understood the awfulness of the Vietnamese situation better when they heard the letter being read, because they saw the pictures projected at the same time. But once the technical possibilities of slides, tapes, etc., are made available, their uses follow naturally.

'The theme used in this production (we called it "*In Our Time*") was peculiarly good for the treatment I used, because the older age-groups in the community could remember what it was about, the television and other media keep the young people constantly informed. (B.B.C.'s *World War I*, Granada's *All Our Yesterdays*, the saturation reporting of Vietnam, Purnell's World War II magazine, etc.). The Blitz and what happened in the War is also a natural "myth" subject for the older generation to pass on to the younger. Also the evidence of War as a disturbing element in civilian life is all round Hoxton, where every new block of flats marks a vanished bombed site.

'The people at Hoxton intend to keep all the elements of the production together – slides, tapes, posters, etc., and add to them day by day.'

DOCUMENTARIES

Since Joan Littlewood made a successful West End entertainment out of documentary material in *Oh What a Lovely War*, documentary theatre has been developed by Companies as far apart as Newcastle and Exeter. At the Victoria Theatre, Stoke-on-Trent, where the most consistent approach to these community-based musical documentaries has been developed, Peter Cheeseman, the Director, realised just how valuable this approach could be in a regional context. 'It's not like the consistent voice of the playwright,' says Cheeseman, 'it feels like life, it feels like history!' ... 'What I should like to see above all is the Theatre accepted as a necessary and useful part of the community – as useful and as necessary as the doctor and the shop on the corner.' At the Vic the life of the Potteries has made a form of theatre with direct relevance for all the people who live in Stoke and thereabouts.

The bread-and-butter of life, the drama of the coal face and the factory floor, of local government and past disputes are the recurring themes; acted and sung in a direct, ballad-type style that reminds us of one of the theatre's traditional functions: that of a living newspaper. While most literary drama deals with the great themes of love and death, community documentaries are at once more specific and mundane, invariably relying for their interest on topicality and immediacy of subject. For amateurs this clearly presents great opportunities: no Aristotelian imitation of the greater passions but a dramatic presentation of life as it is, or has been, lived. The particular, the local, the personal, the documented are what count in this celebration of regional life. At Sheffield, *The Stirrings in Sheffield on Saturday Night*, an account of the saw-grinding trade in the 1860's; at Stoke,[1] *The Knotty*, the birth, life and death of the North Staffordshire Railway Company (researched by Peter Terson); at Newcastle, Alan Plater's *Close the Coalhouse Door*, the story of the miners' fight against the coal-owners in the village of Brockenback, have all 'revealed a willingness on the part of audiences to look squarely at their own history, and to accept a range of theatrical expression way beyond the time-honoured convention of actors exchanging witty badinage about sweet fanny adams in a box set'.[2]

Such a form necessarily relies on intense audience-involvement and draws heavily on every known type of theatrical expression. In *Close the Coalhouse Door* this ranges from straight (fictional) dialogue to pub-banter, sketches, music-hall skits, ventriloquism, historical readings, burlesque, mime, dance and back-projection, in quick succession. In *Six Into One* – about the Federation of the Pottery Towns – 'where practically every word spoken or opinion expressed is taken from the recorded speech or published writing of the people concerned', extracts from local directories and published statistics, as well as speeches which give a basic impression of the Six Towns at the time of Federation, are sung by a tram conductor as the rest of the company mime the jogging movement of the vehicle as it journeys from Longton to Tunstall. Thus the most intractable material is shaped into lively theatre.

Music is an essential ingredient of this kind of total theatre, and folk-song, shanties, music-hall tunes, ballads, jazz, pop and traditional airs all play much the same part as music of the popular idiom did for John Gay's *The Beggar's Opera*. Gay's words were written to fit extant airs, but a composer such as Alex Glasgow who wrote the words and music for the songs in *Coalhouse Door*, where drums, trumpet, accordion, guitar and piano were used as accompaniment, is the ideal (for song scores see

[1] Now issued on Argo.
[2] Alan Plater in an article 'What's Going on Behind the Coalhouse Door'. *Sunday Times*, February 1969.

published edition). Here are the words of one of his most brilliant songs from *Coalhouse*:

JACKIE: When that I was and a little tiny boy,
    Me daddy said to me,
    'The time has come, my bonny bonny bairn
    To learn your ABC'.
    Now Daddy was a Lodge Chairman
    In the coalfields of the Tyne
    And that ABC was different
    From the Enid Blyton kind.
    He sang:

A is for Alienation that made me the man that I am
and B's for the Boss who's a bastard, a bourgeois who don't give a
    damn.
C is for Capitalism, the boss's reactionary creed
and D's for Dictatorship, laddie, but the best proletarian breed.
E is for Exploitation that the workers have suffered so long
and F is for old Ludwig Feuerbach, the first one to see it was wrong.
G is for all Gerrymanderers like Lord Muck and Sir Whatsisname
and H is the Hell that they'll go to, when the workers have kindled
    the flame.
I is for Imperialism and America's kind is the worst
and J is for sweet Jingoism that the Tories all think of first
K is for good old Keir Hardie who fought out the working-class fight
and L is for Vladimir Lenin who showed him the left was all right
M is of course for Karl Marx the daddy and mammy of them all.
and N is for Nationalisation, without it we'd crumble and fall
O is for Over-production that capitalist economy brings.
and P is for all private property – the greatest of all of the sins.
Q is for Quid pro quo that we'll deal out so well and so soon
when R for Revolution is shouted and the Red Flag becomes the top
    tune.
S is for sad Stalinism that gave us all such a bad name
and T is for Trotsky the hero who had to take all of the blame
U's for the Union of workers, the Union will stand to the end.
and V is for Vodka, yes Vodka, the one drink that don't bring the
    bends.

W is for all willing workers and that's where the memory fades
and X Y Z, me dear daddy said, will be written on the street barricades
But now that I'm not a little tiny boy
Me daddy says to me,
'Please try to forget the things that I said
Especially the ABC'
For Daddy's no longer a Union man
And he's had to change his plea.
His alphabet is different now
Since they've made him a Labour MP.

Staging a documentary is invariably a collective process: the director, the actors and composer must be able to work together as a team, to understand each other, take from each other, and give to each other without stint in the exacting but immensely creative work of shaping a documentary from the moment of inception to its final presentation. To date, the genre has been largely associated with professional companies – though the Oxford University's Experimental Theatre Club's *Hang Down Your Head and Die* (an attack on Capital Punishment set in a circus ring) was one of the very first to be conceived. Here is an example by non-professionals from Tavistock in Devon, where a group of teachers (who have not acted before) are developing a production based on the history of the Devon Great Consols Mine. This lies three miles northwest of Tavistock on a hill overlooking the River Tamar. John Butt, the County Drama Adviser, who is directing the project, describes how it arose, was researched and is being developed:

'It started off with a search for material for Children's Theatre work and I presented them with a fantasy play (the usual sort with dinosaurs and monsters) but they weren't particularly interested in this! We then looked at other ideas but they felt that they wanted to do something intimately connected with the place in which they lived and worked. There was, therefore, one solution: I sent them out into the environment to research it. One of the girls went to see the editor of a local newspaper (who was a renowned antiquary) while another, the head of a Junior School, got to work in the Library.

'There were many possibilities (as there are in almost any district), but by far the most obvious was the Great Consols Mine.

'We began by visiting the desolate heaps of waste and the ruins of the arsenic plant on the moors above the town. Then we read histories, investigated reports, unearthed facts, anecdotes, legends, ballads and speeches. We spoke to old men who had worked in the mine. We collected helmets, lanterns, picks and shovels. We discovered the immense power of something which is close to us and the children the teachers are teaching, the children whose grandfathers worked for the mine in the days of its teeming prosperity.

'Then we thought, well, possibly Scene I – the discovery of the ore. There will obviously have to be a contraction in time here. Issuing of the shovels, picks (which were loaned out), candles, powder and fuse for enlarging the old shaft which was dynamited. Two and a half fathoms deeper, there was a sudden rush of water on November 4th, 1844: this was the discovery of the longest and richest unbroken sulphide lode in South Western England. Within hours "glowing piles of golden ore" were lying between the trees at the head of the mine at the top of the shaft, and crowds collected. It was a very exciting thing and for days afterwards, of course, they had nowhere to store and no way to transport the ore, and the golden piles were lying out in the fields.

'By 1850 the shareholders received about £207,000; the Company £300,000 more. But the average wage per miner was 14/- a week. The whole life of Tavistock was bound up with these facts.

'But we also discovered a great deal more which will be woven into the narrative of our production. There is a record, for example, of two men who were working near Lamerton when a large ball of fire arose from one of the shafts and descended on them and passed overhead. They swore to their dying day that this was the devil, though it was in fact one of the gases which ignite on contact with the oxygen in the atmosphere. There are records, too, of the great processions which moved across the moors in darkness, as hundreds of people walked to work each carrying a lantern. And a description of a miner breaking into what he calls a palace which he likened to a Jew's shop in its riches and its wealth and glitter.

'All this material, all these facts, we needed to give a dramatic shape and unity and rhythm. I first prepared a skeletal outline, a tentative scenario broken into scenes which would give us something to work from and adapt as we went along. For example, after the original discovery of the ore in Scene I, I conceived the idea of tracing the fortunes of a miner's family, William Clemo of Ivybridge, one of the three brothers employed in sinking the original shaft, some biographical notes on whom exist in Volume 46 of the *Devonshire Associations Reports*. We gave him a wife, Lucy, and two daughters, Emma and Victoria, who became bal-maidens – they broke ore into small pieces at 1/- a day. Other scenes traced the fortunes of the mine and its various workers.

'We were particularly fortunate in that one of the teachers[1] developed my scenario into a script (some passages from which are quoted below), so that the teachers, only one of whom had acted before, felt the security of a text which they were nevertheless free to knock about as much as they liked as the production developed. This is important. I'm no fanatic about improvisation which can and should be used, but there is much value in a group writing its own text which they can edit and supplant with good powerful improvised work.

'Here, then, is a brief snatch of dialogue from our first scene – as it stands at the moment. Two girls, Emily and Sally Gardiner, are talking together at nightfall on the moor:

EMILY: Eh, Sally, come back, we be nearly there now Emily, come on!

SALLY: But it's dimpsy, dear; and Blanchetown plantation's no place for a maid at this time of the day.

EMILY: What, you 'fraid the Duke will take you for a pheasant and have a pot at you! Come on, we got to get some wood for the bonfire tomorrow night. Think of it, tomorrow's November 5th, Tavistock will be full of bonfires by then, I'll wager. And I want to have mine.

SALLY: T'aint Duke I'm afraid on, he don't shoot deer now anyway since those foreigners come.

EMILY: Foreigners?

SALLY: That Will Clemo and his brothers.

EMILY: Clemo's men, they baint foreigners.

SALLY: They foreigners I tell 'ee, all the way from Ivybridge they come to live 'ere in Tavistock, 'tis shame they can't stay home, gallivanting all over the world like that.

[1] Philip Dyson.

EMILY: Well Sally, look 'ere!

SALLY: What?

EMILY: Careful, Sal. Sal come back 'ere at once, that goosan's crumbly, you'll break your neck.

(*Sally is walking around examining the shaft*)

They bin working some more, this rock is fresh dug. Come back Sally, 'tis not safe, come back or I'll tell Mum and then you'll be for it.

SALLY: You'll tell Mum all right but it'll be good news you'll be telling her, not bad. Look how much they dug out, they must be on to something. Reckon they've dug out another 12 ft. from the bottom of the shaft, must be near 100 ft. down by now.

EMILY: Here, suppose they find copper, we'll all have jobs, proper jobs instead of scraping taters.

SALLY: Work for Dad and for me, my dear, we'll be rich.

EMILY: Garn, we'll never get jobs here, t'would be man's work.

SALLY: No they'd give us jobs, light jobs like; well, breaking up the lumps of rock with a hammer, like this.

(*She dances about doing a mime of breaking up ore*)

EMILY: Garn mate, you'm mazed.

(*A loud shout is heard and the girls freeze*)

SALLY: My God, what was that?

EMILY: Must be the devil.

SALLY: Yes it is. Look there through the trees. Jack O'Lantern.

EMILY: No, no. 'Tis worse than the devil. 'Tis men. 'Tis they foreigners.

SALLY: Oh Emily, what'll we do? They're coming this way.

EMILY: Hide, hide, in behind these pile of rocks. And pray.

And then Captain James Philips, Mine's Manager enters. He hurries up Peter, Jack and William Clemo who also enter. They go down into the shaft and they dig and the water breaks, and then the

*two maids come out and are after jobs, and are given jobs. The scene
continues as follows :*

SALLY: Well, Cap'n, Emily and me was wondering . . . suppose there were
copper, if there would be any chance of jobs for a couple of healthy
maids to work at bal-maidening?

PHILIPS: Be you strong enough to swing a hammer?

SALLY: Yes, Cap'n.

PHILIPS: And be you decent honest God-fearing maids?

EMILY: Well I never. Yes we be, Cap'n.

PHILIPS: Such as will sing hymns at work and pray?

SALLY: Yes, Cap'n, that we be.

PHILIPS: And no such as will be swearing and cursing the like of most
bal-maidens of other mines?

SALLY: The idea!

PHILIPS: Then maybe, and I say maybe, because I doubt if we'll find any
copper at all.

*Then, of course, when the water comes, they panic. Here is some more
dialogue when the ore is actually seen.*

PHILIPS: Hold that lantern, Peter. Now let's have a look.

WILLIAM: Look at the flickering and glitter of it! Look! Like stars in the
Milky Way. Or like candles through a dark forest. Copper. This is
copper ore.

PHILIPS: Right, let's dig out as much as we can, the water's rising. Peter,
keep working that pump and operate the pulley to get the ore out.
Will, you get swinging your pick and Jack, help to load the ore. I'll
go to the top of the shaft and get those two maids to help pile it up.
Work now, work fast before the water beats us. Come on you two
girls, pick it out of the buckets and take it over there. Got it? Go
on I'll help.

'And so on. Later Josiah Hitchins, who instigated the whole thing,
appears and sees the ore. Then you come to the moment where you can

45

bring in the children, when the mine is flooded. Hitchins explains the need for labour. "We'll be able to employ everybody here from the age of seven upwards". The excitement is built up.

'Obviously there's a good deal to work on. It's going to take a long time, I doubt even if we'll get it done for next term. If we are going to do it thoroughly, I want it to take a long time. It may well be that we won't be ready for a performance until the summer term. It will all be done in the round, as Brian Way's plays are, and will be toured to as many schools as we can get to in a given length of time. And at the end of it all I hope to have a text.'

TEXTS

Oh What a Lovely War. Theatre Workshop and Charles Chilton (Methuen)
U.S. Peter Brook (Calder)
Close the Coalhouse Door. Alan Plater (Methuen)
The Hero Rises Up. John Arden and Margaretta D'Arcy (Methuen)
Six into One. An introduction to the show (Victoria Theatre)
Hang Down Your Head and Die (not published)
Portrait of a Queen (French)
The Investigation. Peter Weiss (Calder)
Lee Harvey Oswald. Michael Hastings (Penguin)

MUSIC

Oh What a Lovely War. L.P. of the show with original Theatre Workshop Cast (Decca)
The Beggar's Opera

The number of recorded folk songs now on record is too long to mention here: See catalogues; especially Topic Records Ltd., 27 Nassington Road, London N.W.3.

REFERENCE

Folk Song in England. A. L. Lloyd (Lawrence and Wishart)
The Penguin Book of English Folk Song. R. V. Williams and A. L. Lloyd (Penguin)
Irish Sheet Ballads. C. L. Lochlainn (Constable)
The Common Muse. An Anthology of Popular British Ballad Poetry 15th to 20th century – ed. V. de Sola Pinto and A. E. Rodway (Penguin)

DRAMATISED READINGS

Groups that do not wish to embark on a full-scale production can 'present' a dramatised reading for public performance. Many sources are suitable ranging from scripted plays, 'anthologies' like Peter Weiss's *The Investigation* or John Barton's *The Hollow Crown* to the use of ballads, folk-tales, short stories, novels and film-scenarios, which can be 'produced' with the aid of lighting, sound effects and even a limited use of setting. The B.B.C. continually broadcast new plays and dramatised versions of diaries, letters, etc., of a kind which can be presented in this way. T.V. scripts are also published which can be used.

Shiphay Amateur Dramatic Societies' 'production' of two short stories – *Mrs Bixby and the Colonel's Car* and *The Landlady* – by Ronald Dahl, with sound-effects from a tape recorder on stage and lighting projected, in turn, on those who read, seated on rostra on the stage, is an example of one kind of approach that can be adopted.

FILM MAKING

For children, young people and adults, film making can be an exciting creative adventure. Yet, at the moment, few actors or producers in the amateur movement would even consider the idea of making a film in spite of watching hundreds of hours of cinema and television. The present division between the numerous aspects of dramatic activity is nowhere more saddening than in the almost total lack of interest by amateur dramatic societies in the possibility of making films.

This cannot be a question of money. As a rough guide, a twelve-minute black and white silent film will cost in all between £20 and £30 to produce. Second-hand cameras, light-meters, tripods, and splicers can be purchased for less than £75, or borrowed by members of the Society for Education in Film and Television (see page 50). Best of all the film could be made in co-operation with a local cine club. Technical difficulties, though important, should not be exaggerated. Many people have made highly successful first films with very little initial experience.

A case in point was the film made by Bradford Grammar School pupils. Called *Strike Action*, it was probably the most successful film made by school children in 1963, winning an 'oscar' in the Amateur Cine World

Ten Best Competition. D. M. W. Barker who directed the film gives the background story. '*Strike Action* was the first attempt at fiction film-making at Bradford Grammar School. Previously three documentaries had been made about various aspects of school life but they had had little support. For this new venture we chose a comedy in the hope that the humour would distract people's attention from the technical weaknesses which were inevitable.

The idea of a schoolboy strike, with a procession in front of Bradford Town Hall, walking out from lessons and so on, fired the imagination of many boys and we had little difficulty in obtaining extras. There were about twenty boys involved in the production team which meant we could always guarantee having sufficient for a filming session without there being too many with too little to do.

The first job of the production team was to discuss the original story, completely altering it in the process, but improving it greatly. We found it an impractical ideal to have only one script writer and discovered that open discussion of the story brought out its weaknesses far better than merely reading it. The shooting script was then drawn up on a basis of these discussions. It provided a basis on which to shoot the film but it was altered in many places during a shooting.

Having got a script, we then had to find some equipment with which to make the film. Two members had 8mm cameras but we wanted to use 16mm for presentation purposes, our school hall seating 1,100 people. By chance we contacted a film producer who lent us a single-lens Bell and Howell camera and a tripod. This and some home-built lighting completed our equipment. It was very simple, which was a great advantage as we were all beginners. Even then we had a little trouble with the camera; the governor failed to operate so that as the motor wound down the film slowed down, resulting in speeded up action on projection. We have since been complimented on the 'Charlie Chaplin effect'!

We used negative-positive film stock, which though a little more expensive initially, was well worthwhile. It enabled us to chop the cutting print into shape in the initial stages of editing, without having to worry too much about the celluloid. Having cut and re-cut the film until we were satisfied we then matched the untouched negative to it. From this edited negative we had prints made of the whole film, three 16mm and six 8mm prints, this number more than saving the extra cost of using negative as opposed to reversal stock.

The total stock of *Strike Action* with one completed 16mm print was £40, most of which went on film stock. But although we had to work for a long time to raise this it has since proved an investment. Within nine months of its première the returns were 500 per cent of the original cost.

I don't think anyone need be frightened of the technical details of film-making. We knew nothing when we started. What really matters is the story.'

Notes on equipment

There are two main gauges of film used by amateurs, 8mm and 16mm; the measurements are the width of the film from edge to edge. If the equipment is from official sources it will probably be 16mm. Most private owners have 8mm for home movies. Both are adequate though it must be acknowledged that 16mm, though more expensive, is infinitely more versatile – you get a better picture, the film is easier to edit and it can stand more magnification. Use 16mm if possible – 8mm is primarily for unedited records; for moving pictures rather than for films.

The budget

The basic equipment for film production consists of a camera, tripod, light-meter and splicer (or film joiner), though an animated viewer for editing should be added to this if funds permit. A second-hand camera might cost £50–£70. Never work without a sturdy tripod (ex-Government surveying tripods can be obtained for a few pounds).

Film stock is expensive but not prohibitively so: 100 feet of 16mm black and white film costs about £2, and runs for 4 minutes. Processing costs £1. Allowance must be made for editing, retakes and so on. The actual amount required will be found generally somewhere between 50 per cent and 100 per cent over the length of the finished film.

Colour involves additional problems and expense (probably 40 per cent more) and unless colour is intrinsically essential, stick to black and white or mix the two in different sequences.

The film

What sort of film should be made? Generally, there should be no shortage of ideas from which a story can be selected, and this, of course, should be based on the experience of the group. A film firmly rooted in experience and shot in the local streets or fields is more likely to succeed than something derived at second hand from the cinema or television. The plot should be simple, direct; not too ambitious at first. Once it has been chosen the 'shooting' script is developed. In such a script each sequence is broken down into all its component shots, and every shot will include a careful description of the action and an indication of the camera set-up. This is one way of setting out a shooting script:

Shot	Type	Description
1.	Long shot	General view of room through open window. A figure is seen at the table.
2.	Medium shot	View of table over writer's shoulder.
3.	Close up	Pen moving over letter, words readable.
4.	Close up	The letter is screwed up.
5.	Medium long shot	The writer stands up and camera pans to follow him to the window which he leans out of.
6.	Close up	The writers face. He is quietly crying.

The production unit itself normally consists of a Director, three cameramen (one for the camera, one for exposures, one for the tripod and number board), two lighting crew who are responsible for setting up the lighting, and two for continuity, checking positions of actors in various scenes, clothes, properties etc., so that scenes can be linked together smoothly. At a later stage Film Editors, who arrange the film, will also be needed. This is the really creative process in film-making.

The casting of the main characters may present some difficulties as a good stage actor is not necessarily the most successful performer on the screen.

A book this size cannot begin to go into the best way of making a film. The following organisations are there to help you and should be consulted.

Addresses

Society for Education in Film and Television (s.e.f.t.)
34 Second Avenue, London e.17.

The Society exists to promote and further the education in film and television of children and young people. It distributes information through an advice service, and through its regular publications, *Screen Education*, *Screen Education Yearbook*, *Film and T.V. News*, and *Viewing Panel Reports*. Annual subscription £1.

The British Film Institute (B.F.I.) 81 Dean Street, London w.1.

The Institute's aim is to encourage film as an art and to foster its study and public appreciation. Among its main departments are the National Film Theatre and the National Film Archive. Television is now included within the Institute's scope. The Education Department offers advice, services, and materials to teachers and lecturers. The B.F.I. publishes *Sight and Sound* (quarterly) and the *Monthly Film Bulletin*.

Lectures and courses
Lectures are provided on any aspect of the cinema. Courses range from weekend schools to 24-session courses arranged with extra-mural departments. There is also an annual summer school. Membership open to all individuals and groups costs 25/- a year.

Courses
Summer School of S.E.F.T. 'Education in Film and Television' B.F.I. Summer School. Apply to 70 Old Compton Street, London w.1. For teachers there are also supplementary courses at certain Training Colleges, e.g., Bede College, Durham. L.E.A.'s run courses on films and film making at adult Education centres.

BOOKS
Group Film Making. Robert Ferguson (Studio Vista)
  The best book on the subject.
Young Film Makers. S. Rees and Don Waters (S.E.F.T.)
  A primer on the organisation of young people's film making, but generally indispensable.
The Complete Technique of Making Films. P. Monier (Focal Press)
Making 8mm Movies. Philip Grosset (Fountain Cinebook)
The Simple Art of Making Films. Tony Rose (Focal Press)
Filming in 16mm. Denys Davis (Iliffe Books)

These books cover the whole field of film making. More specialist studies are published by the Focal Press, 31 Fitzroy Square, London W.1. and Fountain Cinebooks, 46–7 Chancery Lane, London W.C.2.

The Screen Education Year Book published annually by S.E.F.T. is also very worth having.

FILMS

Three films worth seeing are:

Fundamentals of Film Making
  Three films produced by Brian Coe for the Kodak Lecture Service. The films are in colour obtainable from *Kodak*.
Film Making in School
  Two films (Planning a Film Script and Shooting the Film) compiled from material shot at Cornwell Secondary Modern School by the B.B.C. Schools Television Service. *Obtainable from the B.F.I.*
Film Workshop
  Film making and screen education at Cornwell Secondary Modern School. A film made for Canadian Television (*obtainable from the B.F.I.*).

A proper understanding of film and film language – story telling in moving pictures – is essential. Learning to operate the equipment is a beginning but the language of film is something which can only be acquired through watching, and analysing films. There are, besides the major films themselves, a number of film extracts for study purposes which are obtainable from the B.F.I. Film Societies exist in most areas and anyone over the age of sixteen can become a member.

HAPPENINGS[1]

Definition. 'I try to make definitions that won't exclude. I would simply say that theatre is something which engages the eye and the ear', *John Cage*.

It is probably positively harmful to try and define Happenings at all; Happenings are already a kind of myth and like other myths they can be useful catalysts without being categorised.

[1] This account was written by John Fox, a more detailed account of whose work, including the description of a Happening, appears as an Appendix to this book (see page 352).

Happenings are difficult to define because, first, their essential lesson is that their inventors should create freely in any media or mixture of media (and to codify such activity would be self-contradictory); secondly, because the Happenings which have occurred have varied enormously; and thirdly, because definition would arbitrarily exclude many activities often basically related such as painting, sculpture, carnivals, mime, festivals, religious ceremonies, pageants, sports days, mediaeval processions, street theatre, circuses, fairgrounds, sideshows, ghost trains, protest marches, riots and pantomimes. Finally Happenings are usually designed specifically for a particular time, country, location and audience and can therefore only really be understood through first-hand experience.

The most helpful definition is perhaps that in Michael Kirby's book *Happenings*.[1] 'A purposefully composed form of theatre in which diverse alogical elements, including non-matrixed performing, are organised in a compartmented structure'.

This usefully brings together a number of characteristics of the Happening: the use of a variety of materials such as films, dance, readings, music etc., programmed together, with activities undertaken simultaneously and separately by groups or individuals, who may act or improvise but who will more usually behave simply as themselves.

Purpose, symbolism, chance and traditional theatre techniques are variously accepted and used; and audiences tend to be provoked to active participation and involvement, or they may be ignored altogether or even non-existent. Programmes can take place in small or extensive, interior or exterior environments, for ten minutes or a month or more. The only rule is to be free to create in any way and place one chooses and to give the maximum liberation to the imagination.

Allan Kaprow was quoted in *Art News*, 1961, 'The Happening would utilise in an environment of total alienation (backyard, kitchen, garage, hanger, supermarket, warehouse) available materials: newspapers, scrap-iron, rags, jam-jars, sundry gadgets or cardboard boxes.

As a matter of historical interest, the word Happening was first used to describe a form of theatre by the American painter Allan Kaprow. Rightly he says 'The name Happening is unfortunate. It was not intended to stand for an art form originally. It was merely a neutral word that was part of my

[1] *Happenings.* Michael Kirby (Sidgwick and Jackson).

projected ideas in 1958–9. It was a word which I thought would get me out of the trouble of calling it "theatre piece", a "performance", a "game", a "total art", or whatever, that would evoke associations with known sports, theatre and so on. But then it was taken up by other artists and the Press to the point where all over the world it is used in conversation by people who are unaware of me and who do not know what a Happening is.'

The production Kaprow had in mind was eventually called 'Eighteen Happenings' in six parts and was presented in the Reuben Gallery, New York, in October 1959. He described it then as a different art, where the artist takes off from life – and where the artist provides some engaging situations. A long loft gallery was divided into three small artificial rooms made with wood and semi-transparent plastic. The six participants were rehearsed very precisely and performed simple formal actions in all accompanied by music, conversation, slides, bells, electronic sounds, coloured lights, loudspeakers and mechanical toys. Although a certain amount of random 'behaviour' was expected and encouraged and the audience occasionally directly involved moving their position according to printed directions, the overall effect must have been close to that of a free form dance performed in a very advanced movement studio.

As we have seen, this event which gave birth to the label Happening, is far removed from certain activities which later artists themselves called Happenings and very far removed indeed from what the Press and public wanted to categorise in the same way. Not that labels matter too much provided the activity is stimulating and enjoyable. Unfortunately though, the word has become debased, the media have used it as a peg on which to hang insensitive assessments of anything a little unusual, by a lunatic fringe of teachers, artists and dealers who gain fame and fortune out of novelty and the jargon of the *avant-garde* – and by wits to describe road accidents, drunken brawls and sundry bust-ups with the wife.

Lebel is perhaps the most eloquent and lucid apologist for Happenings theory. He is largely right when he maintains that it is the total social picture that matters; and that art has become just another product to be bought and sold by the middle classes. Few contemporary artists provide us with any profound experience, and very few of the majority of the populace have the chance to create. The artist is largely a paid hack of the entertainment industry, a sop to the vested interests of investors, dealers, managements, critics, art schools, universities and art administrators.

So creators of Happenings are responding deeply to the great malaise they feel in their own Society and it is essential to understand this if one wants to 'do a Happening'. They are seeking to replace all 'Art', not just theatre, with forms more exciting, more relevant and more accessible to all. Forms free from arbitrary boundaries and rules embodied in academic definitions of Theatre, Painting, Dance, Film, etc. They will use any media to give the most direct expression in the particular environment involved.

Happenings are an attempt to break out from the aesthetic and moral taboos of our impersonal, industrialised, materialised and life-defeating system; they challenge the values of our society; they seek to free the creative potential of every individual. Although their authors may use enormously different tactics they might agree with McLuhan when he says that 'Art as a radar environment takes on the function of indispensable perceptual training rather than the role of a privileged diet for the élite'. Art and life must become free – and perhaps it is through art that life will become less controlled and constricted. Or as Jean Jacques Lebel puts it, 'the function of the creator is to perceive and to let things happen. He helps people to get high. To open their minds and bodies.'

So let things Happen. Create, Create, Create.

IMPROVISED SKETCHES AS THE BASIS OF A DEVELOPED WORK
Improvised work cannot normally hope to be anything more than a short sketch as the unity of structure needed for an extended play can only come if one person has complete control. But it is possible to use a series of improvised sketches, skits or vignettes linked together by an embracing framework, to create a longer work.

The subject or theme should be within the knowledge and experience of the people taking part so that they are unconsciously enabled to contribute something of themselves in a colloquial and unaffected way: Peter Terson's *Zigger Zagger*[1] written for production by the National Youth Theatre used just such a framework, that of a massed football crowd in front of whom a series of cartoon-style home-life sketches were acted out – like scenes from Hogarth's *The Industrious Apprentice*.

[1] Published by Penguin.

A comparable instance of such a production, done with non-actors, was the powerful work *Who Killed Tony Rand?* developed by members of the Haymarket Youth Theatre Workshop in Basingstoke, and first performed in 1965.[1]

This was evolved by John Butt (now County Drama Adviser for Devon) and a group of twenty-five people whose ages ranged from fifteen to twenty-one, including apprentices in local factories – a machine tool fitter, a body-builder, and electrician – an insurance salesman, shop assistants etc. The work's framework, a series of seven narrations describing Tony Rand's progress through school, the factory, the magistrate and finally to prison, was originally written by John Butt – though later much modified by the group in discussion. It served as a linking device for a series of improvised scenes which were acted between the spoken narrative.

One of these takes place in a pub soon after Tony had been condemned to death for killing a girl in a fight. His fiancée, taunted by those who remember her going out with a young man whose photograph is in all the papers, disowns him ('to think, he touched me ... the hands of a murderer'). His sister enters. A violent scene ensues at which, on one occasion at a performance at a Youth Club, the whole audience angrily joined in, shouting and jeering in sympathy with the 'action' on the stage.

Here is the Narration spoken before the previous scene:

NARRATION SIX – WHO KILLED TONY RAND ?
The Magistrate
Who killed Tony Rand ?
I, said the Magistrate, I killed Tony Rand.
He came before me, and my colleagues,
Staring dully at us
From beneath his cowl-like hair.
His eyes
Were blank most of the time.
Occasionally
Flashes of aggression and frightened self-assertion
Flickered and darted towards us,
But most of the time he was sullen.

[1] A fuller account of this Workshop's activities is told in Volume 8, No. 8 of *Youth Service*. Published by the Department of Education and Science.

He came from a reasonable sort of home
His parents seemed to care about him
His school had tried extremely hard
With him
He seemed to make friends easily
He had a good steady job
With prospects.
I simply could not understand
Why he was
So frighteningly anti-social.
Why did he fight in the streets
And break and enter and destroy?
Why was he a vandal?
And a hooligan?
I asked him.
I said to the boy
'Why do you do these things?
Explain to me why
At once'.
There was a silence
He looked at the floor.
'Look at me' I said.
(It is important that they look at you)
There was another silence.
His mother sobbed quietly in the chair across the room.
He waited for his answer
But he did not reply.
I sometimes wonder if there is an answer.
We had no option my colleagues and I
We had given him every chance
Probation – everything.
This was his third and most vicious offence.
And so I sent him to a Borstal.
I put him with dozens of others like him
I performed my function and moved hurriedly to the next case on the list
I, said the Magistrate, I killed Tony Rand.

Another example of a framework into which various short, idiomatic sketches can be slotted is currently being revived by the London Critics

Group, a number of young folk singers from various parts of the British Isles who are trying to recreate the basis for a popular theatre inside the folk idiom. They meet regularly to explore the techniques of folk-music and drama and to see how these can be applied within the folk-music revival. John Faulkner, who has been with the group for some years, explains: 'We are lucky in some ways inasmuch as we have a sort of ready-made audience of a non-theatre going type, in the folk clubs themselves. Undoubtedly our *Mummers Play* and the *Festival of Fools* had a startling impact on the audiences that were exposed to them. Startling in the sense that here we have a piece of entertainment, in theatre form, that the audience really feels involved in. We tried to break down the contradictions of formal theatre so that the play could erupt from the audience itself. Most of the techniques we have used have been quite new to us, and we are still floundering. We are critically examining many of the techniques and structures that have for so long confined the conventional theatre, as we know it, to such a narrow national audience. *The Festival of Fools 1967* incorporated some ancient ritualistic patterns of theatre such as Pace Egging and Turning the World Upside Down as well as the traditional ballad form itself. The group produced, too, a month-by-month satirical account of the year's events ranging from a high society wedding, a scene round a camp fire with Harold Wilson and his boy scout cabinet to tragically moving scenes about the unjust U.S. aggression in Vietnam.' (See plate 2.) These 'political, folk documentaries' are presented annually.

A more recent *Festival of Fools*, which was scripted and produced by Ewan MacColl, began as usual with the election of the Lord of Misrule and the destruction of the old year:

NARRATOR : First, you have to destroy the old year. You see, way back people believed that winter could last forever unless it was driven out in the person of a scapegoat. So they collected things identified with the old year and destroyed them – sacrificed them.

JIM : You mean like the pay freeze?

NARRATOR : Doesn't it need destroying?

ACTOR : There's still Vietnam, of course.

PEGGY : And the race riots in America!

ACTOR: And Enoch Powell . . .

JIM: Of course! The news! What's older than last year's news? Right.
           We're going on a journey, back to January, 1968.

With the help of newspaper cuttings collected throughout the year, each
month is dramatised by a series of sketches which take as their subject the
follies of bureaucracy, racial prejudice, intolerance, etc., as seen in the day-
to-day news stories of the year. This is an attempt to bring to life the
Broadsheet in dramatic form, performed by people and to audiences for
whom the literary theatre is as remote as the Reading Room of the British
Museum, and for whom the issues and subject really matters.

The following extract is from the month of September:

TAPE 60   D'Oliveira left out of tour party. *Guardian,* September 7th. A
          group of M.C.C. members, including former England batsman,
          the Rev. David Sheppard, decided in London last night to call
          for a special meeting of the M.C.C. to discuss the committee's
          handling of the tour of South Africa this winter.

          (*Lights up on Stage 2. Narrator on ladder. A semi-circle of men and
          women all reading newspapers. A batsman stands in the centre*)

NARRATOR: Dolly's playing first-class cricket this afternoon and he's absolutely
          savaging the Sussex attack. He's already made his first century
          and looks all set for making another. Greig is bowling to him, at
          the moment, and here he is with one of his rather fast deliveries.

          (*Crowd claps*)

1ST MAN: Boundary! Bravo, Dolly!

2ND MAN: Lovely, clean stroke!

NARRATOR: Beautifully played. There's Griffiths looking rather discouraged
          as he chases the ball. Another four. Yes, there it is up on the board.
          That's Dolly's thirteenth this innings. I don't think there's much
          doubt that Worcester will . . .
          (*Crowd Claps*)

3RD MAN: Jolly well played.

1ST
  WOMAN: Good old Dolly!

NARRATOR : Greig misjudged that one; placed it rather too high up the field and D'Oliveira stepped up to it with one of those tremendously powerful swipes of his. One of those superb moments when everybody says 'six' the moment the ball makes contact with the bat. It's gone right out of the ground. He's playing with enormous confidence, and with just that touch of bravura the crowd loves. Here's the last ball of the over . . . and . . . yes . . . he's done it again!

(*Crowd claps*)

3RD MAN : A hundred and ninety-eight for three wickets. Good man! Good man!

4TH MAN : Keep it up, Dolly!

NARRATOR : Greig's beginning to look rather tired and now it's Jones' turn to bowl. No . . . Powell's taking his place, Enoch Powell, the formidable fast bowler from Wolverhampton. A very dangerous man, this, full of surprises and . . . Oh! a tremendous ball that . . .

(*Crowd claps*)

1ST MAN : Jolly well bowled!

2ND MAN : Come on, Enoch, get him out!

1ST MAN : Of course, they eat Kit-e-Kat, y'know.

2ND MAN : Sleep on the floor . . .

3RD
  WOMAN : Grinning picaninnies! I was absolutely terrified . . .

NARRATOR : That was a tremendous ball! And now he's . . . fantastic power in that arm.

(*Crowd gasps*)

NARRATOR : He managed to block that one but there's no doubt that he's less confident than he was. In the last few minutes the emotional temperature here has shot up and all the crowd's attention now is on Powell. It's tremendously exciting. And now he's coming down to the bowling line, slower this time, more deliberately . . . and . . .

(*Gasp from crowd*)

4TH MAN: L-B-W! L-B-W! Well bowled, sir!

2ND
 WOMAN: What's up, Sambo? Getting cold feet?

NARRATOR: I don't think it was L.B.W., but we'll know in a moment after the referees have conferred . . .

1ST
 WOMAN: It's not that I object to them but . . . why can't they stay where they belong?

2ND MAN: I think they go a bit far in the States . . . I mean killing them! A bit drastic, I think.

1ST MAN: I was out in Egypt during the war. Fantastically primitive; you could smell some of the villages for miles.

3RD MAN: Grinning picaninnies just terrorising landladies . . .

3RD
 WOMAN: Some of them don't even know what a W.C.'s for!

NARRATOR: The umpires have apparently decided against L.B.W. The coloured batsman from South Africa is looking rather apprehensive . . . and not without cause. Here's another ball from Powell . . . Oh, a beautiful . . .

(*Crowd gasps*)

2ND MAN: You've got the bastard groggy, Enoch! Keep it up!

3RD MAN: I'm open-minded, but there *are* limits! After all, we cater for a rather better class of customer and I just can't afford to serve these people.

2ND
 WOMAN: I mean, Heather's only five and she doesn't know any better. She just plays with them the way she plays with anybody else. But what's going to happen when she gets older?

1ST MAN: Grinning picaninnies! Breed like rabbits!

1ST
 WOMAN: Of course, I realise it's not their fault they're not civilised! It's just . . .

61

4TH MAN: Ought to send 'em back to the jungle, really. We've got enough problems without having to deal with . . .

NARRATOR: That was a very close one indeed; a very tricky ball, just the right amount of edge on it . . . just nicked the corner of the coloured man's bat . . . if Heath, at Silly-mid-off, had been a little more alert, there's no doubt it would have put paid to . . . here he goes again . . . he's on tremendous form!

(*Cry from the crowd*)

1ST MAN: Oh, damned hard luck! Come on, Enoch, show him who's boss!

4TH MAN: Let the bastard have it in the pills!

2ND MAN: Coming here taking our jobs . . .

3RD
WOMAN: NINE of them sleeping in one room! . . . Savages!

3RD MAN: Grinning picaninnies everywhere!

1ST
WOMAN: I mean, it wasn't just a house, it was an investment. We'd worked hard for it all our lives. When the first one came, we didn't bother too much, but then another came, and another . . .

4TH MAN: Breed like rabbits!

1ST
WOMAN: The whole tone of the avenue changed . . . and the value of the property . . . well, it just went down and down . . .

1ST MAN: About time we began to assert ourselves . . .

NARRATOR: Only another three balls of Powell's over to go. The coloured chap's beginning to sweat a little and I wouldn't be at all surprised to see him sent back to the Pavilion in the next few minutes . . . the Wolverhampton bowler's beginning his run . . .

(*Cry from the crowd*)

NARRATOR: Oh, he gets better all the time!

3RD
WOMAN: Bash his head in, Enoch!

1ST MAN: Would you let your daughter marry one of 'em? Would you?

2ND MAN: Breed like rabbits!

3RD MAN: We gave 'em their freedom and now look at 'em. Nothing but trouble.

2ND
 WOMAN: Grinning picaninnies.

4TH MAN: Trouble is, we're spoiling them, getting 'em used to things they don't really appreciate . . .

2ND MAN: Time they were taught their place. Too damned uppity!

1ST
 WOMAN: Eats Kit-e-Kat.

NARRATOR: Enoch's really bang at the top of his form. Enormously stylish bowler! He's already being tipped to captain England's next eleven. Fifth ball coming up now, a tremendously rocket of a bowl . . . that was almost there . . .

(*Crowd roars*)

1ST MAN: Come on, Enoch, old chap!

4TH MAN: Keep the nigger on the run!

3RD MAN: East is east and West is west is what I always sing . . .

1ST
 WOMAN: Up half the night singing and dancing . . . it's like being in the jungle.

2ND MAN: Grinning picaninnies!

2ND
 WOMAN: We gave them their freedom and now look at them! . . .

3RD MAN: Breed like rabbits!

3RD
 WOMAN: You're afraid to walk down the street at night for fear of . . .

4TH MAN: They're all sex-maniacs, of course. The men have all got enormous great . . .

1ST
  WOMAN: Kit-e-Kat! Tins and tins of it!

NARRATOR: Last ball of Powell's over! He's gone well back ... and, he's tearing down towards the bowling line like an Olympic sprinter ... Oh, magnificent! yes ... he's ... out ...

  (*Crowd howls*)

ALL: Out! Out! Kill him!

  (*They begin to strike out at the batsman with rolled up newspapers, umbrellas and handbags. They leap and shriek like hounds at the killing of a fox. The sound is reinforced by following tape*)

TAPE 61 (of a pack of hounds in full flight)

  (*One of the men grabs the bat and as he begins to bring it down on the batsman's head the lights black out*)

MASKS

Masks and make-up are related. They are disguises and can be used in a number of ways; in improvisation, plays, mimes and other entertainments.

There are not only extraordinary and fantastic disguises, but immense carnival heads, masks of stock characters, half masks and comic faces. Their place in theatre is necessarily limited but extraordinarily powerful in effect. For a more detailed discussion of the role of masks see page 283.

THE MASQUE

The masque was a spectacular, aristocratic form of dramatic entertainment which grew out of court revelry. It seems to have evolved from the simple mummers' play and reached its peak of elaboration in the reigns of James I and Charles I.

In the Middle Ages nobles and their ladies liked to while away an evening dancing in elaborate disguise, varying the dance with a suite of songs and rich poetical recitation. The performance usually had some central theme or story, generally allegorical and often cast in the form of an elaborate celebration of the patron of the Festivities, or ruler. In due time these performances became increasingly formal, till under the Tudors and more particularly the Stuarts, the best poets, musicians and designers of the day were employed to provide the material of which these rich

Top RITUAL AND CELEBRATION
A naming ceremony for a child in Rosedale, Yorkshire

Bottom SATIRE AND POLITICAL COMMENT
An episode from the Festival of Fools, 1965

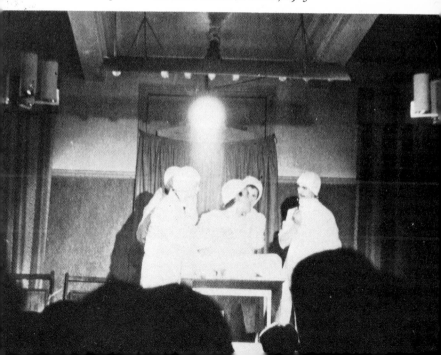

Left :
MYTH AND LEGEND
A Cornish Mystery Play in
Hoxton Hall, London

Below :
STORYTELLING AND
ROMANCE
'The Royal Pardon' in the
Beaford Centre, North Devon

spectacles were composed though the performers (Lords and Ladies of the Court) remained amateurs. The principal geniuses of the masque were Ben Jonson and Inigo Jones, though the poets Thomas Campion, Thomas Carew and James Shirley were among the famous writers for masques. Most of the famous ones were staged at Whitehall under the Stuarts, but they also took place in the great country houses; for example Milton's *Comus*, given in the Great Hall of Ludlow Castle in 1634.

Though the masque as we know it, an expensive whim of an extravagant aristocracy, died a natural death with the Commonwealth, it seems capable of revival in a modified form. The combination of a suite of songs, dances and poetry against a background of rich scenery could be revived with a contemporary theme for there is room for enchantment, magic and fantasy combining words, music and the richest scenic effects in the contemporary theatre.

Perhaps we find this already in a form, Son et Lumière, which has much in common with the original Masques, though adapted to the more democratic and technological processes of our own age.

Son et Lumière, which was introduced into this country from France about eleven years ago, is what its name suggests: first sound, then light, a form of drama in which both play an important part. Using a building or complex of buildings as a broad backcloth, sound plays a major part in the evocation of the historical past and its relationship with the present which is what the form is 'about'. Large dramatic effects are desirable; the script, music and sound effects have to measure up to the impressive unity and monumental eloquence of a building seen under moving light in the dark.

Though the technical and financial problems of a Son et Lumière performance are not inconsiderable they are not impossible on a modest scale. It links documentary drama with the techniques of the Radio Ballad, and both with the life of a community.

A Book of Masques. Various authors (O.U.P.)
Stuart Masques and the Renaissance Stage. A. Nicoll (Harrap)

MIXED MEDIA ANTHOLOGIES
An exciting development of the anthology-programme in which a number of prose-excerpts, poems and dramatic passages are put together and read

(see page 31) is the multi-media anthology in which there is also singing, dancing, music, mime and so on. The basic idea of exploring one theme remains unchanged; the more complex means by which this is developed can include a variety of dramatic activities beyond the scope of the simple readings and dramatised excerpts of an anthology programme. These could include projected slides, film-sequences, sound effects, taped interviews, shadow and rod-puppets, music, songs, readings, improvisations, mime etc.

There is no limit to the kind of theme that can be tackled or the complexity of its development. Nor are there limitations to the number of people taking part: two or three to as many as a hundred; singers, actors, dancers, instrumentalists, readers, technicians all contributing something of their own.

The most extensive development of mixed media work are the Theatre Folk Ballads which Charles Parker has developed with an amateur group, The Leaveners in Birmingham. Excerpts from two works, *Of One Blood* and *Dog in the Manger* are quoted below, because we feel that this affords a better introduction to one aspect of this form than pages of abstract discussion. The Leaveners is a Birmingham group comprising folk-singers and formal singers, folk instrumentalists and formal instrumentalists, experts on tape recording, photography and slide projection, and a dance drama group based in a Birmingham school. The form of both works is a synthesis of song, dance and dramatic action, interspersed with tape recordings and with still and moving picture projection into the auditorium – a form which Charles Parker has been working with in Birmingham for the past ten years.

The first extract, from *Of One Blood*, compiled in 1967, calls for speakers, singers, chorus, caption, tape. *Of One Blood* is a collage of racial prejudice from Rhodesia and South Africa to Birmingham, England and Birmingham, Alabama to Nazi Germany. Here is a typical sequence:

85. SPEAKER: New York, December 27th. Asked in a Television Interview whether Rhodesia was committed to white supremacy, Mr Ian Smith said 'No . . . we are committed to civilisation'.

(Guardian 28/12/66)

86. SPEAKER: Washington, October 17th. President Johnson today left for what he described as a hopeful mission to Asia. 'I shall do

my best to advance the cause of peace and of human progress,'
he said.

(*The Times 18/10/66*)

87. SPEAKER : Johannesburg, September 14th. Mr Vorster tonight offered
friendship to all countries. 'We stand before the world as a
small nation who believes in Christianity and Civilisation.'

(*Guardian 15/9/66*)

88. SINGER : And so throughout the ages,
We have seen how progress marches on its way
No wheel no rack, no Spanish boot
For Alabama's prisoners today . . .

CHORUS : But these are more enlightened days
Cruel men and savage ways
We left long ago,
Now every man may walk his road in peace,
For all are free.

The plague still runs throughout this world today
From Smethwick to Rhodesia and back,
A plague of ignorance and hate, Men
Walk in fear because their skin is black.

CHORUS : But in these more enlightened days,
No room for all these savage ways
Leave them let them go,
Now every man should walk his road in peace,
Let men be free.

89. SINGER : (Freely Verse 1 *The Colour Bar Strike*.)
(a) My Union badge shows two joined hands
With a lighted flame in common fight
But trouble's brewing at the sheds
For both these working hands are white . . .

90. SPEAKER : Wolverhampton, June 8th. Mr James Latham, a chargehand
said 'Their door is only eighteen inches from my door and we
shall be using the same stairs. My wife is frightened of
coloured folk. They are all right to work with but not to live
with.'

(*Guardian 8/6/66*)

91. SINGER: (b) But working hands are white and black
                   And the work they do is all the same
                   But prejudice and fear came in
                   To break that grip and dim that flame.

92. SPEAKER: *Times* August 11th, 1967. A Sikh bus driver who has defied
               Wolverhampton transport department ban on beards and
               turbans, said he was told by a traffic superintendent yesterday,
               to report for afternoon duty without beard and turban – or
               be dismissed.

93. SINGER: (c) The shunters broke that grip one day,
                   The King's Cross Goods-yard went on strike,
                   Not in the fight for better pay
                   But a coloured man they did not like.

               (d) They did not like that coloured man
                   They wouldn't work with him they said;
                   In truth it touched their overtime
                   And to a colour bar it led.

               (e) The colour bar strikers soon went back
                   Jim Figgins led the N.U.R.,
                   And when they asked for his support
                   He said, 'We'll have no colour bar'.

               (f) Jim Figgins said 'Get back to work
                   This is a strike we'll not support,
                   This is the kind of ignorance
                   The unions have always fought.

94. SPEAKER: June 6th. White and coloured tenants marched side by side
               through Islington yesterday. 'We demand council action . . .
               No colour bars here – but £7 for a hovel' . . . said their
               posters.

95. SPEAKER: *Times*, October 5th, 1967. A Barrister appeared in court at
               Inner London Sessions yesterday wearing a white turban
               instead of the more conventional curly horse-hair wig . . .
               he won his case too.

95. SINGER: (g) But though the union won that fight
                   The pressures there are rising higher
                   Smoke rises in the Engine sheds
                   And where there's smoke, there's always fire.

(h) Man don't let smoke get in your eyes,
   Kindle that flame and keep it bright,
   To proud traditions still be true
   And make those joined hands black and white.

96. SPEAKER: *Guardian*, February 5th, 1968. A march by silent Sikhs in Wolverhampton yesterday stretched for more than a mile with demonstrators seven abreast. They carried banners saying, 'Sikhs laid down their lives for Britain wearing beards and turbans'.

97. SPEAKER: Ludwigsour, April 27th. More than seven thousand mourners, mostly men of the former waffen SS or their relatives, today paid their last respects to the former SS General Sepp Dietrich.

98. SPEAKER: *Guardian*. March 3rd, 1967. Letter to the Editor. Sir, a friend tells me that posters are being displayed in Lancashire to persuade good Britons to emigrate to South Africa. I would like to acquaint potential emigrants with some background information.

99. SPEAKER: As the coffin, carried by former generals was lowered into the grave the band played the former soldiers song, 'I had a comrade'.

100. SPEAKER: White South Africans held a cultural rally at Keilbron in the Orange Free State. Thousands crowded round an open air stage one night to hear a voice say that God himself had sent Hendrix Verwoerd to govern South Africa.

101. SPEAKER: Mourners from Belgian, Danish and Austrian waffen SS units were among those who placed wreaths. An Austrian barked out 'Heil Sepp Dietrich. Heil this German soil of yours', as he wept over the grave.

102. SPEAKER: As the voice died away, the Prime Minister of South Africa appeared unexpectedly against the dark night between two blazing torches. While Dr Verwoerd stood motionless during the singing of 'Let the blessing of the Lord descend upon him' the words 'Chosen Leader' and 'Chosen people' shone from the stage in luminous letters.

103. SPEAKER: Bonn, April 5th, 1966. This week 'Der Spiegel' publishes an
                evocative picture of a torchlight procession in Nuremburg
                organised by the local branch of the National Democratic
                Party with the caption 'Has a long day's journey into the
                night begun?'

The second long extract from *Dog in the Manger* 'a Dramatic Commentary upon Christmas 1961' was drawn from the *Coventry Nativity
Play*, *The Wakefield Second Shepherds Play*, English Folk Carols, Contemporary newspaper accounts and the Bible: 'For the past four years,
the Harborne Players have taken a version of the *Coventry Nativity Play*
to hospitals and churches in and around Birmingham. In the process
they have developed a form of music drama in which carols, verse,
dramatic dialogue and slide projection of works of art are integrated into a
unified performance. So that alongside modern dress shepherds, the
audience sees the Crivelli *Adoration of the Shepherds*, and hears an
English mediaeval carol, in an attempt that the combined statement
should give a burningly contemporary meaning to the Nativity story.
In this troubled year, the formation of the Co-ordinating Committee
against Racial Discrimination has fired us to try and extend the form of
this work to embrace the happenings of today. Another element has been
added to the pattern – tape recordings of stories of racial discrimination
and racial harmony, as they are reported almost every day . . .'

160. CHOIR: Lullay, my lyking, my dear son, my sweeting,
                Lullay, my dear heart, my own dear darling.

    SOLO: I that am a maiden sitten and sing
                To lull a little child, a sweete lording

161. LIGHTING: ON   Crib light

    CHOIR: Lullay, my lyking, my dear son, my sweeting,
                Lullay, my dear heart, my own dear darling.
                            (Guitar improvises behind:)

162. LIGHTING: ON   F 2
                            KILL Lantern

163. IST KING: Hail, Lord, that all this world hath wrought,
                Hail, God and man, together in fere.

For Thou hast made all thing of nought
Albeit that Thou liest poorly here.
A cup full of gold here I have Thee brought
In tokening Thou art without peer.

163A. L/SPEAKER: The price of gold fell a little in the London bullion market
    Nave   yesterday, but demand from the Continent and elsewhere
continued on a large scale . . . Near bedlam broke out on the
Johannesburg stock exchange in the scramble to deal in
gold shares. Experienced brokers described market activity
as the most frenzied since the pound sterling was devalued in
1949. One man said, 'This is the nearest thing to organised
mob violence I have ever seen . . .'

                                                      (The Guardian 22/10/60)

164. SOLO: That eternal Lord is He that made alle thing
            Of alle lordes He is Lord, of alle kings King.
                       (Guitar improvises behind:)

165. 2ND KING: Hail be Thou, Lord of high magnificence
            In tokening of priesthood, and dignity of office,
            To Thee I offer a cup full of incense;
            For it behoveth Thee to have such sacrifice.

165A. L/SPEAKER: A Christmas present, 'for the woman who has everything
    Nave   else' was offered for sale today in the 'New York Times': a
diamond and ruby studded gold automatic coffee maker.
The price – £50,000 . . .

                                                      (The Guardian 19/12/60)

166. CHOIR: Lullay, my lyking, my dear son, my sweeting,
            Lullay, my dear heart, my own dear darling.
                       (Guitar improvises behind:)

167. 3RD KING: Hail be Thou, Lord long looked for!
            I have brought Thee myrrh for mortality;
            In tokening those shalt mankind restore
            To life by Thy death upon a tree.

167A. L/SPEAKER: The United States made public today, pictures of the first
    Nave   atomic bombs exploded over Hiroshima and Nagasaki in

1945 ... the 'Little boy' type dropped on Hiroshima, and the 'Fat boy' type which devastated Nagasaki.

(*The Guardian 7/12/60*)

167B. SOLO: There was mickle melody at that child's birth:
                 Although they were in heaven's bliss they made mickle mirth.

   CHOIR: Lullay, my lyking, my dear son, my sweeting
                 Lullay, my dear heart, my own dear darling.

168. MARY: God have mercy, kings, of your goodness!
                 By the guiding of the Godhead hither are ye sent;
                 The provision of my sweet son, your ways home redress,
                 And ghostly reward you for your present.

169. GUITAR: 'bell chimes' intro. (E,D,C,A) for:

170. LANTERN: *Reprise Slide 20 (C.26) Botticelli Angels-detail*

171. LIGHTING: KILL F 2

172. CHOIR: *Angels* bright they sang that night and saiden to that child
                 Blessed be Thou, and so be she, that is so meek and mild.

173. LANTERN: *Reprise Slide 21 (C.25) Botticelli Nativity*
                 (*Exit Mary and Joseph*)

   CHOIR: Lullay, my lyking, my dear son, my sweeting
                 Lullay, my dear heart, my own dear darling.

174. LIGHTING: ON   FY
                           KILL   Crib light, Lantern

A more modest project than this (at Scarsborough College) grew out of the idea of steam locomotion. There were paintings, models, drawings and working engines in a large hall. At the same time a varied entertainment moved round the room, with musicians playing folk songs on a balcony, with poems read to music from a small platform, and sketches about railways, both comic and melodramatic, which were staged amongst the recorded sounds of engines, the blowing of whistles and even the waving of red and green flags.

A further example evoked the day-to-day life in a village, and the continuity of life in a place whose past and present are inextricably interwoven. Slides of old and recent photographs were shown against a recorded background of familiar sounds – (church bells, traffic noises, the steady tread of a herd of cows moving up the lane on their way to milking, the sound of a beat-dance across the meadows) and the recorded voices of the village's youngest and oldest inhabitants talking about their lives. Songs were also included and documents read in this programme which was devised for performance in the village itself.

Such 'entertainments' are one of the most satisfactory ways in which a group can achieve something of dramatic significance. This can be of any length or complication, from the examples we have already described, to the more developed form of such presentations as Joan Littlewood's attack in concert-party/Pierrot style on the horrors of the First World War in *Oh What a Lovely War* or the documentaries described between pages 38 and 46.

MIMES

In Documentaries, mixed-media shows and, indeed, anywhere where non-naturalistic acting is required, mime, which is an aspect of improvisation, can play an important part.

Mime has always been a part of drama; for its origins are so primitive that it can hardly be classed as drama at all. All over the ancient world there were jugglers, acrobats and public entertainers of different kinds who displayed their art in the market-places, at festivals or whenever or wherever they could secure an audience.[1] 'Among these nameless mountebanks there were some with a special gift for mimicry. They could imitate with their voices the neighing of horses, the sound of thunder, and so forth; even more important was their command of gesture, an art carried to a high pitch in the ancient world, involving the active use of every limb and great control of facial expression. Such improvised performances were especially popular among the Doric peoples of Greece.'

From the Roman period until the present day mime has passed through varying degrees of popularity reaching its height at the time of the Commedia dell'Arte (see page 34) when a form of extemporised comedy was in use in which the actors wore masks and employed the spoken word together with mime and gesture. The familiar figure of the

[1] William Beare in the *Oxford Companion to the Theatre*.

73

harlequinade, and much of the traditional word gesture of ballet and traditional mime may be traced to the same source.

Today mime is once more a purely silent art, in which the actor conveys his meaning by gesture, movement and expression. The fight between the two brothers in *Close the Coalhouse Door* (see page 39); the cricket match in the *Festival of Fools* (see page 59) and the actors, in *The Royal Pardon*, furiously rowing across the sea to France on the floor of the acting area, are all instances of the use of mime:

CLOWN: (*sings*)
'For travelling expenses three and fourpence per head
(Rowing rowing over the sea to France)
They'd pay more to the gravediggers when we are dead
(If it blows up a gale we haven't a chance)'

The Kings great Lord Chamberlain found us a boat
(Rowing rowing over the sea to France)
But he couldn't be bothered to see if it would float
(If it blows up a gale we haven't a chance)

CROKE: We must be about in the middle by now. Can you see the lighthouse at Calais?

CLOWN: Not a sign of it, Mr Croke.

WILLIAM: I can't see the Dover lighthouse any longer, that's something anyway.

ESMERALDA: We must be in the middle by now.

CLOWN: Very comforting to hear that, dearie, it's the deepest part just here.

Later, running into a storm they are wrecked. Without the use of properties of any kind, but with lighting and a musical accompaniment, they re-created the disaster as the boat breaks up and they are spilt out into the surf and struggle ashore. Thus mime can be integrated into a production, eclipsing time and suggesting actions which could not possibly be represented on the stage.

MUMMERS' PLAYS
The Mumming plays of rural England, amongst the oldest forms of drama,

were never intended for the stage or for a sophisticated audience. They had their origin in the pagan rituals performed to propitiate the forces of nature, which began with a sword dance, the climax of which was the locking of the swords above the head of the pretended victim to symbolise the death of the spirit of life of the old year.

During the fifteenth century the dance form was expanded into a crude dramatic shape which included character and dialogue. This form still survives. The version varies from place to place, but always follows the pattern laid down by the sword dance. There is a short prologue craving the hearers' attention and announcing the show. The central feature is a fight which brings the hero to the point of death. He is brought back to life by the doctor (the medicine man of the original pagan ritual). The end concludes with general clowning and gaiety. At Marshfield, in Gloucestershire, the play is enacted every Boxing Day (see plate 16). The characters include Old Father Christmas, King William, Little John, Beelzebub the Devil and the Doctor. A modern version of such ritualistic popular drama is the work of the Bread and Puppet Theatre from New York, who perform in the open air, in streets and open spaces (see Street Theatre, page 101). A simple musical prelude – with drum and pipes – a strongly allegorical theme; and a puppet-like style of acting are important elements of such work in the open air.

The Mummers' Play. R. J. E. Tiddy (Oxford, Clarendon Press)
   Contains excellent introduction, and prints 33 extant plays.
The English Festivals. Laurence Whistler (Heinemann)
The English Folk Play. E. K. Chambers (Oxford, Clarendon Press)

The advisory service of the English Folk Dance and Song Society at 2 Regent's Park Road, London N.W.1, is very helpful. From them, too, *The Symondsbury Mumming Play*, is available.

MUSIC HALL

The 1960's have seen something of a revival of interest in Music Hall, starting just where Music Hall did originally, as free entertainment in the bars of working-class pubs.

This Music Hall began modestly enough in the middle of the nineteenth century, soon created its own stars, who travelled incessantly from one town to another, and achieved enviable reputations. Throughout the last decades of the nineteenth century and up to the end of the first World War it provided a uniquely vigorous popular theatre combining variety entertainments, songs and comic turns. Some of the greatest Music Hall artists, in fact, hardly sang at all, devoting themselves to dramatic monologues in which they portrayed and commented on such basic situations as courting, getting married and living with the wife, to audiences drawn from every walk of life. Vesta Tilley, Little Tich, Marie Lloyd, Harry Lauder, George Robey, Gus Elen, Dan Leno and many others were great individuals rather than ensemble actors as we understand the term.

As a form, a loose structure (as *Oh What a Lovely War* so brilliantly showed) it still holds good. If it has a future it lies this way rather than in terms of revival. Nevertheless, as numerous amateur revivals, such as the Tavistock Repertory Company's *Gas Light and Garters* have shown, the Music Hall can still make an audience sing and weep and roar with laughter and go out warmed. Its good humour, its topicality, its bawdy and nostalgic charm, its variety of mood and humour seem irreplaceable. In no comparable way can a group of actors really achieve the same apparently spontaneous and immediate contact with an audience. For the core of the appeal of the Halls did not lie in social convention, but in the confrontation of actor and audience, both manifestly of flesh-and-blood.

MUSIC:
Feldman and Co. Ltd
Lawrence Wright Music Company
Asherberg, Hopwood and Crew Ltd
Francis, Day and Hunter Ltd

TURNS:
Not published. 'Patter', too, is only available on old records or discs or such L.P.'s as:
The Great Days of Music Hall (Music for Pleasure) MFP1146
Top of the Bill (Fidelio) ATL4010

BOOKS:
British Music Hall. Raymond Mander and Joe Mitchenson (Studio Vista)
Sweet Saturday Night. Colin McInnes (MacGibbon and Kee)

MYSTERY PLAYS

By the end of the thirteenth century there was a flourishing tradition of vernacular religious drama in this country. The first liturgical plays were written for performance by priests and choir boys in church, but as more incidents were added, more space was needed, and these were often performed using the whole church as a multiple setting. Little by little, as the plays became more elaborate (and bawdier too) the drama moved from church to churchyard and from churchyard to market place where more secular influences were able to creep in. The most common form was the mystery or miracle play, a series of dramatic scenes on subjects from the Bible, often enlivened with broad humour and grotesque licence. Four[1] cycles survive in England, those of *York* (48 episodes), *Coventry* (42), *Wakefield or Townley* (32) and *Chester* (25) which were performed in the open air either in a static setting (see plate 10) or mounted on two-storey 'pageants' or carts which paraded round the town. Each episode in the cycle became the concern of a particular trade guild, usually one connected with its work; *Noah's Ark* was staged by the shipwrights, *Jonah and the Whale* by the fishmongers (see pages 134–8 for modern editions and list of books of religious drama).

Many successful revivals of the cycles have been mounted. The most notable is at York where the plays are now performed every three years in an open air setting in front of the ruins of St Mary's Abbey. Many hundreds of local amateurs take part though the main parts are played by professionals. They have also been given from carts.

Many groups could either use some of the Mysteries as Charles Parker did in his *Dog in the Manger*, a Dramatic Commentary upon Christmas, 1961, drawn from the Coventry *Nativity Play*, the Wakefield *Second Shepherds Play*, the Bible and English Folk Carols (see pages 70–2) or make use of them as John Bowen did in his own adaptation *The Fall and Redemption of Man* (Faber). Likewise a group, making use of one or other of the Bible stories as a framework for its work, could improvise and develop their own play in the manner described between pages 24 and 29. Such productions could be toured throughout an area from church to church and developed in conjunction with choirs, folk-singers, readers etc.

[1] A fifth cycle, recently discovered, *The Cornish Cycle*, was performed in 1969 at Piran Round.

The use of both Mediaeval and Modern material in juxtaposition could also be introduced by carol singers who might bring small plays into their tours, or into such fossilised rituals as the *Festival of Nine Carols and Lessons* which could be completely rethought in contemporary dramatic terms.

Here is a description of another rather different production (by Roland Miller) of the Cornish Mystery Play *The Making of the World*, which was given in Hoxton Hall in London, August 1965 (see plate 3).

Hoxton Hall, he writes, 'is now run by the Society of Friends as a community centre, and the main part of the building is a Victorian Music Hall which is used for many and varied dramatic activities. I put on the Miracle play with two professional actors playing God and Lucifer, students from a U.N. work camp at the Hall playing angels and other minor parts, and local children and teenagers as animals, birds and fishes in the creation. The décor was gathered from bombsites and scrap heaps in the district, the audience was almost entirely of local people. It was possible to use the whole of the Hall – balconies on two levels, and the auditorium, as well as the stage, for the action, so that the audience was entirely inside the setting, in Hell (on the lowest level) or with the angels in Heaven.'

PAGEANTS, CARNIVALS AND POPULAR ENTERTAINMENT

A great many pageants have been so gruesome – Merrie Englande with rain – the form has earned itself a bad reputation. But there is no reason why this form of entertainment should not be revived and developed along fresh lines.

Originally the word 'pageant' referred to the movable stage on which scenes of mediaeval religious plays were performed; later it came to be applied to the entertainment enacted upon them, and so to its modern usage to describe a procession made up of spectacular tableaux and usually including songs, dances, and dramatic scenes with some bearing on local history. Not always a procession, it also refers to vast spectacles with large crowds of actors which are presented not only out of doors but in settings as diverse as a cathedral, a circus, a civic square or an exhibition hall. A good director can do marvellous work if he enjoys semi-balletic movement of large groups, space, and the use of an exciting setting.

Plate 5 illustrates one kind of Pageant which involved staff, music and drama students, members of the Estate and local school children at Dartington Hall in Devon. The jousting match on hobby-horses pictured here formed the climax of the *Tournament of Ancient Sports*, which was much more than an elaborate reconstruction of a Mediaeval jousting match. The framework of *Ancient Sports* provided a joyful and really festive occasion in which everyone had a chance to contribute some invention of their own.

Local history (documentary drama again), parades, and popular large-scale entertainment of all kinds provide pretexts for the development of the kind of event listed below, all of which we have either been involved in or seen. At first sight, a group used to the comfortable shelter of a proscenium stage, may find our suggestions Utopian or impossibly difficult to achieve. This need not be the case. Think big and you begin to conceive on a larger scale. The police, fire officers, civic authorities, army, St John's Ambulance, etc., are, in our experience, invariably co-operative. Here are some ideas:

A Torch Masque for November 5th including fireworks, bonfires, bell-ringing, scenes of the Conspiracy and the Discovery of Guy Fawkes. A Proclamation read by the Town Crier.

The Anniversary of a town's Charter, a Church's Foundation, a Cathedral's Saint etc., in which local children from primary and secondary schools, musicians, amateur dramatic societies etc., all contribute.

Son et Lumière productions designed for a specific building or event, using tapes, music and light. Amateurs will be limited as far as lighting is concerned but not necessarily in other ways (see page 65).

Giant puppets for street performances (see plate 13).

A Christmas Festival in the Parish Church involving massed local choirs, instrumentalists, readers and musicians. Processions, projected slides, rod-puppets, readings, small 'plays' on a raised stage, hymn, carol and folk singing are all possible.

A children's entertainment on the beach or in a park. This could include music, little plays, dressing-up, treasure trails, painting. Actors can improvise situations invent games, provide a pierrot-type show in a simple booth or a Punch and Judy show and create a festive feeling with bunting, music, colour.

PANTOMIME AND CHILDREN'S THEATRE

Pantomime began life as an appendage to or variation on the Harlequinade, and by the 1800's had developed to the point where it became the main item on the bill, with perhaps a one-act comedy to start, and a vestigial comedy to round things off. Spectacular pantomimes with an exotic and irrational story invariably based on fairy tales but padded out with popular songs of the moment, topical comedy and audience participation routines were the main fare of nineteenth century popular audiences. Even today, though reduced to a tatty shadow of their former glory, the form remains; and a ready-made audience exists without even trying to fine one. If Pantomime has been commercialised out of recognition there seems, nevertheless, no reason why talented amateur groups should not attempt their own versions.

Alternatively plays like John Arden and Margaretta D'Arcy's *The Royal Pardon*; the *Big Noise at Fort Issimo* which was originally devised by Bernard Goss and students of the Rose Bruford College of Speech and Drama and developed by actors at the Northcott in Exeter; or familiar adaptations of *Beauty and the Beast*, Brian Way's *Pinocchio*, and some of the plays Caryl Jenner has presented at the Arts Theatre, all approach the ideal children's show.

The Royal Pardon, which John Arden calls a 'Romantic Pantomime', was developed from bedtime stories which he told his children. Dragons and maidens in distress, clowns and princes, songs and improvised music, are all part of this comical and magic play in which a soldier from the fields of Flanders joins a troupe of travelling actors to escape arrest by a melodramatic moustachioed police constable. The costumes are from the period that belongs to traditional folk-tales only, and the props are:

> 'Cardboard and paper and patches of glue
> Pleated and crumpled and folded in two
> With a pair of white fingers and a little bit of skill
> We make a whole world for the children to kill'.

John and Margaretta Arden's children kept a proprietory eye on *The Royal Pardon* as it was developed from their bedtime stories into a play, and then at rehearsals with the original cast of LAMDA students.

An interesting account of how the *Big Noise at Fort Issimo* was developed

Top PUPPET MAKING
Children make their own plays

Bottom PAGEANT AND CEREMONY
The Tournament of Ancient Sports at Dartington Hall, Totnes

Top COMMUNITY INVOLVEMENT
Moby Dick reconstructed in a Notting Hill playground, 1969.

Bottom A BOOTH STAGE
Pierrots on Scarborough Beach, 1907.

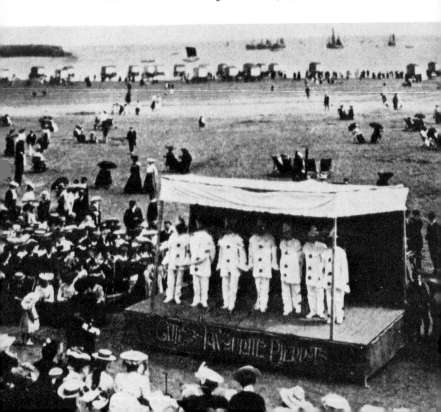

is worth quoting at this point. Bernard Goss, describing the evolution of this unusual but highly entertaining children's play, says: 'We acted out the adventure over and over again, continually finding ways of developing an incident or character. At last we knew we could go no further without a script; until then, we had acted the story spontaneously, using our own words which expressed the thoughts and feelings of our characters. Much of this improvisation had become a vital part of the story, and was written into the script with all the action we had devised – the painting of the toy soldiers, Mr Chuff's journey, etc. The shape of the play was extremely important; we had to sustain interest from the introduction of the soldiers to the discovery of the Big Noise and the Battle of Fort Issimo.

'When we performed the play, the audience reaction was carefully observed. We continually adapted it until we felt our story was a complete whole, and not just a succession of ideas. Soon the performances were almost over; then the unexpected happened. Tony Church, the Director of the Northcott, saw the show and suggested that the play should be presented in his theatre. Suddenly the whole idea was reborn. Sergeant Major Bumble, Fenella Bullbucket and all the others were to be acted by a new company in a brand new theatre. The Big Noise at Fort Issimo was to be heard again – but louder this time!'

This was a full-scale production done in a large new theatre. But children's productions can be just as magically done in a simple manner. This is true of the work of the American group, the Paper Bag Players, whose costumes and props are made out of cardboard and paper. The four players – two men and two women – wear black; they tell the children they have interesting stories to tell, gorgeous games to play. One piece deals with the plight of three fir trees which have been felled by a ruthless forester. A tree angel (with silver cardboard wings) presents the fir trees with the gift of movement. They learn to walk away from danger and discover the primeval joy of movement. 'Now that we have feet we can go anywhere' they chant in delight. Others include a mad tango with cardboard-box feet, a delicate and crazy game of Cowboys and Indians around a brown paper mountainside, and a sketch in which part of a secret message is revealed to the audience. All four players then disappear, returning one by one in weird sheet shape and show head and flowerpot neck disguises, to tell further passwords and sounds which eventually make sense of the nonsense. In the final sketch (of their visit to the Royal Court Theatre) a whole day and night-time was evoked by the power of a cardboard sun and a paper moon.

The value of work of this simplicity is that the children can be encouraged to go away and do it themselves, which is the real measure of success.

To do a children's show can be marvellously rewarding work for amateurs, for its stretches their powers of invention and controlled fantasy, but it should be approached with sincerity and humility if it is to succeed. The vulgar tinselly show is no substitute for real imagination in front of a child audience (see page 115).

Story of Pantomime. A. E. Wilson (Home and Van Thal)

PLAY-MAKING

Improvised drama is the basis of play-making, which sometimes suggests itself almost by accident when a particularly intriguing situation emerges. For every improvisation, however fragmentary, contains the germ or nucleus of a 'play'. There is no formula or rule-of-thumb technique about how this can be developed; different approaches yield different work and the talents, the past experience, the resources and aims of each group play a vital part in giving each 'production' a unique shape. As long as the group has some idea of what it is after, work can be evolved by a process of trial and error, to fresh invention, elimination and experiment. This calls for a really open situation where suggestions, talents, and fresh ideas, are all thrown into the melting pot and valued in relation to what the group feels it is attempting.

Just how valuable improvisation can be as a method of developing a 'play' is shown by one small example out of many, in which Ed Berman worked with children from the Beauchamp Lodge Community Settlement in Paddington who had never done any acting before. Between them they improvised and performed a Christmas entertainment, far removed from the usual nativity play. This account of the plot is from an article in *The Sunday Times*.

'It's the night before Christmas. Super Santa jets into London Airport with a sack full of toys, but runs foul of a grouchy customs man who throws him in jail for smuggling.

'He's not there for long. A gang of girls from the Hippy Den seduce the guards and set him free. Back at the Den they build him a new sledge. Santa's toys are dropped off on schedule, and the Queen of the Hippies is delivered – gift-wrapped – to the customs man. Christmas is a good idea after all, he thinks. Natch.'

The vitality and wit apparent even in the plot obviously derive from the excited imaginations which the children have brought to the theme of Santa Claus. Influences include comics, the pop scene, T.V. thrillers – the immediate interests of lively teenagers (see plate 7).

Ed Berman explains how he set about creating this improvisation at Beauchamp Lodge: 'It seems a very poor area, with a lot of racial trouble. The Warden of the Settlement got a group of kids together, boys and girls aged from thirteen to sixteen, some of whom can't even read and write, and we started with rhythm patterns. We sat around clapping hands, and then I got them to make up stories. Whenever we stopped clapping, some-one took up the tale from there. They agreed they should do a play together. I threw in the idea of Super Santa, split them into smaller groups, and they produced a number of skits which finally comprised the play.'

Obviously the intention of all improvisation of this nature is strongly therapeutical, as Berman points out: 'We want to help people towards self-expression through the arts, although the actual production is merely a by-product. What's important is that they learn to do things together.'

Not all of us want to act for therapeutical reasons. For though a large amount of improvised drama has only a limited communicative quality, and its purpose is largely concerned with providing opportunities to explore various aspects of human nature, personal relationships, or the environment in dramatic terms, most amateurs are still keen to perform before an audience. Too keen perhaps. Yet this is a sound instinct, for drama is concerned with communication to a greater degree than any other art.

The following approaches to the development of improvised work as the basis of play-making are probably the most important.

Work based on a plot

Possibly the easiest way of creating a play is to work on an established plot or story. The range of themes that can be tackled from verse, short stories, novels, ballads, folk-stories, songs, mythology, history or contemporary documentary evidence is limitless; and all of these can be developed in a number of different ways.

Imagine working on the ballad of *The Flying Cloud*, which tells of a young man first apprenticed to a cooper, who becomes a sailor, sails on a slaving vessel from Africa to the West Indies, becomes a pirate on the *Flying Cloud*, and after several adventures is caught, brought to Newgate, and finally hung from Tyburn Tree. Obviously many scenes can be worked out here, and the main character, Edward Holland, can be surrounded by others. It is the sort of story which can be built up into a play, or developed as documentary or anthology drama supplemented by the singing of shanties, the projection of slides, and readings from contemporary documents, journals and poems.

The structure of such a work is invariably chronological, though when the thoughts and feelings of one character are the main focus of interest, this need not be so. Then it can be more impressionistic, though this may demand a more subtle and imaginative insight into human motivation and character.

Work based on character

Another kind of approach, a development of what we have been discussing, is that which has its starting point in the creation of one character – as in, for example, Shakespeare's *Othello* or John Osborne's *Luther*. Here the work develops the conflicts within a character and between him and all the other people with whom he comes in contact. By a process of trial and error the material is explored and sifted until a really satisfactory form begins to emerge.

Work based on themes

Themes can be the basis of a great deal of work, either plays in which, as in Capek's *The Insect Play*, this is the unifying factor, or the mixed-media anthologies we have already discussed (see page 65). In the case of the play, plot and characters are developed solely in order to express or illustrate the theme. If, for example, this is the plight of old people, the group may explore ideas which may take either a documentary or fictional form. In either case the group would begin by a general discussion, followed by visits to old people and general research. Newspapers, magazines, the radio and television are all sources, as well as the old people themselves.

Some of this material will be abandoned, some fed back into improvisations or used in a documentary way; but all will need to be worked upon, edited and linked so that it takes on its own satisfactory dramatic form. The final drama might include a combination of dialogue scenes, recordings, projected photographs, reading and songs illustrating different aspects of old age and the problems of living with it.

The incomplete script

Work can also grow from a written script or scenario which may be an incomplete idea, the beginning, the mere hint of something which has dramatic possibilities. This can be developed by the group working alongside the author, re-writing on the spot (or taping and then re-writing) as each new sequence is explored in turn, and altered in the light of further improvisation. This happened with Frank Norman's *Fings Ain't Wot They Used T'Be* which was developed by Theatre Workshop actors, under Joan Littlewood, as follows:

'Frank sat in at all our rehearsals. He improvised with us as an actor, and when new script was needed, the way it was produced was by Frank improvising it himself on the stage to find out if it was theatrically possible. Sometimes we played our own parts, sometimes he did the acting. And if he felt he could use the lines he wrote while he was improvising, they were in. What Joan was after was the relationship of a scene to some facet of the character playing it. Frank knew far more about criminals and the way they reacted than any of us – he would be able to improvise what he thought a criminal would do in a given situation. That would be taken as a lead. This is a way of working for a unity between actor, author and producer.'

A group from a class of fourteen-year-old schoolchildren at Scarborough College wrote a play in a similar manner. One of them prepared a working script, telling of the revenge by a modern member of the Macdonald clan on his neighbours the Campbells, on the anniversary of the Glencoe massacre. The cast easily developed their own characters, ranging from a shrewish wife to a gormless son who entered gingerly carrying his father's claymore, murmuring 'I wondered what was blocking up the bogs'. The dialogue was invented and improvised during rehearsals. New scenes were added, like that in which the murderer was put into a mad house, and the whole cast became groaning, writhing, possessed madmen (an idea borrowed from the *Marat/Sade*, but carried out with great panache and individuality by a cast that had never seen Peter Brook's production).

When they had developed the original idea to their satisfaction, a new script was written out to fix the play which had emerged. It was a fuller script than the original version, rich with jokes, incidents, characterisation and effects which came from the personalities of the cast themselves. It was remarkable for its theatricality, a quality that was achieved by this particular method of working. One of the cast could play the bagpipes, and it suddenly occurred to them to march him on in full skirl at the moment of the murder. This imaginative and totally successful *coup de théâtre* could only have been conceived in a working atmosphere of freedom and improvisation, where each new idea can be tried, accepted or rejected. The result was a play created by the imaginations and inherent sense of drama of a group of lively children. It was a quite unique achievement; yet any group willing to work with the same freedom could produce something just as personal for themselves.

PLAYREADING AND PERFORMING NEW PLAYS

Many people in the amateur movement do not read plays or go to the theatre. The loss is theirs, for the study of plays as literature as well as in performance is an indispensable part of an actor's training, and something one takes delight in for its own sake. Plays should be read, theatres visited, new dramatists discovered, and familiar ones reassessed in the light of further experience. The two aspects of drama work, the study of plays and performance, are complementary rather than exclusive.

There is no shortage of plays to read during the fallow times when one is not in a production. For example, such 'chamber' plays of Strindberg's as *The Storm* and the *Ghost Sonata* which he wrote between 1907–9 for the Intima Tratern in Stockholm, or plays by Arrabal, Vitrac, Calderón. How many know Marivaux's sophisticated *The Game of Love and Chance*,

Ibsen's last play *When We Dead Awaken* or Pirandello's *Enrico IV*?
How can we know what these are like if we never see them performed?
Is the nine-thousandth revival of *Hay Fever* really justified?

If few groups read plays, even fewer write them or perform new ones. In
the course of their history some of the Little Theatres, notably the
Questors and the Tavistock Repertory Company have found new plays
and courageously produced them. James Saunders, whose first plays were
put on by Stephen Joseph's Theatre in the Round at Scarborough, had
his *Next Time I'll Sing To You*, first produced at the Questors, and
Charles Wood's *Dingo*, later seen at the Royal Court, was first produced
at the Bristol Arts Centre.

Only a tiny percentage of new plays are works of genuine talent and
originality, and of these an even smaller fraction are fully achieved works
of art. It is very unusual for a writer to spring fully equipped to write a
masterpiece for the stage. Playwriting is a complex and difficult art, and
there is no substitute for practical experience of the theatre. This is where
amateur groups could play a significant part. The best groups, such as
the Questors who now have an annual new play Festival, can nourish
writers by encouragement and by giving them the opportunity of seeing
their own plays, in performance. 'I like to find a new play of promise',
writes Stephen Joseph,[1] who did so much to help unknown dramatists,
'merely in the hope that the playwright will develop and write good
plays eventually. Playwriting is a difficult job, and it is wrong to expect
a first play to be good; if it is, the playwright will probably be a one-off
merchant who will never write a better. It may seem a bit heartless
to present an audience with a new play that I know is not good, is no
more than promising merely. It would be so if most of the secondhand
plays that have already been done in London were better. They are not.'

USEFUL BOOKS ON PLAY APPRECIATION (suitable for a group library)

Going to the Theatre. John Allen (Phoenix)
Looking at a Play. Bridges-Adams (Phoenix)
Understanding Drama. D. Brooks and Heilman (Harrap)
You and the Theatre. C. Landstone (Macdonald and Evans)
Watching a Play. C. K. Munro (Gerald Home)

[1] In *Theatre in the Round* (Barrie and Rockliff).

New Directions

The Art of the Play. Herman Ould (Pitman)
The Theory of Drama. Allardyce Nicoll (Harrap)
Drama in Performance. Raymond Williams (Muller)
Study of Drama. H. Granville-Barker (C.U.P.)

PUPPETS

Puppetry can be a part of any dramatic performance. Some scenes in a play might work better with puppets than with human actors, though this, of course, depends on the style of the production. It is always worth experimenting with improvised puppets in rehearsal. Puppets are usually associated with children's entertainment but there is no reason why their particular qualities should not be used to great effect in adult perform-ances; and, in fact, the major surviving puppet traditions (the Sicilian, the Czechoslovakian, and the great Bunraku theatre of Japan) draw their audiences from all sections of the population and are considered serious dramatic forms.

Modern puppetry is best developed with an entirely experimental approach. 'If puppetry is to survive and develop in the modern world,' writes Helen Binyon,[1] 'it is essential that there should be as many serious experiments in as many different directions as possible. Puppetry is not a one-man affair, but the shared creative activity of a group, and the greater the variety of talents available the better.' It is for this reason that we have largely limited this section to examples of modern puppetry which are likely to give a picture of their largely unexplored possibilities.

Puppetry is story-telling or playmaking with dolls – glove, rod, shadow and marionette – and the different ways which have been devised to bring a puppet to life give it its particular character and range of ex-pression.

In this book we cannot hope to describe each type in detail; excellent books on how to make puppets are given at the end of this section. Even though a knowledge of construction is essential the main concern of puppetry is not the puppet: it is the performance. Many bad shows are the result of a mistaken aim on the part of their creators whose concern, as Helen Binyon says, 'is in mechanical ingenuity rather than in any form of drama. They have not given anything like the same thought or know-

---

[1] In *Puppetry Today.* Helen Binyon (Studio Vista).

ledge to the point or planning of the whole show as to the jointing of individual puppets, choosing not only a theme that has been used many times before, but the actual forms and features.'

Shadow Puppets

The shadow puppet is a two-dimensional object casting its shadow on a two-dimensional area of space. There are three essential elements: a screen made of some translucent material (paper, calico) stretched on a frame; a light (perhaps from a slide projector) fixed behind it and projected on to the screen which is surrounded by darkness; and something which can be held and moved about between the light and the screen, so that it casts a moving shadow on the screen. This can be virtually anything, either transparent or opaque, solid or patterned – cardboard, cellophane, perforated zinc, feathers, a scrap of wicker-work etc., which can be held up by rods or wires.

A developed form of shadow puppetry has been evolved by students of the Hochschule für Bildende Kunste in West Berlin who study Puppetry as part of their normal training on a Foundation Course. They came to London in 1962 and gave a most stimulating show at Goldsmith's College. It is described here by A. R. Philpott:[1]

'The show was built up of items each of which was devised by one student. . . . An interesting arrangement of five shadow screens of varying shapes and sizes and elevation were set in an overall position, the width of the hall . . . the vision of the audience was constantly switched from screen to screen as item followed item swiftly, some being extremely brief. The first item was *Spiel mit Glas* and made use of several mirrors (on the marionette stage) the puppets being simply a pink disc on strings, a triangle of glass and a five-sided box-like figure whose sections opened and shut and were each of a different colour, moving in space, with a combination of effects (objects, shadows, reflections) achieved by movement, lighting, effects with appropriate music.

'Item 2 was *Kaleidoscope* – the title being "spelled out" by letters each on a translucent coloured square, like a child's game. A film-like technique employed here, with the whole screen covered with moving patterns and textures and touches of colour by montage.

[1] This account appeared in *The Puppet Master*, Volume 7, No. 3, Spring 1963.

'Item 4 (this is an abridged version of Mr Philpott's report) *Amphibien*
announced by two fantastic coloured shadow fish swimming across the
screen with the title between them. The actual items were three dimen-
sional marionettes, metal-outline figures, moving mouths, rolling ball
eyes, moving fins, with water-noises "off". (Here and in some other items a
white back-drop-cum-screen allowed action behind and in front, first
distorted shadows and then tangible figures throwing shadows from the
front, with front lighting, giving considerable amplification.)

'Item 14 – Paint-brush announcement with painters arms and hands in
silhouette, some finger painting, the final sponge-off with water running
down the screen.'

Glove Puppets

The basis of a glove puppet, and the source of all its movement, is a
human hand; this gives it a different character from the other forms of
puppet. It is worked from below, and the movements it makes with its
head, hands, body and arms (its legs, if it has any, only dangle) have the
qualities of the movements of a human hand (see plate 5).

Traditionally the puppets' heads and hands were carved out of wood
while the 'costume', which is a glove, is sewn together with softer materials.
But the head can be made out of papier mâché or cloth, which is built up
round the tube into which the index finger (which holds the head)
fits. The glove puppeteer is completely identified with his puppet and
should have a talent for spontaneous acting that he can express through
his puppet. The grotesque proportions of the glove puppet (its large
head and short arms, often exaggerated in size compared with its body)
are particularly suited to a rather knock-about parody of human activities
(such as Punch and Judy). An example is given by Helen Binyon: 'It was
in Paris, soon after the war, that I saw a young Puppet Company', she
writes, 'the Comédiens des Champs Elysées, give a most brilliant glove-
puppet show. There were four little plays, all quite different, and all
acted with tremendous style and verve. They were *La Jalousie du Bar-
bouille* by Molière, *Le Petit Retable de Don Christobal* written by Garcia
Lorca specially for puppets – they had a rod-puppet for the poet narrator,
Les Mariés de la Tour Eiffel by Jean Cocteau, and the one I remember the
most vividly, an extract from a farce by Georges Courteline called

Hortense, couche-toi! The situation turned on an old Paris bye-law which said that no landlord could evict a tenant whose wife was just about to have a baby. The scene is the flat of a tenant who has not paid his rent. Sent by the landlord, the furniture removal men arrive, and start to take away the wardrobe, the piano, the chest of drawers. The tenant returns, orders his wife to bed, waves the bye-law at the removal men, who start bringing all the furniture back, and so on. The joy was, of course, the heaving and manoeuvring and groaning of the little furniture men moving the large furniture, all done with a beautiful sense of timing.'

Punch and Judy scripts in D. Holbrook's *Thieves and Angels* (C.U.P.)

Rod Puppets

The rod puppet is held above the puppeteer, so that instead of being on his hand like a glove, it is on the end of a rod supported from below. It has no legs as such (the supporting rod is usually hidden by a long robe) and its arms are moved by two further rods: an arrangement which results in a very beautiful and dignified appearance with great dramatic power. The expressive features are head and arm ones, and the puppet can be moved so that it appears to be walking. Rod puppets are amongst the easiest form of puppet to make, the rod can be a length of dowelling, a broom handle or bamboo and the heads can be made of wood, cloth, papier mâché or even pottery, while almost any kind of material can be used for the costume.

Rod puppet shows are usually given in the same kind of booth as are used for glove. The performances are normally limited to rod puppets but plays can be developed with a combination of human actors and rod puppets as in the Polish Sivierszez Puppet Theatre's production of Stravinsky's *A Soldier's Tale* in which the 'actors' acted in front, while to the beat of music the puppets moved across a wide opening in the booth. This combination of human actors and puppets has been developed, too, by an English troupe, Polka Puppets, founded in 1967 and at productions at the Cannon Hill Centre for young people in Birmingham. Polka's items combine mime and clowning by visible actors who tell stories to the audience while the narrative is enacted by glove, string and rod puppets on a booth puppet-stage behind. The items are taken from the widest possible range of sources; a mummers' play, a Mediaeval morality, and a harlequinade based on a Commedia dell'Arte plot, while one of the actors (in a troupe of three) tells a Japanese story with an origami.

Marionettes

Marionettes are controlled, from above, by strings. There are very simple ones with strings leading only to the head and elaborately jointed puppets with a multitude of strings. Though they are mostly made to represent human beings, they can take widely different forms. The puppet can be made out of jointed and carved wood; or, more simply, like a doll stuffed with stockinette with tapes for joints.

Puppetry Today. Helen Binyon (Studio Vista)
   The best general introduction. Practical but not over-technical. Very well illustrated.
Puppets and Plays. M. Batchelder and V. L. Comer (Faber)
   An excellent introduction on how to create, rehearse and present puppet plays. Creative, practical.
Shadow Puppets. Olive Blackham (Barrie and Rockliff)
Puppets into Actors. Olive Blackham (Barrie and Rockliff)
   On marionettes.
Play with Light and Shadow (the art and techniques of shadow theatre). Herta Schönewolf (Reinhold/Studio)

THE SOUND BALLAD

One of the most significant features of the radio ballad[1] – 'a form of narrative documentary in which the story is told entirely in the words of the actual participants themselves as recorded in real life; in sound effects which are also recorded on the spot, and in songs which are based on these recordings, and which utilise traditional or "folk-song" modes of expression' – is that it dispenses entirely with scripted narration or dramatisation, relying upon the field recordings and the song lyrics to carry the story. Clearly the technique is of value to those shaping their own drama.

The genre was first developed by Charles Parker and Ewan MacColl who were commissioned by the B.B.C. to prepare a documentary radio programme on the life and death of John Axon, an engine driver, who had met his death in a railway accident in February 1957.[1] 'When they arrived

[1] Charles Parker's own definition in the introduction to the folder with the Argo L.P. *The Ballad of John Axon* (Argo RG474).

in Stockport – where John Axon had lived and worked – to talk with his widow and his workmates, they brought with them one of the midget tape recorders which were then becoming available, intending to record their conversations simply as source material for an eventual script . . . it soon became apparent, however, that the material they were beginning to record merited much more than this. Within half an hour of the first visit a next-door-neighbour, himself an engine driver for twenty years, was saying:

'the old railwaymen – it was a tradition. It was part of your life, it went through – railways went through the back of your spine like Blackpool went through rock.'

While it is was perfectly possible – and really much more convenient – simply to incorporate passages like this into script and give them to actors to speak, it seemed illogical to do this when the original utterance had been so powerful and was still immediately available on tape.

Thus was born the first of the Radio Ballads – which include *The Big Hewer* (about coal) the *Song of a Road* (about the building of the M1) and *The Travelling People* (about nomads and tinkers); they depend upon the interaction between field recorded speech and studio performed music which provides the essential dynamic of the radio ballad form.

They have to be heard to appreciate their power of effect; for in all these ballads the music, which is written by Ewan MacColl and improvised by musicians in relation to the speech and effects, plays a part of the greatest importance; heightening the emotion and revealing the epic and heroic in the commonplace.

Ewan MacColl was responsible for a later development of the Radio Ballad – an adaptation of *Romeo and Juliet* which was originally broadcast for schools in the series: *Books, Plays and Poems*, in May 1966 – where passages of improvised 'actuality' dialogue, recorded in the field, replace the field recordings we have already discussed. It is this approach we describe here.

In the case of *Romeo and Juliet*, the 'actuality' sequences were worked out in improvisation sessions by fourteen members of the London Critics Group (see page 57) from a scenario provided by Ewan MacColl. The sessions were recorded on the spot in garages, by the river and in the streets; then edited and juxtaposed between sound effects and songs, which are introduced at moments of heightened emotion, in much the same manner as the documentary Radio Ballads.

This technique provides a framework in which an actor can improvise, and at the same time contribute towards a performance. The embarrassment of experimenting in public is avoided, stage-awkwardness ceases to be a factor, and dramatic activity becomes a possibility for those who fight shy of appearing before an audience. Each person who takes part has a chance to contribute his imagination and his idiom of speech. The vitality of this form comes from its reliance on people's personalities, rather than a literary re-creation: it is designed for the amateur rather than the trained professional.

The story, which is loosely based on Shakespeare, has been brought up to date with the Capleys and Montagues now running a rival garage and automobile repair business in London. Ron Montague falls in love with Capley's daughter, Juliet; and the Ballad sets their love in the context of contemporary London.

The following long excerpt from the final script (quoted by permission of the B.B.C.) taken roughly from the middle of the work, relates the development of Ron and Juliet's passion for each other after they have met for the first time at a dance.

59.	ACTUALITY	Seq. 25 part 2 *Ron and Juliet*

(Ron) I must see you tomorrow. (Juliet) Tomorrow?
(Ron) Yes. (Juliet) I can't. Everybody's at home
Saturday . . . (not clear) doesn't go to the Garage.
(Ron) What garage? (Juliet) Capley garage. Do you know it?
(Ron) Capley garage! (Juliet) Yes. (Ron) I'm Ron Montague
(Juliet) Montague. (Ron) Yeah. (Juliet) So what.
(Ron) Till tomorrow. There's a jazz boat – going up the
river. Back early on Sunday morning. (Juliet) Oh, I
couldn't . I don't know how. (Ron) Try the old baby-sitting
lark. (Juliet) Wait a minute . . . Uncle Larry!
(Ron) Larry! Yeah! Of course! I'll see 'im down the Lane
tomorrow. (Juliet) Will you? (Ron) Yeah. (Juliet) I must
go. (Ron) No. Not yet. (Juliet) Tomorrow. (Ron) Yes.
I'll see Larry and fix it.

60.	EFFECTS	Angel Lane Market

61. SINGER   *Angel Lane on Saturday Morning* (A) (dur: 36″)
                            (Terry Yarnell)
                          (chorus, guitar, autoharp? fiddle)

        Verse 1 and Chorus:
        'Down the Lane on a Saturday morning,
        When the place is on the go,
        Stalls are open and the grafters working,
        Alf and Eddie and May and Jo,

        Chorus: O, you noisy city,
                   O, you sprawling city,
                   O, you're my old city.

62. EFFECTS   Peak and behind:

63. ACTUALITY   (Seq. 26) *Larry.* (dur: 33″)

So – I tells her to slope off into the caf and have a cuppa tea, don't I. And while she's going I see Ron. 'Hallo Larry' he says, er, 'how's things?' So I say, 'Oh, alright Ron old boy – how are you then?' And then he comes across, don't he. He only wants me to fix it up for him so he can take Julie on one of these jazz boats. The more I thinks about it – the more it appeals to me. It's about time Margie was taken down a stop or two, I thinks. So I tells him: 'I phone her up, try and fix something'. Well, why not? The very idea made me feel 10 years younger. . . .

64. SINGER   *Angel Lane on Saturday Morning* (B) (dur: 21″)

        Verse 2 (no chorus)
        'Women pass with their hair in curlers,
        Lads stroll by with hair unshorn,
        And the girls on 5-inch heels go tripping –
        Known 'em all, since they were born.'

65. EFFECTS   Angel Cafe

66. ACTUALITY   (Seq. 27) *Wizz/Benny/Sal/Ron/Larry* (l 15″)

(W) We were at this dance of old Capley's last night. (S) You didn't. (W) Yeah. All of us . . . Ron and all. (S) How did you get in? (W) Well, we were just knocking around a bit 'till they were all canned and then, kinda crawled in round the back ... (S) What was it like? (B) Oh, bags of birds, bags of beer. (W) Fact, we haven't seen Ron since. (B) The great gass. (W) Yeah ... There's big councillors there. You know ... (S) Yeah ... (W) Old Capley's chatting them all up and Mrs Capley's looking like a dog's dinner. (S) Yeah ... (W) I'm not kidding ... (S) What's she got on ... (W) She's walking along – and she had a stoop like the Hunchback of Notre Damme in pearls ... marvellous ... 'hallo.' Where you been then? (R) Hallo lads. I thought I'd take a walk down the lane. (W) Yeah? (R) I come down and looked around and you weren't here. (W) Do me a favour, we were there till it finished. (S) Ron? How was Rosie? (R) Oh, I don't know about her. (S) What? (W) He was dancing with another bird last night. Yeah ... The dark piece. Yeah ... never seen her before, have we, lads? Strange bird. Wonder who she is? (S) One of the Councillor's daughters, or something. (W) I wonder who she is? (B) What's her name, Ron? (R) You'll find out. (W) Get out of it! (General greeting to Larry). (L) Don't stand up, you're gonna tread on Wizz's hair. (Laughs) That's a lovely tablecloth you've got on ... they'll bury you in that one day (more chatter and laughs) ... Er, Ron! How's about it, eh? (R) O.K. then. (L) Excuse me, boys. I'll bring God's gift to women back in a minute. Yeah ... Get the coffee up, Sal. (S) Oh, he's always on.

67. SINGER   *Angel Lane on Saturday Morning* (C) (21″)

      Verse 3 (*no chorus*)
'As you walk on a Saturday morning
Past the fruit and winkle stands
Get the tangy sea smell for a moment
And the breath of distant lands.'

68. ACTUALITY   (Seq. 28a) *Larry*. (dur: 28″)

I thought of stringing him along for a bit ... well, he wasn't in a mood, he was turning somersaults ... so, eventually I gives it to him straight ... I tells him that I've rung up

Marge and she thinks I'm taking Julie down to Henley only, what I'm really going to do is that I'm going to bring Julie to Westminster Pier at 7.30 and that he's got to be at Richmond the following morning with her to stand by the free pigeons . . . I was tickled just looking at him. I reckon I'm wasting my time in book making. I should be in a matchmaking business.

69. SINGER   *Angel Lane on Saturday Morning* (D) (dur: 36″)

    Verse 4 and Chorus
'Down the Lane on a Saturday morning,
Underneath the London sky –
With the city borne upon their shoulders,
Men and women go walking by.

Chorus :   O, you noisy city,
           O, you sprawling city,
           O, you're my old city.

70. EFFECTS   Angel Lane into Westminster Pier.

71. ACTUALITY   (Seq. 29/30)   *Ron and Juliet*   (dur: 28″)
(R) 24 minutes past . . . ah, she'll come. Larry fixed it. He's all right . . . come in a taxi. Lot of people about, though. Be a fine day. Cor, it's hot! Fag? No. Not just . . . Julie!
(J) Hello Ron. (R) Oh, you look great. (J) I'm ready. (R) Good. Let's go, come on, let's go . . .

72. ACTUALITY   (Seq. 31)   *Larry.*   (dur: 18″)

He stood there, grinning from ear to ear and looking at her as if she was made of gold. Then he took her by the hand and they walked up that gangplank like it was the aisle to the altar . . . then the boat moved off and . . . down the river, all lights and music, marvellous . . .

73. SINGER   *Flow Softly, Sweet Thames* (John Faulkner) (44″)
                 (chorus)
                 (dulcimer? guitar, autoharp, concertina)
                   * *This is available on record, sung by*
                   John Faulkner, on Sweet Thames Flow
                   Softly. Argo DA47

'I met my girl at Woolwich pier,
beneath a big crane standing,
And O, the love I felt for her
it passed all understanding.   (13″)

Took her sailing on the river,
Flow, sweet river, flow;
London Town was mine to give her,
Sweet Thames, flow gently.   (28″)

Made the Thames into a crown,
Flow, sweet river, flow,
Made a brooch of Silver Town,
Sweet Thames, flow gently.

At London Yard I held her hand,
at Blackwall Point I faced her,
At the Isle of Dogs I kissed her mouth
and tenderly embraced her.

Heard the bells of Greenwich ringing
Flow, sweet river, flow;
All the time me heart was singing,
Sweet Thames, flow gently.

Limehouse Reach I gave her there,
Flow, sweet river, flow,
As a ribbon for her hair,
Sweet Thames, flow gently.

74. EFFECTS   River boat.

75. ACTUALITY   (Seq. 31) *Ron and Juliet.* (dur: 20″)

(J) laughs (R) You try carrying that lot. Millions of them.
(J) If you look at the land – seem to be hardly moving –
looks a long way away. (R) Do you know what I'm going
to do? (J) What? (R) I'd like to strip off and dive. Can you
swim? (J) Yes. Love swimming. We must do that. Swimming together. (R) We will.

76. SINGER   *Sweet Thames*   C   (dur: 18″)

'From Shadwell dock to Nine Elms Reach,
we cheek-to-cheek were dancing,
Her necklace made of London Bridge
her beauty was enhancing;

Kissed her once again at Wapping,
Flow, sweet river, flow,
After that there was no stopping,
Sweet Thames, flow gently'

77. ACTUALITY   (Seq. 32)   *Juliet.*   (dur: 15″)

I wish this could go on and on – on and on, and on and
never end. Never end. Ever . . .

78. SINGER   *Sweet Thames*   D

'Richmond Park it was her ring,
Flow, sweet river, flow,
I'd have given her anything,
Sweet Thames, flow gently'

79. ACTUALITY   (Seq. 32a)   *Ron.*   (dur: 05″)

Oh, if I could only breathe her in like air.

80. SINGER   *Sweet Thames*   E

'From Rotherhithe to Putney Bridge
me love I was declaring,
And she from Kew to Isleworth
her love to me was swearing,

Love it set me heart a-burning,
Flow, sweet river, flow,
Never saw the tide was turning,
Sweet Thames, flow gently.

Gave her Hampton Court to twist
Flow, sweet river, flow,
Into a bracelet for her wrist,
Sweet Thames, flow gently'

81. EFFECTS   River boat into Angel Lane Street Market, Monday morning.

82. ACTUALITY   (Seq. 33a) *Market Woman.* (dur: 19″)

> I was in my stall that Monday morning and – don't know why, I started thinking about Ron and Julie. He's got an eye on – and she's got an eye on and putting it all on and making out nothing's happened. When she must be feeling on top of the world – to have to cover it all up. With a smashing man like that – the poor kid . . .

Such vivid work as this, with its insolent, anarchic contact with everyday life and its idiomatic freedom of approach, is within the bounds of many groups: amateurs act best when, without entirely realising it, they create from their own personalities a character, completely natural, belonging both to their own experience and to the world of the play. The sound-ballad provides the ideal framework for such activity: the talk, the manner, the values of *Romeo and Juliet* have the surface of life, but cleared of the pretentious phraseology and awkward interpolations of a script, because the actor's normal habits of speech have reasserted themselves.

Much of the material can be recorded in the everyday environment: in the streets, the schools, the factory or pubs; improvised, wherever possible, on the spot. The music should reinforce and emphasise the meaning and quality of the words and action, so that the whole thing becomes a single poetic statement rather than a passage of attractive singing with some dramatic improvisation vaguely attached. Guitar, concertina, fiddle, clarinet and dulcimer accompanied the singing in *Romeo and Juliet*; but other instruments including drums, mouth organ, piano, organ, harmonium, sitar, melodion, tamboura, flute, dilruba, zither and comb and paper are now played by instrumentalists in folk, pop and other groups of all kinds.

Generally speaking there are no fixed rules governing such improvisations – if it works, it works; but the actual process of selection calls for very considerable artistry: the Radio Ballads which last about an hour, were culled from 70 to 80 hours of field recordings of which only about 25 minutes were used. In all this all those who take part, as actors, musicians or technicians, can bring their own personal contribution to the whole. The Director's main function, here as elsewhere, is to work these contributions together until a satisfactory unity results, rather than to preconceive such a unity and then force everyone else to fit themselves into it.

Teaching with Tape. Graham Jones (Focal Press)

STREET THEATRE

Plays can be done anywhere. An audience that has come into a theatre knows beforehand more or less what to expect and is committed to a certain theatrical convention and response. To reach beyond the limits which such expectations necessarily impose, and to reach an audience which has not time for the theatrical convention anyway, certain groups have taken their performances to any public place where they can find an informal and unsuspecting audience already assembled (see plate 7).

The Agitprop groups did this for political purposes in the 1930's; Inter Action and C-A-S-T (Cartoon Archetypical Slogan Theatre) produce floats, plays and speeches for political rallies today. One of the most successful of such groups, certainly the one that has made the most impact, is the Bread and Puppet Theatre from New York, who perform in masks and use puppets up to 18 feet in size. Their visit to England in May 1968 showed us how well plays can be done in the street. Their straight-forward yet intensely moving *A Man says Goodbye to his Mother*, a ten-minute play about Vietnam, was performed on a children's playground in Notting Hill, and held a 'non-theatre' audience in silent concentration until loud applause at the end. The structure and characters were very simple; a man, a woman, a drummer/trumpeter and a narrator. The narrator told the story about the son going to a distant land and bombing a village (played by the mother who changes her mask); the soldier kills the village woman's child, and she kills the soldier with a pair of scissors. The narrator gave the soldier various props, e.g. a gun, a gasmask and a toy aeroplane, while the music on bass drum and kazoo accompanied most actions.

The full text of this, and other of their plays, is published in *Tulane Drama Review* No. 38[1] together with an interview with their director, Peter Schuman. Here are some quotations:

Schuman: – 'I feel that Art in the modern world is generally superfluous.

[1] New York University, Washington Square, New York.

Either we should find a need for it or we should give it up. We named our theatre the Bread and Puppet Theatre because we felt that theatre should be as basic as bread. . . . A theatre is good when it makes sense to people. We have had our best – and sometimes our most stupid – performances in the streets. Sometimes you can make your point because your point is simply to be there in the street. It stops people in their tracks to see those large puppets, to see something theatrical outside of a theatre. They can't take the attitude that they've paid money to go into a theatre to "see something". Suddenly there is this thing in front of them, confronting them. . . . You don't make your point unless a five-year-old girl can understand it. If she gets it the grown-ups will too. The show almost has to be stupid. It has to be tremendously concentrated. You need that intensity on the street much more than in the theatre. Indoors you get by with technique, by sticking to your dialogue, but on the street you come across only if you have your mind on WHAT HAS TO BE DONE. The one space we reject is that of traditional theatre – it is too comfortable, too well known. Its traditions upset us, people are numbed by sitting in the same chairs in the same way. It conditions their reactions. But when you use the space you happen to be in you use it all, the stairs, the windows, the streets, the doors. We'll do any play anywhere – provided we can fit the puppets in. And in each space it will be different. I don't really like the regular theatre much. But there have been theatres that made sense – news reports, religious services, these things communicate. And the Greek theatre, the Egyptian theatre, the Chinese theatre . . . our theatre is still in the thirties. We still hang on to that little cultural revolution.

'The audience which doesn't go to the theatre is always the best audience. Kids and the people that are just usually in a place. At Montreal the best audiences were the people who worked at Expo, the people who swept up, the cops.

'Some of our shows are good and some are bad, but all our shows are for good against evil.'

Thoughts and suggestions for action

1. Was your last committee meeting a more dramatic experience than your last play? If so, why do plays? Or do you prefer the party afterwards?

2. A fifteen-foot penguin from a toy shop fell from the flies in the middle of a housing estate situation. The stage manager strode on to the stage in full view of the audience and demanded that the 'bloody penguin' be removed. This got the biggest laugh of the evening. Chance is often the most interesting member of the cast.

3. Do you need a theatre when you can do plays anywhere? In a dole queue, bus shelter, market, factory, pier, mental hospital or on a beach? In the room you are reading this, maybe? (See plate 7).

4. How many Punch and Judy men get an Arts Council subsidy?

5. Invent plays based on your own environment, local politics, speech days, history, legends, newspapers, letters etc. Analyse issues like planning a by-pass, strikes, unemployment, slum clearance etc. Write about what you care about, let the audience answer back.

6. The rules for amateur drama competitions are an absurd imposition. As with composition-rules for amateur photographers, they are a security device with which to protect the individual with conformity.

7. Re-write ceremonies for weddings, christenings and funerals. These dramatic events are too often sterile and insensitive (see plate 1).

8. Take real situations, e.g. the apprentice's first day in the factory; the club agent comes, a coloured family moves in next door, the juke box is raided . . . and improvise the consequences. Write the script afterwards, or throw it away altogether.

9. Play rounders before you start the rehearsal.

10. Incorporate existing local talent like pop groups, conjurers, folk-singers, gymnasts, etc.

11. Keep it simple. A costume can be a hat, a badge on a T-shirt, a label on a placard.

12. Use a narrator to eliminate boring narrative action and contrivance of plot. Stick to the essentials.

13. Aim at something lasting ten minutes to begin with. Three-act inevitables can be very dreary. Use a band to attract your audience. Do not be afraid to repeat items. The audience will leave if they are bored. A band doesn't need to have virtuoso skill. Try side drums, kazoos, Jew's harps, cymbals. Invent music through new instruments and planned rhythms. Keep a box of scrap instruments handy (e.g. tins and dried peas), so children can join in.

4 The Role of the Director

The conventional theatre's method of co-ordinating the various elements in a play is to use a director. What is today called 'Director's Theatre' describes a situation where the director's contribution has become as important as the dramatist's – the end result is the imposition of his ideas and total conception.

But in some of the ways of performing that we have described, a director may not be necessary at all. A group of students from Rolle College, Exmouth, who produced a highly praised satirical programme called *Raw* for the N.U.S. Drama Festival, emphasised that their work was the result of group collaboration, and that the ideas stemmed from improvised actions rather than the other way round. Group work of this nature is essentially collaborative and the role of the director, if he exists, may be quite minimal. At his best in this situation he is a critical catalyst, rejecting, selecting and stimulating, having a rather more general view of the total effect than other members of the group. In some cases it is possible to use different directors for different scenes – one of the cast without much to do can sit it out and direct. However, in the situation where all members of the group are called upon to contribute their own particular talents and ideas, the director's function is that of an agent who sets up conditions in which work can be undertaken and discoveries made. His role is a creative one; but the actors, the designers and technicians can take part in the creation also.

Stephen Joseph, in a characteristically modest passage in his *Theatre in the Round*,[1] has described this in practice:

'When we started the theatre in the round at Scarborough, as manager and producer I had a busy time during rehearsals; management could not

[1] *Theatre in the Round.* Stephen Joseph (Barrie and Rockliff).

be ignored, and the essential obligation I had to the actors was to encourage them, excite them, stimulate their imaginations. And I found that the best time to do this was during morning coffee-break or at lunch or over a pint of beer in the evening. On reflection, I would say that my only important contribution to the company's eventual performances was to ensure that there was always a good coffee-break during rehearsals. Luckily most of the actors in the company responded to this treatment. The performances were as good as we hoped they might be. Perhaps the company was exceptionally brilliant; though I suspect that most actors, in spite of their fears to the contrary, could work creatively together if given the right stimulus, or merely a fair chance.'

By throwing out ideas, suggestions, ways of approach; by initiating improvisations and encouraging each person to have the courage to make his own contribution; by fanning a group's enthusiasm and interest to fever pitch and then helping them to shape what is thrown up, the director plays a part of special importance. He is co-ordinator, collaborator, clearing-house, sounding-board and inspiration. But as Joan Littlewood says: 'I do not believe in the supremacy of the director, designer, actor or even the writer. It is through collaboration that this knockabout art of the theatre survives and kicks. . . . No one mind or imagination can foresee what a play will become until the physical and intellectual stimuli which are crystallised in the poetry of the author, has been understood by the company, and then tried out in terms of mime, discussion and the precise music of grammar; words and movement allied and integrated.'

DIRECTING A PLAY

The method of direction we have been describing is as applicable to work on a written script as it is to work with improvised beginnings. A group can arrive at an interpretation by common consent or they can rely on a director who does most of the thinking. But in either case it is best to strike a balance between direction which is advanced stage management and direction which is a dictatorship. As Stanislavsky says, 'Simple despotism does not persuade an actor in his inner self'.

The director's main task is to feel his way into a fresh relationship with actors. If he makes a success of this he may get exciting performances, if he does not he may get dull ones; but in either case he should not come to rehearsals with a fixed interpretation containing a precise ground plan and every move worked out.

On the other hand he should not underestimate his own contribution to the performance, for before he can help to shape the whole for others, he must know where he is going and what he is doing himself. The total concept of a production may be largely his; he must work out the play's meaning for himself and see in his mind's eye how each detail fits this concept. He may decide on a quiet, relatively unobstrusive approach, following a straightforward reading of the text; or, on the other hand, he may have some vital, original interpretation which illuminates the text in a new way. In either case, however stimulating his approach may be, it should never be imposed as a production gimmick, a self-indulgent exhibitionist display. A director must relate ideas to the text he is working on, and constantly refer back to see if what he is doing is valid. Only then can his ideas become a new and vital statement of production. Often it is because a director does not trust his play that he feels he must transform it from the outside, and add all manner of fireworks of his own. Indeed it appears a question of humility; a director needs to work from the basis of his text, and make his discoveries, as it were, from the inside so that the play begins to reveal the excitement and power that are already there, and which do not need decoration in production.

It is always dangerous to try to force a play into preconceived ideas and theories about the theatre; that, for example, all theatre must be naturalistic, or that, as Brecht thought, an audience must be 'alienated' from a play. Naturalism in Shakespearean productions of the Victorian and Edwardian periods destroyed swift movement with constant elaborate scene shifts, and Brecht's own plays have been known to lose a great deal if put into the strait-jacket of his own theory, which is still largely misunderstood.

A director must keep open, must consider all ideas as he works towards a concept of the production which is always evolving. His personal view will be a balance between a great number of elements, a matter of emphasis. His final position must be clear to himself, and he must be able to communicate it to his actors; for his position is one in which he sees more sharply than anyone the relationship of every detail to the whole. This is quite separate from the actor's tasks for the latter has to create his own part within the framework of the production, act with others, and project his own ideas and feelings to an audience. Just because he is not involved in an actor's immediate problems, a director is able to focus the whole much more clearly.

1. *Preparation*

The initial work is itself of both a concentrated and a diverse kind. Concentrated, because it demands a detailed knowledge of all the elements in the production; an awareness of rhythm and structure, and an appreciation of climax and character. And diverse because such understanding grows not only through thoughtful reading of the text or a close knowledge of all the factors involved; but through reading other plays or novels of the period, looking at paintings, visiting museums, and soaking oneself in every aspect of the period concerned. Too many amateurs work in a vacuum; they haven't seen enough theatre, they haven't read enough plays, so they have very little to start from. But when the director's detailed knowledge is set in a wider frame, his sensibility is deepened and his awareness of issues sharpened.

Awareness is a key word; it must be carried through all the work on a production. It starts with the director's initial talk with his actors and is a part of the rehearsals which follow in which the actors experiment and develop their own parts within the large framework outlined by the director. The whole pattern takes shape through a complex sharing of experiment, discussion, argument and understanding by the actors, the director and the technical staff.

As director, plan the play as much or as little as you want. Never think that the matter-of-fact business of positioning props, marking entrances etc., is time wasted. It pays off to plan as much as possible, and certainly makes for smooth rehearsals in which time is not wasted. Never become too rigid in your demands. Try and see an actor's viewpoint, and listen to and watch carefully any experiment that is being tried out. It is so easy, once you have your own fixed ideas, to close your mind to anything new, to dismiss it or simply not heed it. A sharing of thoughts and feelings is essential if the rehearsal period is going to be lively and worthwhile. As Adrian Rendle writes:[1] 'If there is too much restriction when rehearsals

[1] In *Everyman and his Theatre*. Adrian Rendle (Pitman).

start there will be no room for the actor to interpret at his own level. However, although the actor must be given adequate freedom, flexibility must not be an excuse for an ill-organised approach to the part. A director's discipline depends on his knowing the measure of his own flexibility.'

2. *Casting*

Avoid casting committees and take complete control yourself. The best actors are rarely the 'actor-types'. They are people who bring a dimension of their lives on to the stage, acting with sincerity and complete candour. Michael Croft, Director of the National Youth Theatre, says: 'He (or she) may never have acted in his life and can't act anyway, but he may have some kind of spark – personality, vitality, sincerity, a bit of fire or feeling about SOMETHING – qualities which you can't pinpoint till you see them and not always then; and if he has a hint of talent, too, so much the better. Often he is too timid to apply; he may be tucked away somewhere in a football team and think acting effeminate. He may have passed unnoticed by the school producer because he can't speak correctly or doesn't look the type. Maybe his school doesn't do plays anyway or maybe he's anti-groups of any kind and wouldn't set foot in the theatre if you paid him.' So do not place too much emphasis on good reading. Many natural actors, even great actors, may give a very poor first reading. Better to improvise a short scene, explore in improvisation the character you are dealing with, or delay casting until the play has been explored through discussions and improvisations. You cannot make your choice until you know your actors really well; and are aware of their various capacities. The good director is continually alive to the inherent potentialities of his group and watches to see the germ of every new development.

3. *Rehearsals*

During rehearsals the actors should become really familiar with the play. Improvisations round a play's theme can help not only to stimulate an actor's imagination, but also lead him to a better understanding of his part. Start with these, or readings, to grasp the main idea and the play's shape; discuss essentials of plot and character, and then explore some of the main situations.

Rehearse short scenes or small sections. A lot can be gained from close study of two or three pages of text rather than from run-throughs of whole acts. For one thing learning by rote is eliminated as memorising comes much more easily this way. And for another, actors begin quickly to see the shape of each section and how it relates to the next one. The quicker scripts are thrown away, the better.

Take scenes not in their real order (e.g. Act I scene I, then II, then III etc.) but try out ones which contrast emotionally, or in which the same group of actors are involved in a different situation. Different ways of seeing scenes can be illuminating. At later rehearsals try longer sections of the play or acts. During final rehearsals concentrate on the continuity of mood and character and the rhythm and tempo of scenes. The basis of everything is rhythm; there must be rhythm in the individual speech, and in the conduct of the whole performance. Try to have a long run through with few interruptions each week. Be careful of interrupting too frequently especially during later rehearsals when, by so doing, you break the rhythm or movement of a scene. Instead, jot down your comments and wait until a natural break occurs.

The technical side of a production is also very important. Technical planning starts before the first rehearsal and these should be planned well in advance – settling the time and the amount of work scheduled is the first necessity. This should be known to everyone in the group. Good organisation in arranging a production is essential, it gives the artistic development a chance.

Be absolutely sure of the technical staging of the scene you are about to rehearse; make a plan of basic entrances and exits, if this helps, though this can be worked out by discussion. From the start use, if you can, the stage intended for the final performance. If this is not available, mark off an area of similar dimensions in a practice room. Use chalk, or tapes pinned down. Mark positions of furniture etc., with tapes or with coloured Sellotape. Keep in close touch with your technicians throughout the period of preparation for a production. Work closely with your designers, scene painters, lighting technicians, and also the public relations side of the production.

DRESS REHEARSALS

Try to have a considerable number of rehearsals in the actual dress that the actors will wear on the first night. But do not, because of this, let the tension slacken or the impetus of rehearsal go. Whatever you do, see that you plan (i) a technical dress rehearsal to give the technical staff a chance to co-ordinate and get everything right, scene changes, sound effects, lighting, props etc. (see page 310), and (ii) a final run-through when the technical side has been perfected and the producer can concentrate on the total shape of the production. The dress rehearsal often highlights weak sections where the rhythms of acting may flag. Seeing the production as a whole may, indeed, suggest ways of improving these parts, and of strengthening the texture of the whole. At such rehearsals always stick to a strict time schedule.

Work at these rehearsals in close touch with your stage manager. Do everything as you will at the first public performance, i.e., start with dimming house lights, and rehearse curtain calls if you intend to have them.

The Producer and the Play. Norman Marshall (Macdonald)
Excellent introduction to direction.
Sense of Direction. John Fernald (Secker and Warburg)
The Play Produced. John Fernald (Deane)
Two of the most indispensable handbooks for the director, and amongst the best general books on the subject.
Directing a Play. James Roose-Evans (Studio Vista)
Imaginative, succinct, open-ended introduction.
Directors on Directing. ed. T. Cole and H. K. Chinoy (Vision/Owen)
Good short history of directing, includes pages of prompt books and personal note books, as well as verbatim transcripts of rehearsals by Stanislavski, Brecht, Elia Kazan and Joan Littlewood.
Play Production. John Allen (Dobson)
An excellent guide, lucid, fresh, very short and well written.
The Empty Space. Peter Brook (MacGibbon & Kee)
A brilliant and thoughtful book. Highly interesting.
Stanislavski Produces Othello. (Bles)
The Present Stage. John Kershaw (Fontana)

5 Choosing the Play

The Lord Chamberlain's Men were a privileged company. They had a resident playwright who could turn out the sort of play they wanted, and with a cast suitable to their acting strength.

This is the ideal situation; but not one to which an amateur company can hope to aspire. So the perennial business of choosing a play involves the same old factors – size of cast, cost of set, suitability for the audience, whether Mrs Robinson can be persuaded to take on Lady Bracknell. . . . But given all the limitations, the choice for any particular group is probably fairly large, if only someone is prepared to research into what is available by reading texts, listening to the radio, watching television, collecting reviews, talking to other people.

Once the range of choice becomes large enough, the process of selection can begin. Personal enthusiasm is bound to be the largest determining factor, and this is as it should be. Unless the director and the group as a whole are committed to the play they are doing, that sense of excitement which is an amateur company's most valuable asset will be missing. Casting is no less important.

But beyond this there are other considerations. A programme of plays should be seen as related, and some sort of balance achieved. Variety is probably the best guide here – of the type of play, of period, of cost. Here, taken almost at random, are some well-balanced programmes by professional and non-professional groups alike, in which a play by a contemporary playwright, a Shakespearian production, another play by a major pre-twentieth-century writer, and one production (either a musical, a documentary or a new play) which the company are giving its first performance, are juxtaposed with telling effect:

BRISTOL ARTS CENTRE   September – November 1968
(non-professional)

The Erpingham Camp	Joe Orton
New Play especially written for the Centre	Charles Wood
The Unquiet Spirit	Jean-Jacques Bernard
Fairy Tales of New York	J. P. Donleavy
A Midsummer Night's Dream	Shakespeare
The Restoration of Arnold Middleton	David Storey
Musical – developed by the Company	

CENTURY THEATRE   North-West tour March – September 1968
(professional)

The Tempest	Shakespeare
Charley's Aunt	Brandon Thomas
Billy Liar	K. Waterhouse and W. Hall
The Birthday Party	Harold Pinter
The Servant of Two Masters	Carlo Goldoni
A Day in the Death of Joe Egg	Peter Nichols

PEOPLE'S THEATRE, NEWCASTLE
(non-professional)

Five Finger Exercise	Peter Shaffer
The Visit	Friedrich Durenmatt
Peer Gynt	Ibsen
Sweeney Todd – a musical based on Victorian melodrama (see page 32)	

TAVISTOCK REPERTORY COMPANY   October – December 1968
(non-professional – presents 14 full length a year)

Love and a Bottle (London première)	George Farquhar
A Doll's House	Ibsen
Richard II	Shakespeare
The Milk Train Doesn't Stop Here (British première)	Tennessee Williams

VICTORIA THEATRE, STOKE-ON-TRENT   August – November 1968
(professional)

The Promise	Aleksei Arbuzov
Othello	Shakespeare
Six into One – Documentary musical created by the Company (see page 39)	
Christopher Pea	Ken Campbell (new play)
Rookery Nook	Ben Travers

WORTHING CONNAUGHT THEATRE   August – November 1967
(professional)

The Beggar's Opera	John Gay
Private Lives	Noel Coward
Andorra	Max Frisch
The Playboy of the Western World	J. M. Synge
A Midsummer Night's Dream	Shakespeare
Hedda Gabler	Ibsen
Little Malcolm and his Struggle Against the Eunuchs	David Halliwell

But even a well-balanced programme is insufficient when there is no urgently felt purpose behind the choice of each particular play. It is right that groups should explore the new frontiers of drama as well as revive those plays, neglected now, which were milestones in their own day; but nothing should be presented as part of a museum policy. A play, once chosen, should mean a great deal to everyone involved; it should have something important to tell us about ourselves today; it should excite us to an unusually passionate degree: if not it is better left alone.

Of course there are good reasons why some plays should not be tackled at all. In our experience amateurs rarely achieve a high standard with Shakespeare, or any of the great classical plays, which, for lack of technique, are so often performed in a derivative manner, indifferently modelled on half-learned skills. But the case for doing Shakespeare rests on the inspiration which contact with a supremely creative mind can give to the performers. Even if they fail, they might have gained more than from a dozen easy successes. Who, after all, are they doing Shakespeare for?

Stylised comedies of manners are probably the most difficult plays for an untrained actor to attempt, almost certainly attended by an inevitable failure to respect the style and language of Vanbrugh, Congreve or Sheridan. Farces, which rely on superb timing as well as highly artificial and stylised acting, can be even more disastrous.

Amateurs succeed with plays within their grasp *as people*. It was no accident that Brecht took many amateurs into his company when he was starting the Berliner Ensemble. His first aim was to avoid the cliché. He said 'I do not want people who look like actors, and I do not want people who behave like actors. We want to have people who have a reality and a personality which is produced by their own lives.' It is the reality of their own lives that amateurs contribute to performances whose scope is within their imaginative and emotional range. Where actors can identify without indulgence or insincerity, where human understanding and personal involvement are paramount there are fine performances. André Obey's *Noah*, Tennessee Williams's *Suddenly Last Summer*, David Cregan's *Three Men for Colverton*, and Strindberg's *Miss Julie*, all of which we have seen brilliantly produced, are invariably, though not necessarily, more successful than, for example, Marlowe's *Tamburlaine* or Shakespeare's *Hamlet*. Thus casting is probably more important than rehearsal.

The following lists which are offered as a convenient guide to the vast range of plays available should be read as clues which might be worth following up. No attempt has been made to make this list exhaustive: we have not listed every one of an author's plays; and we have not read or seen all the plays that have been performed and written. Within such variety each group will have to make its choice determined by its strengths and limitations: no group should attempt a Feydeau farce unless it has a competent technical stage staff which can achieve the effects upon which these plays depend.

We have tried to give some short indications of the dramatic possibilities of the various types of play. The survey is preceded by more detailed lists, which attempt to categorise plays into certain useful groups: Plays written for Children, Plays suitable for performance by Older Boys and Girls, Plays for Women, and Religious Drama. But even these groups should not be regarded as rigid: all of the plays suggested for Older Boys and Girls could be performed by any amateur group with sufficient members. In the end it is only by ignoring categories, by choosing plays for their interest and meaning that the productions themselves become lively. The way to achieve the fullest dramatic experience is to trust the dramatist, and the heart.

PLAYS FOR PERFORMANCE TO CHILDREN

We are certainly opposed to any kind of public performance by children in primary schools. Children of that age should be given every opportunity to express and create in their own way without the pressure of an audience: dramatic play, like movement or painting, should be done for its own sake.

The aim is not the training of young actors but the development of each child's personality and powers of sympathy and communication. Drama in school is closer to children's creative play than to the traditions of the theatre. The activity is the process of learning; the end-product, the performance, is not an aim in itself. When children do wish to share their work with others and to show what they have done – and there are a few occasions when it is right that they should do so – the audience should be small and the occasion as informal as possible.

Our first list, then, is of plays especially written for performance to children. It is incomplete; and, of necessity, of written texts only. Many primary and secondary schools are fortunate enough to receive visits from companies of actors, such as Brian Way's, who bring child-drama and improvised performances which are children's first (and last?) experience of theatre. Why shouldn't older children or experienced adults (under the direction of the County Drama Adviser) occasionally do the same?

How should plays for children be produced? When asked how he would produce a children's play Stanislavsky replied: 'The same as for adults, only better'. 'Playing-down', condescension, insincerity are noticed immediately. Nicholas Stuart Gray writes: 'An intelligent child will not tolerate insincerity of dialogue, plot, or acting; lack of clarity in production; inaudibility in delivery of lines; slowness of action; slip-shod scenery or costumes. They will appreciate style and wit in all these.' The younger the age group, of course, the more unexpected the reactions. Eight and nine-year-olds are slapstick minded. Anything will make them shriek with laughter. Their attention must be held steadily on the plot, and they will co-operate if not played down to. Older children are concerned with emotion, character, subtlety of story, comedy and wit, as well as the custard-pie. For all, the essentials are sincerity and clarity and action.'

The lists are based upon those published by the British Children's Theatre Association, to whom we are most grateful.

PLAYS RECOMMENDED FOR PERFORMANCE TO JUNIOR CHILDREN
Bibliography of Plays (available from: Gerald Tyler, Hon. Secretary, British Children's Theatre Association, County Education Offices, Bond Street, Wakefield. Price 2/6 each.)

William Baines   *The Two Masks**

Myrrha Bantock	*Dragon's Daughter**
Lucia Benedetti	*The Enchanted Cloak* (c/o I.B.E.C.C.) (trans. Claude Vincent)
Melvin Bernhardt	*The Pied Piper of Hamelin* (J. Garnet Miller)
Franklyn Black	*The Heartless Princess* (French)
A. J. Bradbury	*White Doctor**
Janet Brandes and John Temple	*The Magic Snuffbox* (Margaret Ramsay)
Alan Broadhurst	*The Tinder Box* (Children's Theatre Press)
James Ambrose Brown	*Circus Adventure* *Mango-Leaf Magic* *The Three Wishes* (all English Children's Theatre)
Donald Buckley	*Up the Chimney**
Helga Burgess	*Where Do We Go From Here?* (MacDonald and Young)
Charlotte Chorpenning	*Elves and the Shoemaker* (Children's Theatre Press) *Jack and the Beanstalk* (Children's Theatre Press) *Little Black Sambo and the Tiger* (Children's Theatre Press) *Little Red Riding Hood* (Children's Theatre Press) *Radio Rescue* (J. Garnet Miller) *Rumpelstiltskin* (Children's Theatre Press) *Sleeping Beauty* (Children's Theatre Press) *The Three Bears* (Children's Theatre Press)
D. J. Culham	*After October** *Pengarren Cliff**
Alan Cullen	*Hans, the Witch and the Goblin* (French) *King Patch and Mr Simpkin* (Children's Theatre Press) *Niccolo and Nicolette* (Children's Theatre Press)
Marjorie Dawe	*Chinese Charm* (Dobson)
Michael Drin	*The Puppet Prince* (Curtis Brown)

John English	*Brer Rabbit* (French)
	Silver Shilling (International Theatre Service Organisation)
Olive Enoch	*Twilight Forest* (Peter Carroll)
Margery Evernden	*The Frog Princess and the Witch* (J. Garnet Miller)
Eleanor and Herbert Farjeon	*The Glass Slipper* (French)
Eleanor Farjeon	*The Silver Curlew* (French)
Arthur Fauquez	*Reynard the Fox* (Children's Theatre Press)
Richard Franks	*The Brave of Begonia**
E. R. Gard'ner	*The Boy who Wanted to be His Own Master**
	*The Man with a Monkey**
J. T. Gates	*The Ring, The Star and The Music Box**
Jose Geal and Michael Pugh	*Plum Plum and the Dragon* (University of London Press)
Margaret Gibbs	*The Flipperty-Fly-By-Night* in 'Simon the Tart-Eater and Other Plays' (Heinemann)
	Simon the Tart-Eater in 'Simon the Tart-Eater and Other Plays' (Heinemann)
	*The Snoodle's Egg**
	The State Umbrella of the Great Hoo Wi in 'Simon the Tart-Eater and Other Plays' (Heinemann)
	The Whispering Grass (French)
Phyllis May Gill	*Rumpelstiltskin**
Joseph Golden	*Johnny Moonbeam and the Silver Arrow* (Children's Theatre Press)
Nicholas Stuart Gray	*Beauty and the Beast*
	The Hunters and the Hen Wife
	The Marvellous Story of Puss-in-Boots
	The Other Cinderella
	The Tinder Box (all O.U.P.)

R. G. Gregory	*A Play to Pay the Rent* (Hope, Leresche and Steele)
A. Greidanus	*Two Pails of Water* (a comic fantasy available from Netherlands A.I.T.I. Centre – agent Prins & Prins)
Elizabeth Hagen and Philippe Berlyn	*I Wonder What Happened to Able* (Bertha Myers)
Willis Hall	*The Play of the Royal Astrologers* (Heinemann)
Aurand Harris	*Simple Simon* (Children's Theatre Press)
Wilfred Harvey	*The Adventures of Pang* *Master Luck* *Mr Punch at Home* (all English Children's Theatre)
Alick Hayes	*Just William* (MacDonald and Young)
Tom Hendry	*Trapped**
Mary Howarth	*The Proud Princess**
Ted Hughes	*The Coming of the Kings* – a nativity play (in *Listening and Writing*, B.B.C. schools' pamphlet, Autumn 1964)
H. S. James	*Scarecrows**
Ronald James	*The Reluctant Dragon**
Angela Jeans	*Listen to the Wind* (French)
Marian Jonson	*Greensleeves' Magic* (J. Garnet Miller)
John Leeming and G. Bell	*Claudius, the Bee* (French)
Luongo	*The Prince of Air* (Pirandello Society)
Mollie MacArthur	*Seraphino** *The Talking Horse**
Patrick Mace	*Broomsticks* *Cake for the King* *Harlequin Lends a Hand* *The Silver Whistle* *The Tree and the Fountain* *The Witch Queen* (all MacDonald and Young)

Suria Magito and Rudolf Weil	*The Snow Queen* (Heinemann)
O. J. Mahoney	*The Little Tailor**
Donald Mattam	*Tuesday-Monday**
M. J. Matthews and H. Milton	*The King's Mistake**
Nellie McCaslin	*The Little Snow Girl* *The Rabbit Who Wanted Red Wings* (both J. Garnet Miller)
Madge Miller	*Hansel and Gretel* (Dobson) *Heidi* (Children's Theatre Press) *The Land of the Dragon* (Children's Theatre Press) *Pied Piper of Hamelin* (Dobson) *The Princess and the Swineherd* (Children's Theatre Press) *Puss in Boots* (Children's Theatre Press)
Clifford Mills and John Ramsey	*Where the Rainbow Ends* (French)
A. A. Milne	*Make Believe* (French) *Toad of Toad Hall* (Methuen)
Rosemary Musil	*Mystery at the Old Fort* (Children's Theatre Press)
James Norris	*Aladdin and the Wonderful Lamp* (Children's Theatre Press)
David C. Pethybridge	*Do It Yourself**
Jocelyn Powell	*The Slippers of Abu Kasim**
Michael Pugh	*The Mercenary Mandarin**
Corinne Rickert and Frank Whiting	*Huckleberry Finn* (Children's Theatre Press)
Antonia Ridge	*The Poppenkast* (Faber)
Adele Thone	*The Wizard of Oz* (Children's Theatre Press)
Dan Totheroh	*The Stolen Prince* (Thos. Nelson – agent French)

New Directions

Dorothy Turnock	*The Little Mermaid**
Eric Vos	*The Dancing Donkey* (musical fantasy available from the Netherland A.I.T.I. Centre – agent Prins and Prins)
John Readman Walshaw	*The Seventh Dungeon* (O.U.P.) *The Island of Doom* (French)
Evelyne Ward	*The Wizard's Birthday**
Brian Way and Warren Jenkins	*Pinocchio* (Dobson)
Brian Way	*The Storytellers* (Pitman)
Catherine Wilkinson	*Rumpelstiltskin* (Dobson)
Harcourt Williams	*The Emperor's New Clothes* (French)
Anthony Woodhall	*The Enchanted Forest* (Margaret Ramsay)

PLAYS RECOMMENDED FOR PERFORMANCE TO SENIOR CHILDREN

John Arden and Margaretta D'Arcy	*The Royal Pardon* (Methuen)
William Baines	*Smuggler's Bay** *The Roses and the Bear**
Robert Bolt	*The Thwarting of Baron Bolligrew* (Heinemann)
A. J. Bradbury	*David Copperfield or the Villainy of Uriah Heep** *Lighten Their Darkness** *Smuggler's Inn**
Charlotte Chorpenning	*The Adventures of Tom Sawyer* (J. Garnet Miller)
C. W. Cooper	*The Packet Boat Inn**
D. S. Daniell	*Hereward the Wake* *The Gascon Ring* *The Silver Snuffbox* *The Stowaway* (in *More Children's Theatre Plays* – Harrap) *Hide-and-Seek*

	Stand and Deliver
	The Adventure
	The Jester, the Queen and the Hen
	The King's Messenger
	The Queen and Mr Shakespeare
	(in *Children's Theatre Plays* – Harrap)
John English	*Tom Sawyer* (International Theatre Service Organisation)
Ken Etheridge	*The Boy Who Carved Birds* (Evans)
	*Cinderella Boy**
J. A. Fergusson	*The Scarecrow* (Harrap – agent French)
Joan Forman	*Maid in Arms*
	Midwinter Journey (both Evans)
Carlo Goldoni	*The Servant of Two Masters* (Heinemann)
Bernard Goss	*Big Noise at Fort Issimo*
Eunice Hanger	*Short Street* (Greg. Branson)
Wilfred Harvey	*All the Tea in China* (French)
Fred Hoyle	*Rockets in Ursa Major* (G. Hoyle)
Erich Kaestner	*Emil and the Detectives* (French)
J. Kelly	*The Flippant Heroes**
Eugène Labiche and Emily Tyler	*Monsieur Perrichon Goes Abroad**
Patrick Mace	*Jassell*
	No Memorial (both MacDonald and Young)
Louis MacNeice	*The Nose Bag* (published in B.B.C. pamphlet *Listening and Writing* – Autumn 1968)
Jean Baptiste Molière	*The Mock Doctor* (Penguin)
David Moyser	*The Beat of the Drum* (D. E. Adland)
Peter Slade	*Saint Patrick**
Sara Spencer	*Little Women*
	Tom Sawyer (both Children's Theatre Press)

New Directions

J. C. Trewin	*Last Man In*
	So Early in the Morning
	The Silver Rose
	(all in *A Sword for a Prince* and other Plays)
Barbara Willard	*Brother Ass and Brother Lion* (J. Garnet Miller)
Clifford Williams	*The Disguises of Arlecchino**

* indicates play available direct from Author (see *Bibliography of Plays*).

Two very good collections of plays suitable for use with children of secondary school age:

Eight plays edited by Malcolm Stuart Fellows. (Cassell.)

Volume 1

John Arden and Margaretta D'Arcy	*Ars Longa, Vita Brevis*
Bernard Kops	*The Boy Who Wouldn't Play Jesus* (this deals with the world hunger problem)
Jean Morris	*The Spongees*
Alun Owen	*Dare to be a Daniel* (a play which grew out of a happening at school)

Volume 2

Frederic Raphael	*The Island*
Rosemary Anne Sisson	*The Man in the Case*
Gwyn Thomas	*The Loot*
James Yaffe	*This Year's Genie*

and Four Continental Plays edited by John Allen (Heinemann)

> *The Broken Jug* (Kleist)
> *The Jar* (Pirandello)
> *The Wedding* (Chekhov)
> *The Poet* (Niccodemi)

PLAYS FOR PERFORMANCE BY OLDER CHILDREN
AND YOUTH GROUPS

Public performance, improvisation and the school play

Drama in education is not, as we have said, the subject of this book; it needs a book in itself and several have been written already. For the moment our purpose is the relationship of improvisation with the formal production and public performance of a play.

There is no doubt of the value of the improvised work which lies at the heart of school drama. But the main purpose of such work is not aesthetic. It has a limited communicative quality, and can develop into a succession of undeveloped charades which never progress into playmaking (see page 82) and formal play production.

So how can improvisation, drama as therapy, informal drama in the classroom, develop into the considered production of a great play? The problem is discussed in *Drama Education Survey 2*.[1] Its sane and discerning report we quote at length: 'One of the problems facing school drama is that the present emphasis on improvisation is leading to an impoverishment of the literary side of drama and a disregard for dramatic literature... the value of improvisation should not divert attention from the extreme importance of studying plays for their own sake. The use of language, the depiction of character, the expression of ideas, and the development of narrative in dramatic form, are a substantial part of English. Dramatic literature is an art form in its own right.

'Some people believe that the distinction between educational drama and the art of the theatre, involving the actor and producer's responsibility for interpreting a play, is greater than we have suggested. We tend to believe that the former, valid in its own right, is at the same time a corollary of, and even a preparation for, the latter. . . .

'The difficulty for young people of changing from improvised to written dialogue is always acute when classroom improvisation has not been accompanied over the years by practice in reading aloud and speaking. We have constantly emphasised that education in all aspects of English and the arts must proceed on a broad front. If one element is emphasised at the expense of another, sooner or later the lack of balance will become evident. Young people, capable of improvising in the liveliest fashion, often find the

[1] *Drama Education Survey 2*. Department of Education and Science (H.M.S.O.).

greatest difficulty in bringing to life a simple dramatic text. But if they have never read poetry aloud in the classroom, or become practised in using different registers of speech, they can hardly be expected to make music of Shakespeare's verse or to speak a text of Bernard Shaw with understanding of the quality of the language.

'The chosen play must therefore be one that is written in a style the young people can hope to master. The language of the Restoration dramatists, for example, presents even greater difficulties than that of Shakespeare. It must have characters that are reasonably within the emotional and imaginative range of the young people. And perhaps most important of all, it must be a play the young people want to do.'

None of the plays in the list which follows were written for children or young people, and we make no suggestion that any of them are suitable for production by a particular secondary school or youth workshop group. It is very possible that none of these plays suit the requirements of a particular group who might do better and develop their own work. How this might be attempted is discussed in the section on Playmaking (pages 82–7) and throughout Chapter 3.

There are few social comedies, and naturalistic plays have been avoided: stylised and naturalistic acting is invariably unsuccessful. Plays with elements of fantasy and symbolism are often a success however. Most of the plays listed in the remainder of the chapter are also suitable; with the obvious exception of those beyond the technical and imaginative range of adolescents.

Development Through Drama. Brian Way (Cassell)

GREEK PLAYS

Sophocles	*King Oedipus* (Penguin)
Aristophanes	*The Birds* (Penguin)
	The Frogs (Penguin)
	The Clouds (Bantam) trans. Lucas (Dent)
Euripides	*The Trojan Women* (Methuen)
Menander	*The Rape of the Lock* (Allen and Unwin)

CHINESE PLAYS

Anon	*The Circle of Chalk* (13th century) (famous Chinese Plays in a collection of Arlington and Acton (Vetch, Peiping)
Hsiung	*Lady Precious Stream* (French)

JAPANESE PLAYS

The Noh Plays of Japan edited by Arthur Waley (Allen and Unwin)

INDIAN PLAYS

Kalidasa	*Shakuntala* trans. Ryder (Dent)
Sudraka	*The Toy Cart* trans. Symons (Mounsel, Dublin) Both are old Hindu stories
Tagore	*The Sacrifice* (and other plays) (Macmillan)

MEDIAEVAL, ELIZABETHAN AND JACOBEAN PLAYS

Apart from the Miracle and Morality plays (see pages 134 and 155–6) there are:

Sir David Lindsay	*The Satire of the Three Estates* (Heinemann)
Anon	*Gammer Gurton's Needle* (Bantam)
Nicolas Udall	*Ralph Roister Doister* (O.U.P.)
Thomas Dekker	*The Shoemaker's Holiday* (Dent)
Francis Beaumont and John Fletcher	*The Knight of the Burning Pestle* (Longmans)
Ed. J. Allen	*Three Medieval Plays* (Heinemann)
Christopher Marlowe	*Dr Faustus* (Benn)

Shakespeare (only a selection here of some of the most successful to attempt with young people)
Macbeth
Richard II
Julius Caesar
A Midsummer Night's Dream

> *Henry V*
> *Henry IV*, parts 1 and 2
> *The Tempest*
> *Twelfth Night*
> *As You Like It*

THE FRENCH CLASSICAL THEATRE

Molière
> *The Imaginary Invalid*
> *That Scoundrel Scapin*
> *The Would-Be Gentleman*
> *The Misanthrope*
> *The Mock Doctor*
>   (Penguin, o.u.p. etc.)

THE 18TH CENTURY

Oliver Goldsmith
> *She Stoops to Conquer* (many editions: e.g.
>   Heinemann)

R. B. Sheridan
> *The Critic* (MacGibbon and Kee)
> *The School for Scandal* (MacGibbon and Kee)
> *The Rivals* (MacGibbon and Kee)

Beaumarchais
> *The Barber of Seville* (Penguin)
> *The Marriage of Figaro* (Penguin)

Carlo Goldoni
> *A Servant of Two Masters* (Heinemann)
> *The Fan* trans. May (University of Leeds)
> *The Liar* (Heinemann)
> *Mirandolina* (Penguin)
> *It Happened in Venice* (Heinemann)

Carlo Gozzi
> *The Blue Monster* (c.u.p.)

ROMANTICISM

Georg Büchner
> *Danton's Death* (MacGibbon and Kee) also trans.
>   Spender (Faber)

Edmond Rostand
> *Cyrano de Bergerac* (Heinemann)

RUSSIAN 19TH CENTURY PLAYS

Nikolai Gogol	*The Government Inspector* (Heinemann)
Turgenev	*A Month in the Country* (Heinemann)
Andreyev	*He Who Gets Slapped* (Bantam)

SCANDINAVIAN PLAYS

Henrik Ibsen	*Peer Gynt* (Heinemann, O.U.P. etc.) *Brand* (Heinemann)
August Strindberg	*The Bridal Gown* (Cape) *Lucky Peter's Travels* (Cape)

FRENCH FARCES

Eugène Labiche	*An Italian Straw Hat* (edited Bentley, *The Modern Theatre*, vol. 3 – Anchor) *M. Monet's Money* trans. Partridge apply: International Copyright Bureau, 26 Charing Cross Road, London WC2

BELGIAN PLAYS

Maeterlinck	*The Blue Bird* (Methuen) *The Betrothal* (Methuen) *Sister Beatrice* (Allen and Unwin)

THE 20TH CENTURY
America

Arthur Miller	*The Crucible* (Heinemann)
Elmer Rice	*The Adding Machine* (Gollancz)
William Saroyan	*Pullman Car Hiawatha* (French) *My Heart's in the Highlands* (French)
Thornton Wilder	*The Happy Journey* (French) *Our Town* (French)

Britain

John Arden (and M. D'Arcy*)	*The Royal Pardon* (Methuen) *Sergeant Musgrave's Dance* (Methuen)

127

	The Happy Haven (Methuen)
	*Ars Longa, Vita Brevis (Cassell)
W. H. Auden and C. Isherwood	*The Ascent of F6* (Faber)
Robert Bolt	*A Man for all Seasons* (Penguin)
James Bridie	*Tobias and the Angel* (French)
David Campton	*The Laboratory* (and others) (Garnet Miller)
V. C. Clinton	*Baddeley, Nichevo* (French)
Nigel Dennis	*The Making of Moo* (Weidenfeld and Nicolson)
T. S. Eliot	*Murder in the Cathedral* (Faber)
Willis Hall with Keith Waterhouse	*The Long, The Short and the Tall* (Penguin)
Ann Jellicoe	*The Rising Generation* (Hutchinson)
	The Knack (Faber)
John Osborne	*Look Back in Anger* (Faber)
	Luther (Faber)
Alan Plater	*The Mating Season*
	Ted's Cathedral
	apply Margaret Ramsay Ltd, 14A Goodwin's Court, St Martin's Lane, London WC2
N. F. Simpson	*A Resounding Tinkle* (Penguin)
Peter Terson	*Zigger Zagger* (Penguin)
	The Apprentices (Penguin)
Theatre Workshop and Charles Chilton	*Oh What a Lovely War* (Methuen)
Arnold Wesker	*Roots* (Penguin)
	Chips with Everything (Penguin)
John Whiting	*Marching Song* (Penguin)
	Penny for a Song (Heinemann)
Peter Ustinov	*Romanoff and Juliet* (Heinemann)

Czechoslovakia

K. Capek	*R.U.R.* trans. Selver (Oxford)
J. and K. Capek	*Life of the Insects* trans. Selver (Oxford)

France

Jean Anouilh	*Antigone* (Methuen)
	The Lark (Methuen)
Albert Camus	*Caligula* (Penguin)
André Obey	*Noah* (Heinemann)
Marcel Pagnol	*Topaze* (Heinemann)

Germany

Bertolt Brecht	*The Trial of Lucullus* (Methuen)
	The Caucasian Chalk Circle (Methuen)
	The Good Woman of Setzuan (Methuen)
Erich Kaestner	*Emil and the Detectives* adapted Brooks (French)
Carl Zuckmayer	*The Captain of Kopenik* (Bles)

Hungary

Ferenc Molnar	*Liliom* trans. Glazier (Jarrolds)

Italy

Carlo Gozzi	*The Blue Monster* trans. Dent (C.U.P.)
	King Stag trans. May (University of Leeds)
Luigi Pirandello	*Henry IV* (Penguin)
	The Jar trans. May (University of Leeds)

Russia

A. Afinogenev	*Distant Point* trans. Griffin (Pushkin Press)

Spain

Jacinte Benavente	*The Prince Who Learned Everything out of Books* (Scribner)

S. and J. Quintero	*A Hundred Years Old* *Women Have Their Way* *Fortunato* *Peace and Quiet* (all trans. Barker – Sidgwick and Jackson)
Martinez Sierra	*The Kingdom of God* (Sidgwick and Jackson) *Cradle Song* (French)
Garcia Lorca	*Blood Wedding* (Penguin)

Switzerland

Max Frisch	*The Fire Raisers* (Methuen)

PLAYS FOR WOMEN

It is no mere chance that the writers of *Drama for Women*[1] spend their first two chapters lamenting the problems of what to act, for the number of good all-women plays could be counted on the fingers of one hand. These are listed below. Some groups attempt to write or commission a play for themselves or make adaptations from existing plays which were written for men. Others have developed new forms of entertainment derived from historical, documentary or social studies, fable or folk story based on choral speech, songs, mime and improvisation.

Other groups have experimented with the production of formal plays originally written for men where the difference of sex is relatively unimportant. For a Western audience there is some reason why women should be acceptable in male parts if the play has a stylised quality; though when they attempt to play male parts in a naturalistic production the results are disastrous. Productions of *Everyman*, *Lady Precious Stream* or *The Insect Play* are quite possible with all female casts.

Plays for Women

Full length

David Campton	*Point of View* (from 35 Liberty Road, Glenfield, Leicester)

[1] *Drama for Women*. A. Graham-Campbell and Frank Lambe (Bell).

	The Manipulator (Miller)
Jean Genet	*The Maids* (Faber)
Garcia Lorca	*The House of Bernarda Alba* (Penguin)
Frank Marcus	*The Killing of Sister George* (French)

Shorter than full length or one-act plays

Samuel Beckett	*Come and Go* (Calder)
Harold Brighouse	*A Bit of War* (French)
	Albert Gates (French)
	Smoke Screens (French)
David Campton	*Two Leaves and a Stalk* (Garnet Miller)
	Incident (Garnet Miller)
	Silence on the Battlefield (Garnet Miller)
	Funeral Dance (Garnet Miller)
Charles Causley	*How Pleasant to Know Mr Lear* (Garnet Miller)
Ludwig Holberg	*The Changed Bridegroom* (published in Seven One-Act Plays by Princeton University Press)
John Mortimer	*Conference* (French)
J. Niggli	*Miracle at Blaise* (French)
Harold Pinter	*Trouble in the Works* (French)
	The Black and White (French)
N. F. Simpson	*Can You Hear Me?* (French)
August Strindberg	*The Stronger* (Bantam Classics)
Ted Willis	*George Come Home* (French)

Other plays that could be adapted for all-women casts:

| Anon | *Everyman* (Heinemann) |
| John Arden | *The Happy Haven* (Methuen) |

Samuel Beckett	*Waiting for Godot* (Faber)
Karel Capek	*The Insect Play* (Oxford)
S. I. Hsiung	*Lady Precious Stream* (Methuen)

There is also a sketch for all-women cast in *On Stage* (seventeen sketches and one monologue) by David Campton published by Garnet Miller.

Also see: *Out of this Wood* by Robert Gittings (Heinemann), a five play country sequence.

Thursday's Child, a pageant devised by E. Martin Brown, with words by Christopher Fry and music by Martin Shaw. Devised for and published by the Girls' Friendly Society, Townsend House, Greycoat Place, London s.w.1.

The Triumph of Harmony by James Kirkup, a pageant available in typescript from the Girls' Friendly Society.

With This Sword, a modern masque devised by Martin Jay and Alison Graham-Campbell with music by John Carol Case. (National Union of Townswomen's Guilds and Garnet Miller.)

A City not Forsaken by Margaret Turner (Deane).

The Brilliant and the Dark, an operatic sequence for women's voices by Malcolm Williamson (Joseph Weinberger).

RELIGIOUS DRAMA

During this century not only have the miracle and morality plays been more frequently performed than at any time since the sixteenth century, but writers have tackled seriously the problem of the modern religious play. The greatest impact was made by E. Martin Browne's production of Eliot's *Murder in the Cathedral* at the 1936 Canterbury Festival. This play succeeded in speaking about martyrdom and a man's belief in a fresh and vigorous way, avoiding the meaningless clichés of so many sermonisers.

Other experiments followed. Ronald Duncan wrote *This Way to the Tomb*, Anne Ridler *The Shadow Factory* and Norman Nicholson *The Old Man of the Mountains* which sought to set the story of Elijah among the poet's native Cumbrian hills. But the attempts of these writers to create new poetic drama was not entirely successful. Christopher Fry's lyrical statements seem already dated, and Eliot himself turned away from the specific religious subject of *Murder in the Cathedral* to explore a contemporary scene, the drawing-room. Beneath the brittle surface of 'comedies' like *The Cocktail Party* and *The Confidential Clerk* there is, however, a spiritual theme which gives meaning to the whole. Through such plays Eliot sought to broaden the area of the 'religious play' so that more men and women could grasp something of what the Church seeks to teach in its own language.

Modern experiments to broaden and deepen the experience of the religious play have led to most interesting developments. Benjamin Britten in *Curlew River* casts a Japanese 'Noh' play in the form of a medieval drama, whilst his *Noye's Fludde* uses the words of the Chester mystery play as the libretto of a delightful opera in which children take a great number of the parts. Writers like Obey have retold the same story through their own experience, whilst groups such as Negro Theatre Workshop use dance, acting and song to interpret afresh what they think and feel about Christ's life and death.

Work and experiment of this kind can be the activity not just of a solitary group but of a whole area of groups working to develop a single theme, as in the case of the women of County Durham who took the story of Christ's Passion and 'produced' this as a cycle of plays in church at Eastertide. Each group worked at part of the story in its own way, and then each individual contribution to the central theme was moulded to all the other 'plays'. Such a bringing together of work by many groups, be it Mothers' Union, Girl Guides or Scouts, makes a tremendous impact in a cathedral or in an out-of-doors setting.

Equally important is the developing of religious themes not specifically associated with the Christian myth. For example, hunger, darkness and light, poverty, heroism, healing and faith can form subjects for exploration. They can be tackled not only by older groups but by children of many ages, for the experience of religious truth is, in this way, seen and felt through the physical world, and through the problems we encounter in daily living. Such themes can be explored by painting, poetry, dance and word in a much freer way than is possible with many specific Bible stories. These, however, can be used by actors to illustrate their themes, so that modern incident and historical or biblical material are juxtaposed in striking ways. The central theme opens out with new meaning, and the 'entertainment' not only involves those acting in it in soul and body but strikes vividly at any audience that comes to share in it.

The Church, as in the Middle Ages, can again be in the forefront of experiment with drama and festival. At that time, plays took place in church as part of services, as well as out-of-doors on carts and pageants. Today we can use all these acting areas afresh, and many new ones besides; we can take our 'plays' to parks, hospitals, old people's homes, pubs, and prisons, as well as into the streets. Older groups can learn from younger ones about the power of improvisations around great themes; festivals can be fashioned anew; and the whole tradition of Christian drama refreshed and strengthened.

Much work has already been done by the Religious Drama Society and other groups, but far more must be tackled and tried out. This book aims to show how this can be done. The experiments of one part of the theatre (whether amateur or professional) can be taken up and used creatively by other groups. In this way religious plays and entertainments will speak vividly again to a wide audience, and drama itself come to be the expression of wide areas of our society, not just of cliques and small isolated groups within it.

The lists of scripted religious plays which follow are necessarily limited to those dealing with Biblical themes, the lives of saints, Miracle and Morality plays etc. This does not mean that a group should restrict itself in this narrow way, for, as we have shown, the field for exploration is immense.

Religious Plays for Children

Many producers will find that children are extremely keen to create their own plays from the stories of the Bible and the stories of saints. But it is nevertheless useful to have plays that can be adapted to children's needs. These may fire off the children's imaginations so that they begin to improvise on their own. The following list may prove useful in this way:

The Chester Shepherds' Play
The Chester 'Noye's Fludde' (in Chester Mystery Plays: Heinemann)
The Wakefield Nativity Play (in 3 Townley Plays: Heinemann) (also Evans)
The Mystery Play of Abraham and Isaac (Arnold)

St George and the Dragon (Nelson or Dent)
The Nativity Play of Cerne (Eleanor Hall, apply to British Drama League)
Three Medieval Plays edited by John Allen (Heinemann)
Seven Shrovetide Plays by Hans Sachs trans. E. U. Ouless (Deans)
The Little Plays of St Benedict. Anon. (Blackwell)

Also the following modern plays:

Freda Collins	*The Centurion* (Nelson)
Margaret Cropper	*The Legend of St Christopher* (S.P.C.K.)
A. H. Debenham	*The Green Hill* (French)
Everett Glass	*The Tumbler* (Winter)
Laurence Housman	*Brother Wolf etc.* *The Little Plays of St Francis* (Sidgwick and Jackson)
Miles Malleson	*Michael* (Nelson)
H. D. C. Pepler	*St. Martin* (St. Dominic's Press, Ditchling)
Charles Williams	*The Rite of the Passion* (Milford)
J. E. Flecker	*Joseph and Mary* (a Christmas play)

FOR OLDER CHILDREN, YOUTH CLUB MEMBERS AND ADULTS

The Chester Cycle of Mystery Plays selected and modernised by Maurice Hussey (Heinemann)

The Wakefield Cycle of Mystery Plays edited and slightly modernised by Martial Rose (Evans)

The York Cycle of Mystery Plays edited and slightly modernised by J. S. Purvis (S.P.C.K.)

Andreyev	*Samson in Chains* (Brentano's)
John Arden	*The Business of Good Government* (Methuen)
James Bridie	*Tobias and the Angel* (French) *Jonah and the Whale* (French)
Marc Connelly	*Green Pastures* (Gollancz)

Petrus Van Diest	*Everyman* (a 15th-century Belgian morality adapted by John Allen) (Heinemann)
T. S. Eliot	*Murder in the Cathedral* (Faber)

Everyman and Medieval Miracle Plays edited by A. C. Cawley (Dent)

J. E. Flecker	*Masque of the Magi* (Heinemann)
Joan Forman	*Midwinter Journey* (Evans)
Christopher Fry	*The Boy with a Cart* (Miller)
	Thor, with Angels (Oxford)
	The Firstborn (Oxford)
	A Sleep of Prisoners (Oxford)
Michel de Ghelderode	*The Women at the Tomb* trans. G. Hauger (University of Leeds)
Henri Ghéon	*Christmas in the Market Place* (Miller)
	Farce of the Devil's Bridge (Miller)
	Journey of the Three Kings (Miller)
	The Marvellous History of Saint Bernard (Sheed)
Arnoul Greban	*The True Mystery of the Passion* trans. by James Kirkup (Oxford)
Willis Hall	*The Day's Beginning, an Easter play* (Heinemann)

The Harvard Dramatic Club Miracle Plays edited by D. F. Robinson (French, New York). These include:

> *The Benediktbeuren Play*
> *The Hessian Christmas Play*
> *The Maastricht Play*
> *The Nativity*
> *The Star*
> *The Townley Play*
> *The Wisemen*

Christopher Hassall	*Christ's Comet* (Heinemann)
Laurence Housman	*The Little Plays of Saint Francis* (Sidgwick and Jackson)
	The Interlude of Youth (Gowans and Gray)

Ted Hughes	*The Coming of the Kings* (in *Listening and Writing*, B.B.C. booklet for schools Autumn 1964)
Ewan Hooper and E. Marvin	*A Man Dies*, a dramatisation for our times of the Passion and Crucifixion (Darton, Longman and Todd Ltd)
Maeterlinck	*The Miracle of Saint Anthony* (Methuen)
Louis MacNeice	*One for the Grave* (Faber)
John Masefield	*The Coming of Christ* (Heinemann) *Easter* (Heinemann) *Good Friday* (Heinemann)
André Obey	*Noah* (Heinemann)
Dorothy L. Sayers	*The Zeal of Thy House* (Gollancz)
G. B. Shaw	*Saint Joan* (Penguin)
Sudermann	*John the Baptist* (John Lane)
Tagore	*The Post Office*, an Indian miracle play (Macmillan)
Charles Williams	*The House by the Stable* (Oxford)

FOR ADULT GROUPS (in addition to the previous list)

F. E. M. Agnew	*Prelude*, a Nativity play (English Theatre Guild)
Jean Anouilh	*The Lark*, a play about St Joan (French)
Robert Bolt	*A Man for All Seasons* (Penguin)

The Play of Mary the Mother adapted by E. Martin Browne (P. Allan)

The Mysteries, made from the *Lincoln Cycle of Mystery Plays* by E. Martin Browne (French)

John Bowen	*The Fall and Redemption of Man.* Selected, arranged and rendered into modern English from the *Chester, Coventry, Lincoln, Norwich, Wakefield and York Mystery Plays* (Faber)
P. D. Cummings	*A Time to be Born* (Deane)
Campbell Dixon and Dermot Morrah	*Caesar's Friend* (French)

John Drinkwater	*A Man's House* (French)
Ronald Duncan	*This Way to the Tomb* (Faber)
	Our Lady's Tumbler (Faber)
E. and H. Fargeon	*A Room at the Inn* (French)
Christopher Fry	*A Sleep of Prisoners* (Oxford)
Henri Ghéon	*The Comedian* (Sheed and Ward)
	The Marriage of St Francis (Sheed and Ward)
Gordon Honeycombe	*The Redemption* (Methuen)
Norman Nicholson	*The Old Man of the Mountains* (Faber)
André Obey	*Frost at Midnight* (French)
John Osborne	*Luther* (Faber)
Denis Potter	*Son of Man*
Anne Ridler	*The Shadow Factory* (Faber)
	The Trial of Thomas Cranmer (Faber)
Dorothy L. Sayers	*The Man Born to be King* (Gollancz)
Mona Swann	*At the Well in Bethlehem* (British Drama League)
T. C. Thomas	*The Lonely Road* (Deane)
Charles Williams	*Thomas Cranmer of Canterbury* (Penguin)

ONE-ACT AND SHORT PLAYS

Since the Forties the one-act or short play has become a major force in the Theatre. New and progressive theatres broke away from the commercial, hidebound tradition of three acts and two bar intervals, and were prepared to experiment with new forms, and to listen to new voices in the theatre. So it was that George Devine staged Ionesco's *The Chairs* and *The Lesson* at the Royal Court Theatre in 1958, and gave opportunities to a young generation of British playwrights. Many have followed his lead. The Arts Theatre Club in London has made a success of the short play or two plays at lunchtime with a snack-bar handy, and the Edinburgh Traverse Theatre has presented many successful evenings of short plays (see the Penguin *Traverse Plays*). Audiences accustomed to radio and T.V. plays have grown to enjoy such fresh forms of entertainment with their contrasts and variety. No longer does the term 'one-act' suggest *The Monkey's Paw* performed by amateurs in the village institute, but rather *The Dumb Waiter*, *Zoo Story* and some of the most powerful modern plays. The poetry of a Pinter play, just as some of the late Yeats' plays, seems to need the concentration of a short form; certainly Ionesco's power is felt more strongly in *The Chairs* than in *Rhinoceros* – where his phantom dreams thin out when stretched over three acts.

The rise of the short play is a real revolution in theatre, marking new discoveries about the nature of a play, the breakaway from the traditional pattern of exposition/development/dénouement in three acts, and the opening up of areas of experiment and exploration – previously left out of 'dramatic' entertainment. *America Hurrah*, for example, which consists of five short plays by Van Itallie – not all of which need be performed at one time – is one of the best known of the off-off-Broadway productions which are connected with the young ensemble theatre groups like La Mama and Living Theatre. The short, formal, and rather physical nature of these plays is the result of close collaboration between writer and ensemble, the final script being a crystallisation of much improvised work. Sam Shepeard, and Megan Terry are two further writers associated with this way of working.

MEDIEVAL

See Plays in the Medieval Cycles (pages 134–5 and 155–6)

Everyman and Medieval Miracle Plays (Dent)

Three Medieval Plays edited by John Allen (including *Farce of Master Pierre Pathelin*, *The Summoning of Everyman* and *The Coventry Nativity Play*) (Heinemann)

Hans Sachs   *Seven Shrovetide Plays* (Deane)

17TH AND 18TH CENTURIES

Molière   *The Sicilian* (Penguin)
                              Sganarelle, a farce built around typical Commedia
                                 dell'Arte characters (French)

New Directions

Ludwig Holberg	*The Arabian Powder*
	The Healing Spring
	(three plays trans. Spink, published by Heinemann)
	The Talkative Barber
	The Peasant in Pawn
	(both Seven One-Act Plays published by Princeton University Press)
David Garrick	*The Lying Valet* (O.U.P.)
Henry Fielding	*The Mock Doctor – a Molière adaptation* (Nelson)

19TH CENTURY

Pushkin	*The Stone Guest* (in 19th Century Russian Drama by M. Slonim) (Bantam Books)
Turgenev	*The Provincial Lady* (French)
Chekhov	*The Bear* (Chatto and Windus)
	The Proposal (Chatto and Windus)
	The Anniversary (Chatto and Windus)
	On the Highroad (Chatto and Windus)
	A Wedding (Duckworth)
	Swan Song (Chatto and Windus)
	The Harmfulness of Tobacco (Dent)
	A Jubilee (Chatto and Windus)
Gogol	*The Gamblers* (Chatto and Windus)
H. Von Kleist	*The Broken Pitcher* (Heinemann)
Eugene Labiche	*Troubles*, trans. Partridge (International Copyright Bureau, 26 Charing Cross Road, WC2)
	90° in the Shade (French)
	How He Lied to Her Husband (Heinemann)
G. B. Shaw	*The Dark Lady of the Sonnets* (Constable)
	The Man of Destiny (Constable)
	O'Flaherty V.C. (Constable)
	A Village Wooing (Constable)
	The Glimpse of Reality (Heinemann)
	Augustus Does His Bit (Heinemann)

	The Shewing-up of Blanco Posnet (Constable)
	Passion, Poison and Petrification (Constable)
	The Fascinating Foundling (Heinemann)
	(Penguin and Constable publish Shaw)
A. Strindberg	*Playing with Fire* (French)
	The Stronger (Heinemann)
	The Bond (Bantam)
	Comrades (Bantam)
	The First Warning (Cape)
	The Ghost Sonata (Heinemann)
	The Great Highway (Constable)
	Creditors (Cape)
	(Cape publish many Strindberg plays)
H. Sudermann	*The Young Hussar* (Evans)
	The Far-away Princess (Duckworth)
J. M. Synge	*Riders to the Sea* (Heinemann)
	The Shadow of the Glen (Oxford World's Classics)
Leo Tolstoi	*Michael* (adapted by Miles Malleson) (French)
Oscar Wilde	*Salome* (Penguin)

20TH CENTURY
America

Marc Conelly	*Little David – from 'Green Pastures'* (contained in J. Marriott – Best One-Act Plays of 1937)
Clifford Odets	*Waiting for Lefty* (Gollancz)
O'Neill	*In the Zone*
	The Rope
	The Dreamy Kid
	Bound East for Cardiff
	The Long Voyage Home
	In the Lone
	The Moon of the Caribees
	Before Breakfast
	(Jonathan Cape publish all O'Neill plays)
William Saroyan	*Hello Out There* (Faber)
	The Oyster and the Pearl (Longmans)

New Directions

Thornton Wilder

The Happy Journey (French)
The Long Christmas Dinner (French)
Queens of France (Longmans, Green)
Love and How to Cure It (French)
The Pullman Car Hiawatha (French)

Tennessee Williams

The Last of My Solid Gold Watches
Auto-Da-Fe
The Long Goodbye
Portrait of a Madonna
The Strangest Kind of Romance
Twenty-seven Wagons Full of Cotton
   (all in one volume – John Lehmann)

Belgium

Michel de Ghelderode

Chronicles of Hell
Barabbas
The Woman at the Tomb
Pantagleize
The Blind Men
Three Actors and Their Drama
Lord Halewyn (Seven Plays – Vol. 1)
Red Magic
Signor!
The Death of Doctor Faust
Christopher Columbus
A Night of Pity
Piet Bouteille
(Seven Plays – Vol 2) (MacGibbon and Kee)

Maurice Maeterlinck

The Interior (Allen and Unwin)

China

Cheng-Chin Hsiung

Mencius was a Bad Boy (in 8 New Plays for Children) (Dickson)
The Thrice-promised Bride (French)

Denmark

Kaj Munk

Before Cannae trans. Keigwin (Routledge)

France

Yves Cabrol   *The Fish* (Rylee)

Jean Cocteau   *The Wedding on the Eiffel Tower* (in Modern French Plays, Benedikt & Wellworth, Faber)

Henri Ghéon   *Farce of the Devil's Bridge* (Miller)

Sacha Guitry   *Villa for Sale* (French)

Germany

Bertolt Brecht   *The Measures Taken* (in Jewish Wife and Other Short Plays, Grove Press)
The Exception and the Rule (in Jewish Wife and Other Short Plays, Grove Press)
The Trial of Lucullus (Methuen)

F. Wedekind   *The Tenor* (Stewart Kidd, Cincinnati – 50 Contemporary One-Act Plays)

Franz Kafka and others   See 7 German Expressionist Plays (Calder) which contains scripts by Oscar Kokoschka, Ernst Barlach, August Stramm etc.

Hungary

Lajos Biro   *The Bridegroom* – a comedy translated by Recht in 25 Short Plays (edited by F. Shay)

India

Tagore   *The Post Office* (Macmillan)

Ireland

Lady Gregory   *Dave* (Putnam)
The Gaol Gate (Putnam)
The Jackdaw (Putnam)
The Rising of the Moon (Putnam)
Spreading the News (French)
Workhouse Ward (French)
On the Race Course (Putnam)
   (Putnam publish Lady Gregory's collected plays)

Sean O'Casey	*The End of the Beginning*
	A Pound on Demand
	Behind the Green Curtains
	Figuro in the Night
	The Moon Shines on Kylenamoe
	Bedtime Story
	Time to Go
	Hall of Healing
	(Macmillan publishes O'Casey plays)
Synge	*The Well of the Saints* (Dent)
	Riders to the Sea (Nelson)
	The Tinker's Wedding (Dent)
	The Shadow of the Glen (Longmans)
Yeats	*Purgatory*
	The King's Threshold
	Cathleen Ni Houlihan
	Deidre
	The Green Helmet
	The Hour Glass
	On Baile's Strand
	The Player Queen
	The Euchulain Plays
	The Pot of Broth
	The Shadowy Waters
	The Unicorn from the Stars
	(Macmillan publish Yeats's collected plays)

Italy

Pirandello	*Sicilian Limes* (Dutton, New York)
	At the Gate (Dutton, New York)
	Our Lord of the Ship (Dutton, New York)
	The Man with the Flower in his Mouth (Dutton, New York)
	The Other Son (Dutton, New York)
	The Jar (Heinemann)

Japan

Kwan Kikuchi	*Madman on the Roof* (Hokuseido, Tokyo)

S. Obata	*The Melon Thief* (French, New York)

Russia

Afinogenev	*The Passer-by* trans. by Marshall in Soviet One-Act Plays (Pilot)
Andreyev	*The Dear Departing* (Macmillan)

Spain

Benavente	*No Smoking* *An Enchanted Hour* *Don Juan's Servant* *His Widow's Husband* (all Scribner)
Garcia Lorca	*Don Perlimplin and Belissa in the Garden* (in E. Bentley: From the Modern Repertoire, Indiana University Press)
S. and J. Quintero	*Fortunato* (Sidgwick and Jackson) *A Sunny Morning* (Stewart Kidd, Cincinnati – 50 Contemporary One-Act Plays)
G. M. Sierra	*The Lover* (Chatto) *Poor John* (Chatto)

Britain

James Barrie	*The Will* (French) *The Twelve Pound Look* (French) *Shall We Join the Ladies?* (French) *The Old Lady Shows Her Medals* (French)
James Bridie	*The Kitchen Comedy* (Constable) *Paradise Enow* (Constable) *The Sign of the Prophet Jonah* (Constable)
Harold Brighouse	*The Stoker* (French) *Lonesome-like* (French) *Oak Settle* (French) *The Price of Coal* (French) and 47 others
Harold Chaplin	*Augustus in Search of a Father* (Harrap) *It's the Poor that 'elp the Poor* (Harrap)

Noel Coward	*Astonished Heart*
	Family Album
	Fumed Oak
	Hands Across the Sea
	Red Peppers
	Still Life
	Ways and Means
	We Were Dancing (all French)
John Drinkwater	$X = O$ (a verse play about Troy) (Sidgwick)
T. S. Eliot	*Sweeney Agonistes* (Faber)
Christopher Fry	*The Boy with a Cart* (O.U.P.)
	A Phoenix Too Frequent (Hollis and Carter)
	Thor with Angels (Oxford)
John Galsworthy	*The Silver Fox* (Duckworth)
Stanley Houghton	*The Dear Departed* (French)
	Fancy Free (Constable)
	The Master of the House (Constable)
	The Fifth Commandment (Constable)
Terence Rattigan	*Harlequinade* (French)
	The Browning Version (French)
Charles Williams	*The House by the Stable* (Oxford)

FROM ABOUT 1950 ONWARDS

Paul Ableman	*Tests* (Methuen)
Arthur Adamov	*Professor Taranne* (Penguin)
Edward Albee	*The Zoo Story* (Penguin)
	The American Dream (French)
	The Sand Box (Longmans)
	Death of Bessie Smith (French)
Jean Anouilh	*Madame de . . .* (French)
	Cecile, or the School for Fathers (in Eric Bentley: From the Modern Repertoire, Series III) (Indiana University Press)

John Arden
Squire Jonathan
Soldier, Soldier (Methuen)
Ars Longa, Vita Brevis (Cassell)
Wet Fish (Methuen)
When is a door not a door? (Methuen)

Fernando Arrabal
Fando and Lis (Calder)
The Two Executioners (Penguin) (Calder)
Orison (Calder)
The Car Cemetery (Calder)
Picnic in the Battlefield (Calder)

Samuel Beckett
Come and Go (Calder)
Play (Faber)
Embers (Faber)
Words and Music (Faber)
Krapp's Last Tape (Faber)
Act Without Words (Faber)

Saul Bellow
A Wen (Penguin)
Orange Soufflé (Penguin)

John Bowen
Trevor (Methuen)
Coffee Lace (Methuen)
Silver Wedding (Methuen)
The Essay Prize (Faber)
A Holiday Abroad (Faber)
The Candidate (Faber)

David Campton
Funeral Dance (Miller)
Little Brother : Little Sister (Methuen)
Out of the Frying Pan (Methuen)
Silence on the Battlefield
The Laboratory (Garnet Miller)
Sunshine on the Righteous
A Smell of Burning[1]
Memento Mori[1]
Getting and Spending[1]
Soldiers from the Wars Return

[1] Other one-act plays are available from the author, 35 Liberty Road, Glenfield, Leicester, LE3 8JF.

	Then (in Theatre Today – Longmans) *Don't Wait for Me* (Blackie)
Giles Cooper	*Before the Monday* *The Disagreeable Oyster* *Mathray Beacon* (and others in Six Plays for Radio)
David Creegan	*Transcending* (Methuen) *The Dancers* (Methuen)
Marguerite Duras	*La Musica* (Penguin)
J. P. Donleavy	*The Interview* (and other plays from *Fairy Tales of New York* (Penguin))
Jennifer Dawson	*The Ha-Ha*
Jean Genet	*The Maids* (Faber) *Deathwatch* (Faber)
Brian Friel	*Lovers : Winners and Losers* – a double bill (Faber)
Jean Giraudoux	*The Apollo de Bellac* (French)
Gunter Grass	*On Ten Minutes to Buffalo* (Secker and Warburg)
Willis Hall	*A Glimpse of the Sea* (3 one-act plays) (Evans) *Final at Furnell* (Evans)
Ionesco	*Improvisation* *Maid to Marry* *The Future is in Eggs* *The Leader* *The Lesson* (French) *The Foursome* *The Motor Show* *Exit the King* (long one-act) (French) *Jacques, or Obedience* *The Victims of Duty* *The New Tenant* *The Picture* *The Shepherd's Chameleon* (Calder publishes Ionesco's plays)

Jakov Lind	*The Silver Foxes* (Methuen)
Henry Livings	*Kelly's Eye* (Methuen)
	Big Soft Nellie (Methuen)
	The Day Dumbfounded got his Pylon (Blackie)
William Wellington Mackey	*Family Meeting* (Louisiana State University Press)
Wolf Mankowitz	*The Bespoke Overcoat* (Dent, Evans)
	It Should Happen to a Dog (Longmans)
Frank Marcus	*The Window*
John Mortimer	*Lunch Hour* (French)
	The Dock Brief (Elek)
	Collect Your Hand Baggage (French)
	What Shall We Tell Caroline? (French)
	I Spy (French)
Bill Naughton	*She'll Make Trouble* (Blackie)
Joe Orton	*The Erpingham Camp* (Methuen)
	The Ruffian on the Stair (Methuen)
John Osborne	*Under Plain Cover* (Faber)
	The Blood of the Bambergs (Faber)
Alun Owen	*Dare to be a Daniel* (Cassell)
	Shelter (French)
	George's Room (French)
Robert Pinget	*The Old Tune* (Penguin)
Harold Pinter	*The Dumb Waiter* (Penguin)
	The Collection (French)
	A Night Out (French)
	The Room (French)
	A Slight Ache (French)
	The Lover (French)
	Landscape (Methuen)
	The Basement (Methuen)
	The Black and White (Longmans)
	Last to Go (Longmans)
	Tea Party (Methuen)

	The Dwarves (Methuen)
	Night School (Methuen)
	Silence (Methuen)
Alan Plater	*The Mating Season* (Blackie)
	See the Pretty Lights (apply Margaret Ramsay Ltd)
James Saunders	*Barnstable* (French)
	Double, Double (French)
	Alas, poor Fred (Heinemann)
	Triangle (Deutsch)
	Neighbours (Deutsch)
Jean-Paul Sartre	*In Camera* (Penguin)
	The Respectable Prostitute (Penguin)
Peter Shaffer	*The Private Ear* (French)
	The Public Eye (French)
	Black Comedy (French)
	The White Liars (French)
Sam Shepard	*Chicago* (Faber)
	Melodrama Play (Faber)
	Red Cross (Faber)
	Fourteen Hundred Thousand (Faber)
	Icarus's Mother (Faber)
N. F. Simpson	*The Hole* (French)
	A Resounding Tinkle (French)
	The Form (French)
Norman Smithson	*The Three Lodgers* (apply Margaret Ramsay Ltd)
Tom Stoppard	*The Real Inspector Hound* (Faber)
Jean Tardieu	*The Underground Lover* (Allen & Unwin)
Cecil Taylor	*Allergy* (Penguin)
Dylan Thomas	*Return Journey* (Hutchinson Educational)
Van Itallie	*War* (Penguin)
	Almost Like Being (Penguin)
	Interview (Penguin)
	I'm Really Here (Bantam)

	Hotel (Penguin)
	T.V. (Penguin)
John Whiting	*No Why* (French)
Charles Wood	*Escort* (Penguin)
	John Thomas (Penguin)
	Spare (Penguin)

The following short radio-plays are also worth considering:

Barry Bermange	*No Quarter* (Penguin)
Caryl Churchill	*The Ants* (Penguin)
Giles Cooper	*The Object* (Penguin)
Jeremy Sandford	*The Whelks and the Chromium* (2 acts) (Penguin)
Alan Sharp	*The Long Distance Piano Player* (Penguin)
Cecil P. Taylor	*Happy Days are Here Again* (Penguin)
Tom Stoppard	*Albert's Bridge* (Faber)
	I'll be Frank (Faber)

A SURVEY OF DRAMA
Greek Plays

The texts have come down to us with little indication of the music and dancing which were an integral part of each play. So one of the main problems for a producer is the job of creation or re-creation of the chorus-work. Music will need writing or improvising, and drums, cymbals or pipes can form a rhythmic background to movement. This should be treated freely; slavish imitation of the formal gestures of some other production is useless. Greek National Theatre productions like *The Persians* are exciting because they make no concession to classical convention and treat the plays as if they had just been thought up for the Palladium.

AESCHYLUS (c.525–456 B.C.)

Prometheus Bound
The Agamemnon
The Choephori

The Eumenides
The Persians
Seven Against Thebes
The Suppliants (all Penguin etc.)

Prometheus Bound – An epic and largely static play. There are tremendous choruses.

The Orestian Trilogy – Aeschylus explores the theme of justice in which revenge is replaced by judicial law.

The Agamemnon – The story of Clytemnestra's revenge and the murder of her husband, Agamemnon.

The Choephori or *The Libation-Bearers* – Orestes, son to Agamemnon and Clytemnestra, is commanded by Apollo to kill his mother in revenge for his father.

The Eumenides – His heroic suffering brings about the expiation of the curse laid upon him, so that violence in the shape of the Eumenides withdraws and 'holy Persuasion' wins the day, reconciling revenge with justice.

The Persians – The only Greek play based on an historic event. The messenger gives a vivid account of the Battle of Salamis where Athens triumphed over the Persian fleet. The scenes are full of brilliant pageantry.

Seven Against Thebes—A play with little action, almost one third of its length being taken by the messenger's description of warriors, their weapons and characters.

SOPHOCLES (496–406 B.C.)

Antigone
King Oedipus
Oedipus at Colonnus
Electra
Philoctetes
Ajax
Women of Trachis (all Penguin etc.)

With Sophocles dramatic action becomes more realistic, but the Chorus still has an essential part to play both as an actor in the drama, and as a lyric 'presenter' of its main theme.

Antigone – The play presents a simple conflict between compassion and piety on the one hand, and political expediency on the other; and between them the King's son torn by conflicting loyalties.

King Oedipus – This has since Aristotle's time been considered Sophocles' masterpiece. It presents the tragedy of a complacent and self-sufficient man driven by chance to a terrible agony of soul and body, and shows how he finally raises himself chastened and ennobled. Listen to Stravinsky's *Oedipus Rex* which is a great modern expression in music of Sophocles' theme.

Oedipus at Colonnus – A ritual drama with little movement or spectacle.

EURIPIDES (484–407 B.C.)

Hippolytus
Iphigenia in Tauris
Alcestis
Trojan Women
The Bacchae
Medea
Andromache
Hecabe
Heracles (all Penguin etc.)

In many ways the most modern of the Greek playwrights, Euripides seems unable to accept ready-made religious answers to the problems of good and evil. His character portrayal is ruthless, passionate and subtle and though he remains finally pessimistic about human endeavour, he still believes it right to pursue goodness and kindness despite the hostility of the gods. In *Hippolytus* sexual passion sweeps aside any rational power, as Phaedra, suffering her illicit passion for her stepson, is caught by forces beyond her control and understanding. In *The Bacchae*, probably his greatest play, a destructive madness seizes hold of women desiring to be at one with Nature. Most of these plays are available in *Penguin Classics*, but groups may prefer to work with other translations, e.g. Gilbert Murray's (published by Allen & Unwin) which have a dramatic rhythm and beauty of their own. The poetry seems now too close to Swinburne in its romanticism, and this may deter some people from these fine translations.

Greek and Roman Comedy

ARISTOPHANES (c.445–c.385 B.C.)

The Clouds (Bantam)
The Wasps (Penguin Classics)
The Frogs (Penguin Classics)
The Acharnians (Longmans)
Lysistrata (Faber)
The Birds (Allen and Unwin)
The Poet and the Women (Penguin Classics)

The great representative of the 'Old' Attic Comedy is Aristophanes. He is a highly original genius and his plays, despite all their references to people and events of Aristophanes' own day are still very much alive, very full of vitality and humour, fun and satire.

The 'Old' style comedy of the 5th century was replaced during the 4th century by the 'New' comedy of Menander and other playwrights. This type emphasised plot and construction and it had a repertoire of the kind of stock situations and characters which were later used by Plautus, Terence and the Commedia dell'Arte, even Molière and Jonson.

MENANDER (c.342–c.290 B.C.)

The Rape of the Lock (Allen and Unwin)
Dyskolos (Menander's Plays and Fragments published by Penguin)

PLAUTUS (c.254–184 B.C.)

The Pot of Gold
The Brothers Menaechmus
The Swaggering Soldier
The Rope
The Prisoners
Pseudolus (all Penguin etc.)

The Pot of Gold – The character of the old miser must have existed in 'New' comedy but there is no direct forerunner of this play known.
The Brothers Menaechmus – This, though not one of Plautus' best plays, is notable as having been the original for the plot of Shakespeare's *The Comedy of Errors*.

The Swaggering Soldier – Plautus' most biting satire on the military type.

These rank highly amongst his plays. Some of Plautus' best-drawn characters are his slaves, and it was through such entertaining portrayals that he set the style of 'low' characters in much later comedy.

TERENCE (185 B.C. – 159 B.C.)

The Brothers (Penguin)
The Eunuch (Penguin)
The Woman of Andros
The Mother-in-Law (Penguin)
Phormio (Bell)

His plays have none of the rollicking fun of Plautus and they often seem to have been written for a small gathering of cultivated aristocrats and friends. He discards the farce found in a Plautus play and instead gives his audience a far subtler plot with well-developed characters and elegant economical dialogue. Though he took over a great deal from the 'New' comedy he was no slavish imitator.

Medieval Plays

These were often given the most varied forms of production for a play could take place on a cart, in an inn yard, out-of-doors, in-the-round or practically anywhere. And the plays were as varied and full of vigour as the people who made them; particularly so in the case of many of the miracle plays for performance by various guilds on the feast of Corpus Christi.

Today they can still be performed and still make their impact; the vitality of the language can move an audience and the simple, strong emotions come through as freshly as ever.

Amongst available folk-plays are:

The Symondsbury Mumming Play (No. 6 Journal of the Folk Song Society)
St George and the Turkish Knight (St Dominic's Press, Ditchling)
See *The Mummer's Play*, ed. R. J. E. Tiddy (Oxford, Clarendon Press), which reprints 33 extant plays.

Then there are separate Passion Plays such as:

The Norwich Passion Play (obtainable from the Maddermarket Theatre, Norwich)

The main Mystery cycles are those of *Chester*, *York* and *Wakefield*. The best modern translations of these are:

The Wakefield Mystery Plays (ed. Martial Rose, Evans)

These can be obtained either in a single volume or in four separate parts. The most famous of the plays is the *Second Shepherds' Play*.

The Chester Cycle of Plays (ed. Maurice Hussey, Heinemann)

Noye's Fludde, one of the most lively of the series, has been set to music by Benjamin Britten.

The York Cycle of Plays (ed. J. S. Purvis, S.P.C.K.)

There is also a shorter version by Dr Purvis. It is interesting to note that the language here is quite close to modern North and East Riding dialects.

The True Mystery of the Passion – James Kirkup (Oxford)
Three Medieval Plays – John Allen (Heinemann)
Everyman (Dent)

The True Mystery of the Passion – This is a recent translation of a French series of plays and is very well worth looking at and reading.
Everyman – This can be found in several editions among them *Everyman and Medieval Miracle Plays* (Dent) *English Miracle Plays, Moralities and Interludes* edited by A. W. Pollard (University of London Press).

A useful collection of miracle plays is *Seven Miracle Plays* adapted by Alexander Franklin and published by the Oxford University Press. It includes *Noah's Flood*, *The Adoration of the Shepherds*, and the *Slaying of the Innocents* from the Chester Cycle; the Townley play of the *Killing of Abel*, the *Coming of the Three Kings* and the *Adoration from the York Cycle*; a version of *Abraham and Isaac* made from the Brome and Dublin manuscripts and the Norwich play of *Adam and Eve*.

Another adaptation *The Redemption* by Gordon Honeycomble (Methuen) includes parts of the Medieval Mystery Plays of York, Townley and Chester, the *Ludus Coventriae* and the *Coventry Corpus Christi plays*.

The Renaissance in Italy

NICCOLO MACHIAVELLI (1469–1527)
Mandragola (Jonas). A witty piece of social comment in the form of a classic Italian comedy of intrigue is particularly interesting.

Elizabethan England

WILLIAM SHAKESPEARE (1564–1616)

Do not choose Shakespeare, as so many amateur groups do, because it is suitably 'cultural'; there is no easier way to kill drama stone dead. Choose a Shakespeare play because it means something to you and to your actors.

There is little need to say anything more about Shakespeare's plays but perhaps the following might be attempted:

Macbeth
Julius Caesar
As You Like It
A Midsummer Night's Dream
Richard II
The Merchant of Venice
Henry V

More difficult plays include:

Henry VIII
Romeo and Juliet
Hamlet
Lear
Othello
Cymbeline
Richard III
Twelfth Night
The Tempest
The Winter's Tale

Amongst the many editions of Shakespeare's plays the Arden Shakespeare (Methuen), the New Cambridge (C.U.P.), and the New Penguin Shakespeare are three of the best.

Other Elizabethan and Jacobean Playwrights

CHRISTOPHER MARLOWE (1564–1593)

Dr Faustus
Tamburlaine

Edward II
The Jew of Malta   (Oxford World's Classics: Penguin)

Tamburlaine is a grand heroic theme and the play possesses fine poetry even if the plot becomes monotonous. *Edward II* is better constructed than, for example, *Faustus* which is one of the greatest Elizabethan plays that still plays magnificently.

BEN JONSON (1572–1637)

Volpone (Oxford World Classics, Penguin)
The Alchemist (MacGibbon & Kee)
The Silent Woman (Benn)
Bartholomew Fair (Penguin)

These magnificent plays are rough, witty, humorous, cynical and fantastical, they have vitality and originality with the scene usually set in contemporary England, except for *Volpone* which takes place in Venice. The language is robust, vivid and strikingly fresh; and the whole plot of a Jonson comedy moves with great drive and directness towards the inevitable climax.

JOHN MARSTON (1576–1634)

The Malcontent (Arnold)

Martson's plays have something of Jonson's satirical vein. The *Malcontent* has an elaborate plot and the central figure of Malevole is close in conception to those other malcontent figures, Iago and Bosola (*The Duchess of Malfi*).

THOMAS MIDDLETON (1580–1627)

The Changeling (Penguin)
Women Beware Women (Benn)
A Game of Chess (O.U.P.)

CYRIL TOURNEUR (1580?–1626)

The Revenger's Tragedy (Penguin)
The Atheist's Tragedy (Methuen)

The Revenger's Tragedy is a play of unremitting sardonic power with a burning passionate intensity about it. It certainly ranks much higher than Tourneur's rather feeble second play, *The Atheist's Tragedy*.

THOMAS DEKKER (1572–1632)

The Shoemaker's Holiday (O.U.P.)

This romping Elizabethan comedy is exceedingly good-humoured in tone, robust and altogether delightful. The setting is contemporary London and the story centres around Simon Eyre, the shoemaker, with any number of sub-plots.

FRANCIS BEAUMONT (1588–1616) AND JOHN FLETCHER (1579–1625)

The Knight of the Burning Pestle (Longmans)

A gay farce set among London apprentices and owing much to *Don Quixote*.

THOMAS HEYWOOD (1570–1641)

A Woman Killed with Kindness (Methuen, Revel Plays)

This is a forerunner of the domestic problem play. Though at times naïve, the play is concerned with the husband's dilemma at his wife's infidelity. Frankford, the husband, is revealed with some real insight.

GEORGE CHAPMAN (1559–1634)

The Tragedy of Bussy d'Ambois (Methuen: Benn)

Chapman's dramas are too overloaded with moralising to be successful in the theatre today. But he remains an interesting playwright, nevertheless.

JOHN WEBSTER (1577–1634)

The White Devil (Methuen, Revel Plays)
The Duchess of Malfi (Benn: New Mermaid Series)

Webster was a far better dramatist than Chapman; his plots are exciting, memorable melodramas. The world in which his characters move is cruel, fierce and dark: men are close to animals in their violent and consuming passions. His great scenes have a brooding poetic intensity which makes him outstanding among Jacobean playwrights.

PHILIP MASSINGER (1583–1640)

A New Way to Pay Old Debts (Benn)

ANONYMOUS

Arden of Faversham (Benn: Penguin)

This play, published in 1592, is the first middle-class tragedy. It is a clearly-told murder story and the character of the wife-murderess, Alice, is strong and well-conceived with her direct passionate hatred of her husband, Arden, and her equally passionate love for Mosbie.

JOHN FORD (1586–?)

'Tis Pity She's a Whore (Benn: Dent)
The Broken Heart (Benn: Dent)

Amongst Jacobean dramatists Ford is the last to show really great qualities. His plots have simplicity and compactness and through them he shows a penetrating understanding of emotion and thought, particularly of such qualities as courage and chivalry.

The Great Ages of Drama in Spain and France

The Spanish Siglo de Oro coincided with our own Elizabethan Age and there was the same enthusiasm for the theatre amongst Spaniards of the time as amongst Englishmen. Especially popular were the plays of Lope de Vega, Tirso de Molina and Calderón. But though they were magnificent creators of plot, they only developed character in a limited way. Usually honour was set against loyalty in some form and the whole action turned on point of the elaborate and stylised code of behaviour that had been evolved. It is because of this artificial background that most of these plays seem doomed to being treated mainly as museum pieces. Also the poetry loses a very great deal in translation. This is particularly the case with the wonderfully rich and symbolic verse of Calderón's Autos Sacramentales which grew from religious themes. His best-known plays (e.g. *The Mayor of Zalamea*) are careful rewritings of plays by Lope and Tirso. Lope wrote over 1500 plays, and Tirso has the honour of inventing the original Don Juan character.

The French Classical Theatre grew to maturity later, during the reign of Louis XIV. With Corneille and Racine we discover dramatists very alien to English traditions which stem from Shakespeare. Their closely-argued tragedies seem to take place always in ante-rooms of the palace of Versailles; they are lacking in variety and action to most English tastes.

French comedy in the hands of Molière is far more universal in its impact; it appeals equally on both sides of the Channel. Molière makes no attempt to create comic characters in-the-round like Falstaff; instead we see only one or two aspects of a character like Tartuffe, but yet such characters remain universal types. Molière's satirical wit attacked every kind of pretension from that of affected society women, to would-be fashionable bourgeois and pompous doctors. He is superbly theatrical and extremely amusing. Amongst his greatest plays are *Tartuffe*, *The Imaginary Invalid*, and *Le Misanthrope*. It is interesting to remember that Molière first worked with a group of the Italian Commedia dell'Arte in which improvisations around such characters as Punchinello and Harlequin and the foolish old Pantaloon were the regular stock-in-trade of performance. From this background came some of his own stock comic characters (e.g. the roguish servant) marvellously developed in his great plays.

French Plays

PIERRE CORNEILLE (1606–1684)

El Cid

This is Cornielle's most famous play about the great Spanish hero. It has the usual classical theme of the struggle between love and honour. See *The Chief Plays of Corneille* translated by L. Lockett (Princeton, O.U.P).

JEAN RACINE (1639–1699)

Andromache (Penguin)
Phaèdra (Penguin)
Athaliah (Penguin)
Bérénice (Penguin)

Britannicus (Penguin)
Iphigenia

Though Racine remains one of the world's greatest tragic poets successful productions in English are rare.

JEAN-BAPTISTE MOLIÈRE (1622–1673)

The Miser (Penguin)
Tartuffe (Penguin)
Misanthrope (Penguin)
The Imaginary Invalid (Penguin)
The Scoundrel Scapin (Penguin)
The Would-be Gentleman (Penguin)
A Doctor in Spite of Himself (Penguin)
Don Juan (Penguin)

These comic masterpieces (often verging on tragic possibilities) require an impeccable sense of style if they are to succeed with amateurs. But Molière ran his own company, and his writing is marvellously theatrical. Human vices and weaknesses are ruthlessly exposed.

Spanish Plays

LOPE DE VEGA (1562–1625)

He really created Spanish theatre, writing about 2,000 plays. Usually his characterisation is straightforward and lively; he left a share to the actor who could build up his own character from the lightly sketched-in idea of the playwright. In Lope's hands Spanish drama became 'a rapid, improvised affair of action and lyric poetry'. It lacked depth.

Fuenteovejuna
Peribanez
The Dog in the Manger
The Knight from Olmedo
Justice without Revenge (all MacGibbon and Kee)

Fuenteovejuna – Perhaps his finest play, though a number are of almost equal quality. It tells of a village rising against a tyrant, how he was killed, and finally how the King pardoned the villagers for their crime.

TIRSO DE MOLINA (1584–1648)

The Rogue of Seville (Bantam Classics)

This play, which introduces for the first time Don Juan, has a greater concentrated power than any written by Lope. It works up slowly to the tremendous macabre climax of Don Juan's dinner with the ghost of the Comendador. Don Juan himself seems driven on by superhuman energy to destroy love; yet there is a great dynamic attraction about him. He carries the whole play to its masterly climax.

ALARCÓN (1581–1639)

The Truth Suspected (Bantam Classics)

This is a fine example of the Spanish comedy of character. It was adapted by Corneille in his *Le Menteur*.

CALDERÓN (1600–1681)

Secret Vengeance for Secret Insult
Devotion to the Cross
The Mayor of Zalamea
The Phantom Lady (all MacGibbon and Kee)
Life's a Dream (Bantam Classics)

Calderón's career marks the decline of Spanish drama. It had made its greatest contribution during Lope's lifetime, and with Calderón it exhausts itself. At his death, there is nothing left. Yet he is a great baroque writer and his plays have a firmer form and concentration of power which Lope's so obviously lack. Not only this for he was a more religious man, a deeper thinker, sometimes melancholy but noble and passionate. Calderón also wrote many autos sacramentales, religious plays sometimes with passages of tremendous poetry. Amongst these are *La Cena de Baltasar* and *El Gran Teatro del Mundo*. This latter play is a moving representation of Catholic thought of the time on social inequality. Calderón, unlike Lope, gives his plays a critical social content at times, as for example in *The Mayor of Zalamea*.
The Mayor of Zalamea – This play based on a plot of Lope's is one of Calderón's finest. He shows his power of creating a memorable character

in the peasant, Pedro Crespo who rises to be mayor. The theme is unique in dealing with the honour of a rich peasant whose daughter is violated by a Captain of militia.

Restoration plays and the 18th century at home and abroad

The artificial comedy of manners that started off in Charles II's reign with Congreve and Wycherley lasted until Sheridan. It is a rather difficult tradition for a group to experiment with, because the portrayal of an elaborate code of social behaviour so foreign to today's manners can prove extremely cramping, especially to young people. The elaborate artifice of movement and gesture is often learnt parrot-fashion, but perhaps far more could be done to experiment freely with this tradition.

Congreve's style and wit are magnificent in such a play as *The Way of the World*, but better merely as a constructor of plays was Wycherley. A playwright who has proved extremely successful with modern audiences is Farquhar (*The Recruiting Officer* and *The Beaux' Stratagem*) for he began to create characters in the round, and he brought a freshness into the Restoration theatre with his own breezy humour. Vanbrugh's and Garrick's plays have been little performed yet they, too, deserve an airing as they are well written and perhaps not as dry as Sheridan. Goldsmith's *She Stoops to Conquer* has a delightful vein of humour and it has retained its popularity ever since its first performance in 1773.

Abroad there is Goldoni with his clever bustle of lively intrigue very well contrived, and in more serious theatre, Goethe and Schiller.

JOHN DRYDEN (1631–1700)

Aureng-zebe (a tragedy)
All for Love (Antony and Cleopatra remade) (Benn)

GEORGE ETHEREGE (1634–1691)

The Comical Revenge
She Would if She Could
The Man of Mode (Dent) (Collected Plays: Blackwell: Oxford)

Etherege was the first to realise that French comedy in the style of Molière would be popular on the English stage.

WILLIAM WYCHERLEY (1640–1716)

Love in a Wood (Benn)
The Gentleman Dancing-Master (Fisher Unwin)
The Country Wife (Arnold)
The Plain Dealer (Fisher Unwin)

Wycherley followed up Etherege's success. His *The Country Wife* and *The Plain Dealer* (the last of his plays) have better plots than the rest. *The Plain Dealer* is free from the obscenities of its predecessors; it is based on Molière's *Le Misanthrope*.

WILLIAM CONGREVE (1670–1729)

The Old Bachelor
The Double Dealer
Love for Love
The Way of the World (Oxford World Classics) (MacGibbon and Kee)

Congreve is the greatest of the Restoration playwrights. In his earliest play *The Old Bachelor* the plot is needlessly complicated. In fact, this failure to construct good plots troubled Congreve very much and he made great efforts to improve the intrigue in *The Double Dealer* and even more successfully in *Love for Love*. His tremendous ear for the vernacular and a certain intelligent pessimism enabled him to release toughness, a critical harshness, into quick, talkative naughty fun.

GEORGE FARQUHAR (1678–1707)

The Recruiting Officer (MacGibbon and Kee)
The Beaux' Stratagem (MacGibbon and Kee)

These are the only two mature comedies that Farquhar wrote. They have a realistic interest in background, e.g. the opening scene at the Lichfield Inn in *The Beaux' Stratagem* and the recruiting scene in *The Recruiting Officer* which links Farquhar with the great 18th century novelists – and Hogarth.

THOMAS OTWAY (1652–1685)

The Soldier's Fortune (Fisher Unwin)
Venice Preserved (Oxford World's Classics)

JOHN VANBRUGH (1664–1726)

The Relapse : or *Virtue in Danger*
The Provok'd Wife (Benn)
The Confederacy (Benn)

Vanbrugh makes more use of farce than did Congreve and the dialogue has not the same quality of wit. But the plots are well sustained and the character-drawing shows lively observation.

JOHN GAY (1685–1732)

The Beggar's Opera (Constable)

This was one of the most original achievements of the early 18th century. It had immense popularity and remains delightful and fresh whenever revived today.

OLIVER GOLDSMITH (1728–1774)

She Stoops to Conquer

RICHARD SHERIDAN (1751–1816)

The Rivals (MacGibbon and Kee)
The School for Scandal (MacGibbon and Kee)
The Critic (MacGibbon and Kee)

The Rivals was a miraculous first play. It introduced among others, Mrs Malaprop, and has lively, farcical elements that give variety to the texture in a way which is absent from *The School for Scandal* however brilliant and subtle that later masterpiece may be. *The Critic* is a delightful burlesque on the absurdities of heroic plays, sentimental dramas etc. Sheridan's delicate, dissembling lines have an underlying seriousness, for while sentimental on the surface the comedies of Sheridan were directed against the sentimental foppishness of the day.

DAVID GARRICK (1717–1779)

The Clandestine Marriage (French)

Garrick shows a good observation of his characters and the dialogue is lively, the play well constructed.

The 18th century abroad: France and Italy

MARIVAUX (1688–1763)

Le Jeu de l'Amour et du Hasard (French, New York)

Marivaux rejected the strong masculine quality of classical comedy, and, with almost a womanly sensibility, developed an odd style of his own (marivaudage) in which to reflect and express the behaviour of young lovers. His most successful comedy is *Le Jeu de l'Amour et du Hasard*.

BEAUMARCHAIS (1732–1799)

The Barber of Seville (Penguin)
The Marriage of Figaro (Penguin)

He wrote comedies of intrigue which are not original in pattern but have tremendous vitality and brilliance. There is impudent social criticism and a gaiety and delight about his characters, often basic types but which Beaumarchais lifts into individuality.

CARLO GOLDONI (1707–1793)

The Liar (Heinemann)
Mine Hostess (Cecil Palmer)
The Servant of Two Masters (Heinemann)
It Happened in Venice (Heinemann)
The Coffee House (French, New York)
The Impressario from Smyrna (Cecil Palmer)
The Fan (Yale University Dramatic Association)
The Good-Humoured Ladies (Beaumont)
The Venetian Twins (Penguin)
The Artful Widow (Penguin)
Mirandolina (Penguin)
The Superior Residence (Penguin)

Goldoni attempted to substitute a real human social comedy for the fantasy of the Commedia dell'Arte. He followed in Molière's footsteps and set his plays in his own Venice. His best plays are written in Venetian dialect for when he comes to write in literary Italian he becomes insipid. The plays which are known best in England, such as *The Servant of Two*

Masters, are all rather delightful and good-humoured but they lack any cutting edge.

19th Century Romanticism

The Romantics were far weaker as dramatists than as poets; they made little lasting impact on the stage, though they began to discover much that was new and illuminating about Shakespeare's work in the theatre. It was also an age of the great actor or actress with such names as Edmund Kean, John Kemble and Mrs Siddons.

Best of all the plays of the time were Musset's short and delightful comedies which have a freshness and a lightness of touch which completely escaped the 'heavyweight' tragedians like Hugo.

In Germany the Romantic playwrights were deeply influenced by Shakespeare, and often developed historical themes.

WOLFGANG VON GOETHE (1749–1832)

Faust – Parts 1 and 2 (Penguin etc.)
Götz von Berlichingen trans. Arden as *Ironhand* (Methuen)
Iphigenia in Tauris (Manchester University Press)

GOTTHOLD LESSING (1729–1781)

Emilia Golotti (Constable: Penguin)
Nathan the Wise (Constable)
Minna von Barnhelm (Dent)

FRIEDRICH SCHILLER (1759–1805)

Wallenstein
Mary Stuart (Penguin)
William Tell
Don Carlos (Anchor)
(Constable publish translations of Schiller's plays)

Though rather academic in quality Schiller's plays are still effective theatre today.

HEINRICH VON KLEIST (1771–1811)

The Prince of Homburg (Jonas)
Penthesilea (Anchor: Penguin)

FRANZ GRILLPARZA (1791–1872)

Sappho (in *Works*, vol. 2, published by Rudolf Francz, Leipzig)
Weh' dem, der lugt (as above, vol. 5)
Das Meeres und der Liebe Wellen (as above, vol. 3)
Der Traum, ein Leben (as above, vol. 5)
Medea (Penguin)

GEORG BÜCHNER (1813–1837)

Woyzeck (Penguin)
Danton's Death (MacGibbon and Kee and Methuen)

Georg Büchner reacted against the classical refinement of Goethe and Schiller and wrote in a rough popular idiom in *Woyzeck*, which is a far more 'modern' play than any other of the same period; it shows us a man enslaved by a scientific society, not a great hero in the classical sense. Its technique is almost cinematic, its vision disturbing and prophetic. Büchner also wrote *Danton's Death*. Both plays are extraordinarily exciting and most certainly worth reviving.

Ibsen, Chekhov and Strindberg

Towards the end of the century Realism makes its mark in the theatre, and in this tradition of play-writing stand Ibsen and Chekhov. Strindberg, their contemporary, has been slower to make an impact, and many of his plays remain almost unknown in this country. He wrote many historical dramas, also plays for children, and the main realistic plays in which he revolted against the stuffy conventions of his contemporary theatre.

HENRIK IBSEN (1828–1906)

Peer Gynt
Brand
The Wild Duck
The Master Builder
Rosmersholm
An Enemy of the People
Hedda Gabler
Ghosts
A Doll's House

New Directions

Pillars of Society
Little Eyolf
The Lady from the Sea
John Gabriel Borkman
Emperor and Galilean
When We Dead Awaken (Oxford, MacGibbon and Kee, and many editions)

ANTON CHEKHOV (1860–1904)

The Cherry Orchard
The Three Sisters
The Seagull
Uncle Vanya
Ivanov
The Wood Demon (Penguin and many editions)

Chekhov's characters could not be more unlike those of Ibsen; they have none of the latter's driving force and they seem strangely blind to anything taking place outside themselves. 'A brief brushing of lips is as close as anyone gets to another's beautiful and moving soul' writes Kenneth Tynan. In plays like *The Cherry Orchard* and *The Three Sisters* it is the subtle changing of mood, now wise, now funny, tender or sad, that makes great demands on producer and actors alike. They are not easy plays for their poetry seems at times intangible, and the delicate balance of tragedy and comedy is mysterious and elusive.

AUGUST STRINDBERG (1849–1912)

Lucky Peter's Travels (Cape)
The Father (Penguin)
Miss Julie (Penguin)
Easter (Penguin)
Swanwhite (Anchor)
A Dream Play (Cape, Duckworth)
The Dance of Death (Anchor)
The Ghost Sonata (Heinemann)
The Storm (Duckworth)
The Road to Damascus (Cape)
The Creditor (Hendersons)
Crimes and Crimes (Bantam)

(Jonathan Cape publish many Strindberg plays)
(See also *Twelve Plays of Strindberg* trans. E. Sprigg. Constable)

Strindberg wrote more than fifty plays of which at least a dozen remain in the International repertory and nearly all of which are worth reviving. His first plays, largely historical dramas and farcical tales are, except for *The Wanderings of Lucky Peter* (1882), largely forgotten. In the 1880's he wrote the violently volcanic and hysterical studies of domestic tyranny and hatred in which the implacable emnity of the sexes is a war which women always seem bound to win – *The Father* and *Miss Julie* as well as the one-act play *Playing with Fire*. Then in 1898 emerged the first two sections of his vast symbolic drama *To Damascus*, while over the next decade Strindberg produced with feverish energy no less than 28 plays in a variety of styles, which include a group of strange symbolic dramas *The Dream Play* and *The Ghost Sonata*; *Advent* and *Dance of Death* take up the sort of subject he had dealt with in *The Father* but now heavy with symbolic and religious overtones. His last plays include *The Storm*. Strindberg's plays are a fascinating and largely undeveloped field. They are well worth studying and producing.

19th Century Russian Plays

NIKOLAI GOGOL (1809–1852)

The Inspector General (Heinemann)
The Marriage (Anchor)

The former is one of the greatest of all comedies, telling of the corruption and inefficiency of a small provincial town. The play is superbly constructed.

IVAN TURGENEV (1818–1883)

A Month in the Country (MacGibbon and Kee)
A Provincial Lady (MacGibbon and Kee)
A Poor Gentleman (MacGibbon and Kee)

MAXIM GORKI (1868–1936)

The Lowest Depths (Yale)

Enemies (Yale)
The Zykovs (Yale)

Gorki's plays are a grim study of poverty and suffering in pre-revolutionary Russia.

ALEXANDER OSTROVSKY (1823–1886)

The Storm (Duckworth)

In this his most famous play, Ostrovsky portrays Moscow merchants of his own day. He also wrote historical dramas.

LEONID ANDREYEV (1871–1919)

The Life of Man (Allen & Unwin)
Samson in Chains (Brentano's)
He Who Gets Slapped (Brentano's)
King Hunger
Anathema (Andreyev plays are published by Duckworth)

Andreyev was a philosophical writer who seems to have had a horror of living; this sense of terror permeates his work.

French Farce

In France at the end of the century we have the delightful farces of Georges Feydeau who is irresistibly comic. His wild coincidences and improbabilities are superbly stylised theatre. 'In tragedy, one is stifled with horror. In Feydeau, one is suffocated with laughter' – Marcel Achard. See *Let's Get a Divorce*, a fine selection of French farce, edited by Eric Bentley (MacGibbon and Kee) which includes Labiche and Martin's *A Trip Abroad*, Labiche and Delacour's *Clemaire*, Prevert's *A United Family* and Sardov and Narjac's *Let's Get a Divorce*.

GEORGES FEYDEAU (1862–1921)

L'Hôtel Paradiso (Heinemann)
Look after Lulu (Heinemann)
A Flea in her Ear (French)
Keep an Eye on Amélie (MacGibbon and Kee)

The 19th Century in England

Little need be said about the first half of the century which is one of the dullest periods in the history of the English theatre. Often the greatest virtue of the numerous melodramas, sentimental comedies, comedies of manners and social dramas of the period is their craftsmanship. See *Nineteenth Century Plays*, ed. George Rowell (Oxford) which contains, amongst others, Douglas Jerrold's *Black Ey'd Susan*, C. Hazlewood's *Lady Audley's Secret*, Tom Taylor's *The Ticket-of-Leave Man*, T. W. Robertson's *Caste* and Leopold Lewis's famous melodrama *The Bells*. The two volumes of Michael Booth's *English Plays of the Nineteenth Century* (Oxford) should also be investigated.

The term melodrama became used for romantic and sensational plays with music during the late eighteenth and throughout the nineteenth centuries. Such plays as George Dibdin Pitt's *Sweeney Todd*, which hovers between cold horror and humour and which contains a whole gallery of Dickensian-type characters, provide a completely new experience of theatre. Those interested should consult Michael Booth's excellent *English Melodrama* (Jenkins) and *Hiss the Villain*, ed. Michael Booth (Eyre and Spottiswoode) which contains *Ten Nights in the Bar Room*, *Under the Gaslight* and *The Miller and His Men*.

Other popular melodramas include:

GEORGE DIBDIN PITT   *Sweeney Todd* or *The Demon Barber of Fleet Street* (John Lane: The Bodley Head)

LEOPOLD LEWIS   *The Bells* (French)

ANON   *Maria Marten* or *Murder in the Red Barn* (Cambridge – with reservations)

JOHN BUXTONE   *Luke the Labourer* (French)

ISSAC POCOCK   *The Miller and His Men* (Eyre and Spottiswoode)

W. T. MONCRIEF   *Cataract of the Ganges* (Richardson)

The Late 19th Century and the Early 20th Century in England, Ireland, France, America, Germany, Spain, Belgium and Italy

ARTHUR PINERO (1855–1934)

Dandy Dick (Heinemann)
The Magistrate (Heinemann)
Trelawney of the 'Wells' (French)
The Second Mrs Tanqueray (French)

Trelawney of the 'Wells' – This has a quality and vigour remarkable for its period. Certainly a play that succeeds whenever it is revived.
The Second Mrs Tanqueray – Pinero had, by this time, learnt a great deal about plot construction from his reading of Ibsen. This new-found skill is seen at its best in this social problem play.

OSCAR WILDE (1854–1900)

Lady Windermere's Fan
A Woman of No Importance
An Ideal Husband
The Importance of Being Earnest (Collected Plays in Penguin)

In spirit Wilde returns to the world of Congreve with these elegant, witty plays. There is a sense of fun and gaiety about them which makes one overlook any deficiencies of plot or characterisation. They seem absolutely Wilde, and quite inimitable.

GEORGE BERNARD SHAW (1856–1950)

Despite all his shortcomings as a playwright (e.g. his lack of character range, or depth, his reliance on set techniques and forms, and his relative inability to deal with life on instinctive or irrational levels) despite all this, Shaw remains one of our greatest comic writers. His early plays which challenged ephemeral social ideas have proved themselves to have lasting qualities, owing particularly to their high spirits, gaiety and fun. His middle-period plays dazzle with theatricality and dashes of ideas exploding all over the place. Early plays dealing with social evils include:

Widowers' Houses (slum landlordism)
Mrs Warren's Profession (prostitution)
Arms and the Man (the romantic idea of the soldier)

Then followed plays with historical themes:

The Man of Destiny
The Devil's Disciple
Caesar and Cleopatra

The Man of Destiny – a satirical portrait of Napoleon as a young man.
The Devil's Disciple – set during the American war, this melodrama again turns on a serious intellectual argument.
Caesar and Cleopatra – which in a very amusing way, however shallow, deals with the theme of the great lovers.

Man and Superman
The Shewing-up of Blanco Posnet
Back to Methuselah
Androcles and the Lion
John Bull's Other Island
Major Barbara
You Never Can Tell
Pygmalion
Heartbreak House
St Joan
The Apple Cart
The Millionairess
(Most of Shaw's works are in Penguins; Collected Works: Constable)

Shaw then explores philosophical problems in *Back to Methuselah*, *Man and Superman* and *The Shewing-Up of Blanco Posnet* and the nature of religious faith in *Androcles and the Lion*. He tackles the Irish question in *John Bull's Other Island*, and the Salvation Army together with big-business men in the munitions industry in *Major Barbara*. *You Never Can Tell* is delightfully high-spirited and shows all the Irish brilliance which Wilde had earlier displayed in *The Importance of being Earnest*. *Pygmalion* remains one of Shaw's most lasting plays for it is a modern fairy-tale. *Heartbreak House* is a satiric comedy modelled on Chekhov's *The Cherry Orchard* whilst *St. Joan* succeeds in being at the same time a more human and moving play than many he wrote. His last plays which include *The Apple Cart* and *The Millionairess* are lesser works. Plot as such hardly exists at times and only the skilful dialogue holds the interest.

HARLEY GRANVILLE-BARKER (1877–1946)

The Voysey Inheritance (Sidgwick and Jackson)
The Madras House (Sidgwick and Jackson)
Waste (Sidgwick and Jackson)

The Voysey Inheritance – This deserves to stand with the best of Shaw's plays. It has wit, invention and is beautifully planned and characterised. Its condemnation of Edwardian materialism is still tremendous.

D. H. LAWRENCE (1885–1930)

A Collier's Friday Night (Penguin)
The Daughter-in-Law (Penguin)
The Widowing of Mrs Holroyd (Penguin)

The idea that Lawrence, the dramatist, may be safely ignored no longer holds water. These passionate, powerful and sensitively observed plays of working-class life are amongst the most remarkable of their period.

English Comedies and Farces (1881–1913)

W. SOMERSET MAUGHAM (1874–1965)

The Circle (French)
The Constant Wife (French)
The Breadwinner (French)
Our Betters (Penguin)
Sheppey (Penguin)
Home and Beauty (French)

Maugham's great period as a dramatist was in the 1920's, when he wrote in quick succession several of the wittiest and most elegant comedies of manners in the English language. Their wit and acuteness of observation keep them permanently fresh and attractive.

STANLEY HOUGHTON (1881–1913)

Hindle Wakes (Constable)

HAROLD BRIGHOUSE (1883–1958)

Hobson's Choice (Heinemann)

Both are well-made, realistic plays set in the provincial atmosphere of

Manchester and Salford at the beginning of this century. They revive well.

BEN TRAVERS (b. 1886)

Rookery Nook (French)
The Cuckoo in the Nest (French)
Thark (French)
Turkey Time (Bickers & Son Ltd)
Plunder (Bickers & Son Ltd)

These farces were written in the 1920's for the Ralph Lynn, Tom Walls, Yvonne Arnaud group at the Aldwych Theatre.

BRANDON THOMAS (1857–1914)

Charley's Aunt (French)

This classic farce is beloved of actors for the comic possibilities of its transvestite central role.

NOEL COWARD (b. 1899)

Private Lives
Fallen Angels
Hay Fever
Still Life
Blithe Spirit
Present Laughter (French publishes many Coward Plays)

The cavalcade of plays which Coward produced in the thirties and early forties are airy, stylish, elegantly written and irresistibly amusing with a delightful, crisp and frivolous kind of dialogue.

W. H. AUDEN (b. 1907) AND CHRISTOPHER ISHERWOOD (b. 1904)

Ascent of F.6 (Faber)
On the Frontier (Faber)
The Dog Beneath the Skin (Faber)

These three verse-plays, written in the middle thirties, were interesting experiments well worth reviving today.

J. B. PRIESTLEY (b. 1894)

Dangerous Corner (French)	*When we are Married* (Penguin)
Time and the Conways (Penguin)	*Laburnum Grove* (Heinemann)
Johnson over Jordan (Heinemann)	*They Came to a City* (Heinemann)
The Linden Tree (Penguin)	*Home is Tomorrow* (Heinemann)
Music at Night (French)	*Summer Day's Dream* (Heinemann)
Eden End (Heinemann)	*I have been here Before* (Penguin)
An Inspector Calls (Penguin)	

His early plays in the thirties were his most successful. His experiments with philosophical ideas about time never seemed wholly convincing in dramatic terms; yet they remain an honest and striking achievement. (Priestley's Collected Plays are published by Heinemann.)

JAMES BRIDIE (1818–1951)

He could be most compelling, humorous, witty, macabre and humane. His best plays are probably:

The Anatomist (French)
Tobias and the Angel (French)
Jonah and the Whale (French)
Susanna and the Elders (Constable)
(Bridie's plays are published by Constable)

T. S. ELIOT (1888–1965)

Murder in the Cathedral (Faber)
Family Reunion (Faber)
The Cocktail Party (Faber)
The Confidential Clerk (Faber)
The Elder Statesman (Faber)

Eliot's plays remain part of a serious experiment to revive poetic drama. He may have failed in what he did, but such an effort was needed at the time he wrote.

GRAHAM GREENE (b. 1904)

The Living Room (Heinemann)
The Complaisant Lover (French)
The Potting Shed (French)

TERRENCE RATTIGAN (b. 1911)

The Winslow Boy (French)
The Deep Blue Sea (French)
The Browning Version (French)
French Without Tears—a farce (French)

Though at the moment Rattigan may be unfashionable he is one of the finest writers in the English theatre today. *The Deep Blue Sea* is particularly memorable. *French Without Tears* is one of the best social comedies of the century.

CHRISTOPHER FRY (b. 1907)

A Phoenix too Frequent (Oxford)
The Boy with a Cart (Oxford)
The Lady's not for Burning (Oxford)
Venus Observed (Oxford)
A Sleep of Prisoners (Oxford)

Intoxicating but rather frothy, Fry's delight with words and images makes his plays worth discovering and acting.

RONALD DUNCAN (b. 1918)

The Catalyst (Rebel Press)
This Way to the Tomb (Faber)

ANNE RIDLER (b. 1912)

The Shadow Factory (Faber)

Irish Plays

W. B. YEATS (1865–1939)

The Land of Heart's Desire (Macmillan)
The Countess Cathleen (Penguin)
The Shadowy Waters (Macmillan)
Purgatory (Macmillan)

Yeats remained a lyrical poet even in the theatre, and his early plays are certainly more remarkable for their beauty of language than for their dramatic power. However, in his later plays, his language becomes firmer, more condensed, and he has learnt much from the ritual and ceremony of the 'Noh' play. Finally in his brief monodrama, *Purgatory*, he achieves an intense power that was to have its impact on Beckett, Genet, Pinter and Ionesco.

JAMES JOYCE (1882–1941)

Exiles (Signet)

J. M. SYNGE (1871–1909)

The Shadow of the Glen
The Playboy of the Western World (Penguin)
The Tinker's Wedding
Riders to the Sea
Deidre of the Sorrows
The Well of the Saints (Dent, Oxford, Methuen etc.)

Synge's tragic plays may now seem a little self-conscious but his comedies are as fresh and magnificently alive as ever they were.

SEAN O'CASEY (1880–1964)

Juno and the Paycock (Macmillan)
The Shadow of a Gunman (Macmillan)
The Plough and the Stars (Macmillan)
The Silver Tassie (Macmillan)
Cock-a-Doodle Dandy (Penguin)

Sean O'Casey's early plays are a strange and rather heady mixture of realism and romance. His prose, like Synge's, has a wonderful poetic quality but, whereas Synge turned to the West of Ireland for his settings, O'Casey sets his dramas in Dublin. Despite their grim themes, there is a rich vein of humour and vitality in his work.

German Plays

GERHARDT HAUPTMANN (1862–1946)

Before Dawn (Penguin)
The Weavers (5 Plays: Bantam Classics)

The Weavers is Hauptmann's greatest play. It shows the miserable conditions of the weavers who revolted against their masters in 1844.

FRANK WEDEKIND (1864–1918)

Spring Awakening (Calder)
Earth Spirit (Calder)

Wedekind was deeply influenced in style and subject matter by Strindberg. The sensibility of his writing makes his frank treatment of sexual problems convincing drama. His technique, especially the use of short scenes, influenced Brecht, and is particularly suited to amateur production.

ERNST TOLLER (1893–1939)

Pastor Hall trans. Spender (John Lane)
Draw the Fires (John Lane)
Masses and Man (John Lane)

Toller was a socialist dramatist whose revolutionary dramas and his new theatrical technique greatly influenced the Russian Theatre.

Belgian Plays

MAURICE MAETERLINCK (1862–1949)

Pélleas and Mélisande
The Betrothal
The Blue Bird
Sister Beatrice (Allen and Unwin publish Maeterlinck plays)

He evokes a dream world of fantasy and escape.

Spanish Plays

JACINTO BENAVENTE (1866–1954)

Los Intereses Creados (*The Bonds of Interest*)

One of his best plays built on a Commedia dell'Arte frame.

La Gobernadora (*The Governor's Wife*)
Lo Cursi (*Vulgarity*)
Mas Fuerte Que el Amor (*Stronger than Love*)

In these he satirises various aspects of society.

The Prince Who Learned Everything Out of Books trans. Underhill
(Scribners publish Benavente plays)

G. MARTINEZ SIERRA (1881–1947)

Canción de Cuna (Cradle Song) (French)
Kingdom of God
The Shepherds
The Romantic Young Lady (both these are light, gently satirical plays)

Canción de Cuna – A good-humoured play that succeeds in avoiding
sentimentality.
Kingdom of God – A tragi-comedy translated by Granville-Barker.

(Chatto and Windus publish Sierra Plays)

S. AND J. QUINTERO (1871–1938) AND (1873–1944)

A Hundred Years Old
The Lady from Alfaqueque
Women Have Their Way
Fortunato
Peace and Quiet
(Most of these were also translated by Harley Granville-Barker, and published
   by Sidgwick and Jackson)

The Quintero Brothers wrote many good-humoured comedies about
Spanish life at the beginning of the century. Like Benevente and Sierra
there is a kindliness of feeling and a gentle tolerance about the satire.

F. GARCIA LORCA (1898–1936)

Blood Wedding (Penguin)
Yerma (Penguin)
The House of Bernarda Alba (Penguin)

His first major play was *Blood Wedding*, a savage story of family feuds,
illicit love and sudden death. *Yerma*, written in 1934, is a powerful play
about a woman torn between a passionate desire for the children her
husband cannot give her and her inflexible code of honour which will not
allow her to find another father for them. Lorca's final and finest play, *The
House of Bernarda Alba* is also a study of female frustration, in which a

whole household of sisters are ruled over by a bigoted and tyrannical mother whose dominating maternalism they try to escape. Lorca's plays, because of their essentially Spanish passions and situations, are particularly difficult for amateurs to present effectively.

Italian Plays

LUIGI PIRANDELLO (1867–1936)

With Brecht, he has been a very great influence, exploring relentlessly what lies below our usual ideas of reality. His is a disconcerting world where we move away from firm ground into a trackless labyrinth, until the only certainty we can know seems in the past. Yet despite this despondent vision there is a sense of human values in his plays and a sense of human charity. His main plays include:

Six Characters in Search of an Author (Heinemann)
Henry IV (Penguin)
Right You Are If You Think So (Penguin)
All for the Best (Penguin)
The Rules of the Game (Penguin)
The Life I Gave You (Penguin)
Lazarus (Penguin)

All for the Best – This has a richly comic opening yet its ending is as grave and tragic as his ending to Six Characters.
The Life I Gave You – A study of resurrection in which life is passed on through the medium of love from one person to another.
Lazarus – This is in many ways complementary to the last play, and gives the most complete expression of his religious views; our business in this world is with the here and now, not with the hereafter; with the purity of Nature and the joys of human life rather than the hope of a future heaven.

UGO BETTI (1892–1953)

The Queen and the Rebels (Penguin)
Crime on Goat Island (French)

Betti's recurrent concern is with responsibility and identity, which is expressed with a flair for theatrical effect.

New Directions

Soviet Plays

Amongst modern Russian writers are the following:

Alexander Afinogenev (1904–41)	*Distant Point* trans. Griffin (Pushkin Press)
Aleksei Arbuzov (b. 1908)	*The Promise* (Oxford) *Confessions at Night*
Vladimir Mayakovsky (1893–1930)	*The Bedbug* (Penguin) *The Bathhouse* (Bantam Books)
Isaac Babel (1894–1941)	*Marya* (Penguin)
Eugene Schwartz (1897–1960)	*The Dragon* (Penguin)

The Nineteen Forties and Fifties

The Plays of the Forties and Fifties are set out under the headings of different countries as follows:

United States of America

Thornton Wilder (b. 1897)	*Our Town* (Penguin) *The Matchmaker* (Penguin) *The Skin of our Teeth* (Penguin)
Eugene O'Neill (1888–1953)	*Mourning Becomes Electra* (Jonathan Cape) *Long Day's Journey into Night* (Jonathan Cape) *Desire under the Elms* (Jonathan Cape) *The Iceman Cometh* (Jonathan Cape) (Jonathan Cape publish O'Neill plays)

Out of a ghastly life dominated by drink and three disastrous marriages, O'Neill tore a succession of gigantic and ambitious works that constantly overreach themselves. His stature is less certain than that of any other major twentieth-century playwright. His numerous plays, though often clumsily constructed, have great dramatic and emotional power.

Tennessee Williams (b. 1914)	*The Glass Menagerie* (Penguin) *A Streetcar Named Desire* (Penguin) *Summer and Smoke* (Secker and Warburg)

      The Rose Tattoo (Penguin)
      Cat on a Hot Tin Roof (Secker and Warburg)
      Camino Real (Penguin)

His early plays are the most poetic and subtle. Violent characterisation has taken the place of their delicate, evocative quality in his later dramas which are worth revival nevertheless.

Arthur Miller (b. 1915)	*After the Fall* (Penguin)
	All my Sons (Penguin)
	Death of a Salesman (Penguin)
	The Crucible (Penguin)
	View from the Bridge (Penguin)
	Incident at Vichy (Penguin)
	The Price (Secker and Warburg)

In his plays, Miller shows himself not only keenly interested in social problems, but aware of the predicament and tragedy of the individual.

William Saroyan (b. 1908)	*The Cave Dwellers* (Faber)
	Sam, the Highest Jumper of Them All (Faber)

Clifford Odets (1906–63)	*Golden Boy* (Penguin)
	Awake and Sing (Penguin)
	The Big Knife (Penguin)

France

Jean Giraudoux (1822–1944)	*Amphitryon* (Methuen)
	Ondine (Methuen)
	Tiger at the Gates (Methuen)
	The Mad Woman of Chaillot (Random House)

Unlike his early plays which were rather lightweight, *Tiger at the Gates* is a biting satire. It shows how Hector's attempts to save the peace are thwarted by false idealism and false ideas of heroism and glory.

Jean Anouilh (b. 1910)	*Point of Departure* (Methuen)
	Antigone (Methuen)
	Romeo and Jeannette (Methuen)
	Medea (Methuen)

Anouilh wrote these during the forties. In them he explores such themes as the struggle between idealism and expediency, true love and mere physical comfort. Other plays include:

	The Lark (Methuen)
	Poor Bitos (French)
	The Rehearsal (French)
	Becket (French)
	Ring Round the Moon (French)
	Waltz of the Toreadors (French)
Jean Cocteau (1889–1963)	*Orphée* (Oxford)
	La Machine Infernale (Oxford)
	Les Parents Terribles (MacGibbon and Kee)
Jean-Paul Sartre (b. 1905)	*The Flies* (Penguin)
	Altona (Penguin)
	Huis Clos (Penguin)
	Crime Passionel (Methuen)
	Men Without Shadows (Penguin)
	Lucifer and the Lord (Penguin)
	The Respectable Prostitute (Penguin)
	Nekrassov (Penguin)
	The Trojan Women (Penguin)
	Kean (Penguin)
Albert Camus (1913–60)	*Caligula* (Penguin)
	Le Malentendu (*Cross Purpose*) (Penguin)
	Les Justes (Penguin)
	(collected plays published by Hamish Hamilton)

In 1942 Camus first formulated the idea of the Absurd which was to have such an effect on Ionesco, Adamov, Genet etc. Man's relation with his world is 'absurd'; it is incongruous, and there is no easy way of escaping the conflict, 'the harrowing and marvellous wager of the absurd'. Yet man must choose, he must accept his own destiny; it is the greatest thing he can do.

The Theatre of the Absurd
Whereas Sartre and Camus had tried to 'contain' the idea of the Absurd, and control it, the European and American playwrights who succeeded them during the Fifties were content to abandon themselves to it. There is

no longer any controlling reason or any sense of direction, only the anguish of the drama. Fantasy, violence and murder are at the centre of many of their plays.

Samuel Beckett (b. 1906)	*Waiting for Godot* *Endgame* *Happy Days* *All That Fall* *Embers* (Faber publish most Beckett Plays)

Eugène Ionesco
(b. 1912)
	The Chairs (Penguin)
	Rhinoceros (Penguin)
	The Bald Prima Donna (French)
	Exit the King (French)
	Amedée or How to Get Rid of It (Penguin)
	   (Ionesco's collected plays are published by
	   Calder)

Arthur Adamov (b. 1908)	*Professor Taranne* (Penguin) *Ping Pong* (Calder) *Paalo Paoli* (Calder)
Jean Genet (b. 1910)	*The Maids* (Faber) *The Blacks* (Faber) *The Balcony* (Faber) *The Screens* (Faber)

Those interested in modern French plays, the beginnings of surrealist and 'Absurd' drama should study the work of the following playwrights:

Alfred Jarry
(1873–1907)
	The Ubu Plays (Methuen)
	   Ubu Roi
	   Ubu Cocu
	   Ubu Enchaîné

Guillaume Apollinaire (1880–1918)	*Les Mamelles de Tirésias* (Modern French Plays) (Faber)

Roger Vitrac (1899–1952)   *Victor ou Les Enfants au Pouvoir* (Calder)

In this play the world is seen through the eyes of a nine-year-old child, immensely clever and of giant stature.

Antonin Artaud	*Jet of Blood* (Modern French Plays) (Faber)
(1896–1948)	*The Cenci* (Calder)

Artaud is one of the great seminal influences of the Contemporary Theatre and is more famous for his idea of the 'Theatre of Cruelty' than for his actual plays; he set out to disturb his audience into a full awareness of man's condition today. His important work on the theory of theatre, *Theatre and Its Double* (Evergreen Books) should be studied.

Armand Salacrou (b. 1899)
Salacrou is still little known in this country. His best work includes:

Les Nuits de la Colère (translated as 'Men of Wrath') (O.U.P.)
The World is Round (University of Minnesota Press)
When the Music Stops (University of Minnesota Press)
Marguerite (University of Minnesota Press)

Marguerite Duras	*Days in the Trees* (Calder)
	The Square (Calder)
	The Little Horses of Tarquinia (Calder)
Henri de Montherlant (b. 1896)	*The Civil War* (Penguin)
Georges Schéhadé (b. 1910)	*Vasco* (Penguin)
Boris Vian (1920–1959)	*The General's Tea Party* (Penguin)

Germany

Bertolt Brecht	*In the Jungle of the Cities*
(1898–1956)	*St Joan of the Stockyards*
	The Life of Galileo
	Herr Puntila and his Servant Matti
	The Good Person of Szechwan
	The Caucasian Chalk Circle
	Mother Courage
	The Trial of Lucullus
	Schweik in the Second World War
	The Resistible Rise of Arturo Ui
	(Methuen publish Brecht's plays)

Poland

Stanislaw Witkiewicz   *The Madman and the Nun*
                        The Water Hen
                        The Shoemakers
                            (all 3 in a collection published by University of
                            Washington Press)

Switzerland

Friedrich Durrenmatt   *The Physicists*
   (b. 1921)   *The Marriage of Mr Mississippi*
                        The Angel Comes to Babylon
                        Romulus the Great
                        The Visit
                            (Jonathan Cape publish Durrenmatt's plays)

Max Frisch (b. 1911)   *The Fire Raisers*
                        Andorra
                        Count Oederland
                        The Great Wall of China
                        Don Juan, or *The Love of Geometry*
                        Philip Hotz's Fury
                        Biography: A Game
                            (Methuen publish Max Frisch's plays)

Theatre in Britain in the Fifties

It was at the Royal Court Theatre in May 1956 that a 'new wave' of
English dramatists first made its mark with Osborne's *Look Back In Anger*,
while other dramatists who first made a name at the Court were Ann
Jellicoe, N. F. Simpson, Nigel Dennis, John Arden and Arnold Wesker.

It has become a theatrical legend, created by the press, that in 1956 John
Osborne's *Look Back in Anger* caused a theatrical revolution. This is
clearly untrue, as a reading of that play will show. *Look Back in Anger* is a
drawing-room comedy set in a kitchen, and firmly in the tradition of the
contrived well-made play. John Osborne is less revolutionary than Noel
Coward.

The real revolution in contemporary theatre occurred five years earlier
with Samuel Beckett's *Waiting for Godot*. The revolution was in the

189

language, and in the rhythms of speech, as much as in the material. The emphasis moved from the rhetorical to the unspoken, from the over-stated to the suggestive. Beckett achieved a genuine dramatic poetry where Eliot's verse dramas had failed. His was the great influence on the new talents such as Pinter.

John Osborne	*Look Back in Anger* (Faber)
	The Entertainer (Faber)
	Epitaph for George Dillon (with Anthony Creighton) (Penguin)
	Inadmissible Evidence (Faber)
	Luther (Faber)
	A Patriot for Me (Faber)
	A Subject for Scandal and Concern (Faber)
	Time Present (Faber)
	The Hotel in Amsterdam (Faber)
Ann Jellicoe	*The Knack* (Faber)
	The Sport of My Mad Mother (Faber)
	The Rising Generation (Hutchinson)
	Shelley (Faber)
N. F. Simpson	*A Resounding Tinkle* (Penguin)
	One Way Pendulum (Methuen)
	The Cresta Run (Faber)
	The Hole (Faber)
	See also: *Some Tall Tinkles* (Faber). 3 Short T.V Plays
Nigel Dennis	*Cards of Identity* (Weidenfeld and Nicolson)
	The Making of Moo (Weidenfeld and Nicolson)
	August for the People (Penguin)
John Arden	*Live Like Pigs* (Penguin)
	Serjeant Musgrave's Dance (Methuen)
	Armstrong's Last Goodnight (Methuen)
	The Happy Haven (Methuen)
	The Business of Good Government (Methuen)[1]
	The Workhouse Donkey (Methuen)
	The Royal Pardon (Methuen)[1]
	The Hero Rises Up (Methuen)[1]

[1] In collaboration with Margaretta D'Arcy.

Arnold Wesker   *The Kitchen*
                       Chicken Soup with Barley
                       I'm Talking about Jerusalem
                       Roots
                       Chips with Everything
                       The Four Seasons
                       Their Very Own and Golden City
                           (all in Penguin books)

Another centre of creative work that merged in the fifties was Joan Littlewood's Theatre Workshop. From it there came Shelagh Delaney, Brendan Behan, and the influential *O What a Lovely War* (1963), wellspring of innumerable musical documentaries.

Shelagh Delaney   *A Taste of Honey* (Methuen)
                        The Lion in Love (Methuen)

Brendan Behan   *The Hostage* (Methuen)
                        The Quare Fellow (Methuen)

Stephen Lewis   *Sparrers Can't Sing* (Evans)

Charles Chilton and the *Oh What a Lovely War* (Methuen)
Theatre Workshop
Company

During the fifties also John Whiting and Harold Pinter were first heard of.

Harold Pinter   *The Birthday Party*
                        The Caretaker
                        The Homecoming (all Methuen)

John Whiting   *Saints Day* (Heinemann)
                        Penny for a Song (Heinemann)
                        Marching Song (Penguin)
                        The Devils (based on Huxley's book *The Devils of Loudun*) (Penguin)

THE CONTEMPORARY SCENE
BRITAIN

Paul Ableman   *Blue Comedy* (Methuen)
                       Green Julia (Methuen)

New Directions

Alan Ayckbourn	*Relatively Speaking* (Evans)
Peter Barnes	*The Ruling Class* (Heinemann)
Alan Bennett	*Forty Years On* (Faber)
Bridget Boland	*The Prisoner* (Elek Books) *Cockpit* (Elek Books)
Robert Bolt	*A Man for all Seasons* (Penguin) *Tiger and the Horse* (French) *Flowering Cherry* (French)
Edward Bond	*Saved* (Methuen) *Narrow Road to the Deep North* (Methuen) *Early Morning* (Calder)
John Bowen	*After the Rain* (Faber)
Harry Chapman	*You Won't Always Be On Top* (Methuen)
Giles Cooper	*Everything in the Garden* (Penguin) *Happy Family* (Penguin) *The Object* (Penguin) Six plays for radio: *Mathry Beacon* *The Disagreeable Oyster* *Without the Grail* *Under the Loofah Tree* *Unman Wittering and Zigo* *Before the Monday* (B.B.C. Publications)
David Creegan	*Three Men for Colverton* (Methuen) *The Houses by the Green* (Methuen)
Charles Dyer	*Staircase* (Penguin)
Barry England	*Conduct Unbecoming*
Patrick Garland	*Brief Lives of John Aubrey* (Faber)
Simon Gray	*Wise Child* (Faber) See also a T.V. play: *Sleeping Dog* (Faber)

192

Willis Hall and Keith Waterhouse	*Billy Liar* (Evans) *The Long, the Short and the Tall* (Penguin) *Celebration* (Evans)
David Halliwell	*Little Malcolm and His Struggle Against the Eunuchs* (Faber)
Christopher Hampton	*When Did You Last See My Mother* (Faber) *Total Eclipse* (Faber)
Donald Howarth	*A Lily in Little India* (Penguin) *All Good Children* (French)
Errol John	*Moon on a Rainbow Shawl* (Faber) *Force Majeure* *The Dispossessed* } 3 Screenplays (Faber) *Hasta Luego*
Bernard Kops	*The Dream of Peter Mann* (Penguin) *The Hamlet of Stepney Green* (Penguin)
Hugh Leonard	*Stephen D.* (Evans)
Henry Livings	*Kelly's Eye* (Methuen) *Big Soft Nellie* (Methuen) *Stop It, Whoever You Are* (Penguin) *Nil Carborundum* (Penguin) *Eh?* (Methuen) *Good Grief!* (Methuen)
Peter Luke	*Hadrian VII* (Penguin)
Frank Marcus	*The Killing of Sister George* (French) (Hamish Hamilton) *Cleo* *The Formation Dancers* (Elek Books) *Studies in the Nude* *Mrs Mouse Are You Within?* (Elek Books)
John McGrath	*Events While Guarding the Bofors Gun* (Methuen)
John Mortimer	*The Wrong Side of the Park* (Methuen) *Call Me a Liar* (Methuen) *David and Broccoli* (Methuen) *Two Stars for Comfort* (Methuen) *The Judge* (Methuen)

David Mercer	*The Governor's Lady* (Methuen)
	Ride a Cock Horse (Calder)
	Belcher's Luck (Calder)
	See also David Mercer's plays for T.V.; published by Calder:
	A Suitable Case for Treatment
	For Tea on Sunday
	And Did Those Feet
	The Parachute
	In Two Minds
	Let's Murder Vivaldi
	Where the Difference Begins
	A Climate of Fear
	The Birth of a Private Man
Bill Naughton	*My Flesh, My Blood* (French)
	Alfie (French)
	All in Good Time (French)
	Spring and Port Wine (French)
Peter Nichols	*A Day in the Death of Joe Egg* (Faber)
	The National Health (Faber)
Joe Orton	*Entertaining Mr Sloane* (Penguin)
	Loot (Methuen)
	What the Butler Saw (Methuen)
Alun Owen	*Progress in the Park* (Penguin)
	The Rough and Ready Lot (Encore)
	See also Three T.V. Plays:
	No Trains to Lime Street
	After the Funeral
	Lena, Oh My Lena
Alan Plater	*Close the Coalhouse Door* (Methuen)
David Pinner	*Dickon* (Penguin)
	Fanghorn (Penguin)
	The Drums of Snow (Penguin)
Barry Reckord	*Skyvers* (Faber)

Michael Rosen	*Backbone* (Faber)
David Rudkin	*Afore Night Come* (Penguin)
James Saunders	*Next Time I'll Sing to You* (Heinemann)
	A Scent of Flowers (Heinemann)
Peter Shaffer	*Five Finger Exercise* (French)
	The Royal Hunt of the Sun (French) (Hamish Hamilton)
Muriel Spark	*Doctors of Philosophy* (Penguin)
Johnny Speight	*If There Weren't Any Blacks You'd Have To Invent Them* (Methuen)
John Spurling	*Macrune's Guevara* (Calder)
Tom Stoppard	*Enter a Free Man* (Faber)
	Rosencrantz and Guildenstern are Dead (Faber)
	The Real Inspector Hound (Faber)
David Storey	*The Restoration of Arnold Middleton* (French)
	In Celebration (in *Plays and Players*, June 1969)
	The Contractor (in *Plays and Players*, December 1969)
Cecil Taylor	*Bread and Butter* (Penguin)
	The Ballachulish Beat (Rapp and Carroll)
Peter Terson	*Zigger-Zagger* (Penguin)
	The Mighty Reservoy (in *Plays and Players*, August 1967)
	The Apprentices (Penguin)
	A Night to Make the Angels Weep (Penguin)
	Mooney and his Caravans (Penguin)
Dylan Thomas	*Under Milk Wood* (Dent)
David Turner	*Semi-detached* (Evans)
John Wilson	*Hamp* (Evans)
Charles Wood	*Fill the Stage with Happy Hours* (Penguin)
	Dingo (Penguin)
	H : or Monologues at Front of Burning Cities

New Directions

Collections worth noting:
New Granada Plays (Faber)

Rhys Adrian	*The Protest*
Philip Callow	*The Honeymooners*
Richard Cottrell	*Marking Time*

New Radio Drama (B.B.C. Publications)

Colin Finbow	*Tonight is Friday*
Ian Rodger	*A Voice Like Thunder*
Rhys Adrian	*A Nice Clean Sheet of Paper*
Stephen Grenfell	*Sixteen Lives of the Drunken Dreamer*
Joe Orton	*The Ruffian on the Stair*
Simon Raven	*The Sconcing Stoup*

AMERICA

Edward Albee	*Who's Afraid of Virginia Woolf?* (Penguin) *Tiny Alice* (Jonathan Cape) *A Delicate Balance* (Jonathan Cape)
James Baldwin	*The Amen Corner* (Michael Joseph) *Blues for Mr Charlie* (Michael Joseph)
Kenneth H. Brown	*The Brig* (Methuen)
Jules Feiffer	*God Bless* (in *Plays and Players*, January 1969) *Little Murders*
Jack Gelber	*The Connection* (Faber)
Lorraine Hansberry	*The Sign in Sidney Brustein's Window* (Penguin)
Langston Hughes	*Mulatto* (Penguin)
Leroi Jones	*Dutchman* (Faber) *The Slave* (Faber)
Heinar Kipphardt	*In the Matter of J. Robert Oppenheimer* (Methuen)

Arthur L. Kopit	*Oh Dad, Poor Dad* (Methuen) *Indians* (Methuen)
Jack Richardson	*Gallows Humour* (Penguin)
Murray Schisgal	*The Typists* (Penguin)
Lanford Wilson	*Home Free!* (Methuen) *The Madness of Lady Bright* (Methuen)

BULGARIA

| Georgi Dzhagarov | *The Public Prosecutor* (Peter Owen Ltd) |

FRANCE

| Georges Michel | *The Sunday Walk* (Methuen) |

GERMANY

Günter Grass	*Flood* (Secker and Warburg) *Onkel, Onkel* (Secker and Warburg) *The Wicked Cooks* (Secker and Warburg)
Rolf Hochhuth	*The Representative* (Methuen) *Soldiers* (André Deutsch)
Martin Sperr	*Tales from Landshut* (Methuen)
Martin Walser	*The Rabbit Race* (Calder) *The Detour* (Calder)
Peter Weiss	*Night with Guests* *The Investigation* (Calder) *The Persecution and Assassination of Marat as performed by the inmates of the Asylum of Charenton under the direction of the Marquis de Sade* (Calder)

IRELAND

| Brian Friel | *Philadelphia, Here I Come!* (Faber)
The Loves of Cass McGuire (Faber) |

197

New Directions

POLAND

Witold Gombrowicz   *Princess Ivona* (Calder)

Slawomir Mrozek   *Tango*
The Police   } Short plays or parables expressed
The Party   in terms of the Theatre of the
Out at Sea   } Absurd
    Six plays (Jonathan Cape)

RUSSIA

Alexander Solzhenitsyn   *The Love-Girl and the Innocent* (Bodley Head)

NIGERIA

Wole Soyinka   *A Dance of the Forests*
The Lion and the Jewel
The Road
The Swamp Dwellers
The Strong Breed
The Trials of Brother Jero (all Oxford)

WEST AFRICA

Guillaume Oyono-Mbia   *Three Suitors; one husband* (Methuen)
Until Further Notice (Methuen)

SOUTH AFRICA

Athol Fugard   *Blood Knot* (Penguin)

AUSTRALIA

Ray Lawler   *The Summer of the Seventeenth Doll* (Fontana)

Rodney Millgate   *A Refined Look at Existence* (Methuen)

Hal Porter   *The Tower* (Penguin)
The Professor (Faber)

Alan Seymour   *The One Day in the Year* (Penguin)

Douglas Stewart   *Ned Kelly* (Penguin)

The following T.V. scripts are also worth studying (see page 196 for list of Radio Plays):

Conflicting Generations (Longmans)
   5 T.V. Plays by John Hopkins, David Turner, Ronald Eyre, John Mortimer, Paddy Chayefsky
Z Cars (Longmans)
   4 Television Scripts by Ronald Eyre, Alan Plater and John Hopkins

6 Staging and Setting

99·9 per cent of the theatres we are used to in England are large public buildings constructed in the nineteenth century. They have a curved horse-shoe shaped auditorium with circles and a gallery facing a large opening, the proscenium arch, behind which the stage is set and the actors perform. Even the simplest village hall is modelled on the same arrangement: it is long, with a flat floor, and at one end a raised stage is set behind an opening, curtained off from the rest of the hall, in imitation of the conventional proscenium theatre. Most multi-purpose buildings follow the same pattern and put the audience in rows facing the proscenium arch: an arrangement which has been accepted for so long now that any other seems unthinkable. Yet other arrangements are possible, and each is permissible provided it really suits the play.

There is a thrust stage, in which the acting area juts out into the auditorium allowing the spectators to watch from three sides. There is theatre in the round where the audience sits all round the acting area like spectators at a boxing match. There is also the proscenium stage which we have discussed. But there are other forms which we should not overlook: the curved auditorium of the Greek theatre, the Kabuki theatre of Japan, the Medieval Cart, the travelling circus's big tent, the pierrots' booth stage. All these evolved at different times as needs arose; all of them are valid 'theatre' even though they flow from a specially constructed theatre building into the streets. For amateurs they offer theatrical opportunities which should be explored.

Ideally each dramatic performance should determine its own scale/ shape/staging/setting. This rarely happens in the contemporary professional theatre where every kind of play has to be presented on the same stage. But amateurs who can use different environments – the Parish

Church for *Murder in the Cathedral*, a Barn for *Maria Marten*, the Pannier market for a Pageant, the Beach for a Happening – have much more freedom to explore new actor/audience relationships.

They can use every kind of space besides the Hall or Theatre where they normally work: churches, parks and other open spaces, the market square and public buildings of all kinds, country houses, factory canteens, schools, drill-halls, even the streets. Ed Berman, the young American director and playwright has even written a play, *Pisces*, to be performed in a swimming pool. 'There are more swimming pools than theatres,' he says. 'The audience will sit in the banked seating or actually in the water – depending on how many we can get to bring swimming costumes. . . . The biggest mistake we can make is to think that a change in subject matter is a new departure. Unless you change the form, the structure, you will never achieve any significant artistic advance. The Theatre is decades behind the other art forms precisely because the others are using new techniques to examine our contemporary scene. The Theatre drags far behind because of the nature of its tradition.'[1]

In this chapter we take a look at some of the many different forms of staging and setting in turn.

DIFFERENT FORMS OF INDOOR STAGING

Start with an empty room. Define your acting area by arranging chairs round it, leaving gaps by the doors for actors and audiences alike. This is a 'theatre'. This is a place where actors can act in front of an audience. Acting is the primary business. Next come audiences. They want to be able to see what is going on, they want to be involved; but the unpredictable communication between living human beings, upon which the art of the theatre rests, can occur almost anywhere – in the street, on a playground, in a warehouse or, best of all, in an enclosed room.

In this case the acting area cannot normally be much less than twelve by fifteen feet and the room itself some twenty by thirty feet which, allowing for one doorway, might seat about seventy-five people. This is an admirable size for a great deal of work. The Brighton Combination has a room approximately this size where their resident company of eight perform plays to audiences of about sixty people. The Traverse

[1] In an interview in *Plays and Players*, December 1968.

in Edinburgh holds sixty, too. The basement 'theatre' at the Ambiance in Queensway, an irregular shape some eighteen by forty feet, held a varying number, often as few as thirty people if the play demanded this. In these cases the shape of the acting area and the arrangement of the seating are determined by the needs of the production itself. At Brighton the whole environment – walls, rostra and floor – is often re-painted for each production.

Much smaller rooms, say twenty feet square, are a perfectly practical theatre for the performance of every kind of play except those involving largish casts.

Such a 'theatre' is radically different from the familiar proscenium type, not so much because of its lack of facilities (which could, to some extent, be fixed up) but because the acting area is in the same space as the auditorium. The proscenium theatre, which is characterised by its picture-frame stage and auditorium space (stalls, circle, gallery), has two 'houses' divided by the proscenium wall; the open stage has one, and its different forms, the thrust stage, the end stage and theatre in the round, are now defined below:

The thrust stage, of which the Chichester Theatre (seating 1,360) is a good example, consists of an acting area which is either a flat area of the

auditorium floor or a raised platform projecting forward from one wall. The audience sit on three sides of the acting area and actors either enter through aisles between the audience or directly onto the 'stage' from the stage wall. This is the theatre Shakespeare wrote for.

A second form, end staging, is also important. In this case the acting area is placed across one end wall of the auditorium, with the audience

seated before it. The arrangement is similar to the proscenium theatre except that the acting area and audience are contained within the same room. Actors' entrances can be made through the audience or through the end wall directly onto the acting area which is often raised.

In another arrangement, theatre in the round (or arena theatre) the audience more or less surrounds a central stage. This is usually either circular or rectangular, though it can be virtually any size or shape. If an actor stands in the middle and turns round he always has as many people behind him as in front of him, as in a boxing ring. Examples include the Octagon in Bolton and the Library Theatre, Scarborough (seating 200). (See plate 11.)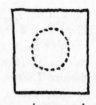

There is also a fourth, a two-sided arrangement of great interest, the traverse stage, where the acting area is in the middle with the audience facing one another on opposite sides as at the pocket sized Traverse in Edinburgh which seats 60 – a fact which has dictated both its problems and its whole artistic policy from the very outset. (See plate 14.)

All these forms of open staging, which bring the actor into a much more informal relationship with his audience, require performances of absolute candour. Rather than relying on a technique that has been developed to project from the tableau framed by the proscenium arch, the actor must interpret the play and his character with a convincing sincerity: the closer the audience is, the more easily will it penetrate facile tricks of stage convention.

To the untrained actor, whose greatest advantage is his enthusiasm and sincerity, this less formal type of theatre clearly offers valuable possibilities and a framework in which he can best exploit his natural assets.

To free oneself from an imitation of the West End, the most effective step is to free onself from the dictates of the proscenium arch and work on a small scale. Small wonder that Rabindranath Tagore wrote: 'The Theatres which have been set up in India today, in imitation of the West, are too elaborate to be brought to the door of all. In them the creative richness of the poet and player is overshadowed by the mechanical wealth of the capitalist. If the Hindu spectator has not been too far infected with the greed for realism; if the Hindu artist has any respect for his own craft and skill, the best thing they can do for themselves is to regain their freedom by making a clean sweep of the costly rubbish that has accumulated and is now clogging the stage.'

THE PRODUCER'S PROBLEMS

There must always be a first time for open stage production and the wise producer might attempt to see one first, before taking the plunge. Try and see performances at Chichester, the Mermaid in London, the Phoenix Theatre, Leicester, the Victoria Theatre, Stoke-on-Trent, the Octagon, Bolton, or at the Traverse in Edinburgh.

Read *Theatre in the Round* by Stephen Joseph (Barrie and Rockliff) and *Central and Flexible Staging* by Walter P. Boyle (University of California Press, distributed by the Cambridge University Press) which cover every aspect of the subject including suggestions for suitable plays, the problems of lighting, style of acting, production and much else which there is no room to go into here. Richard Southern's *The Open Stage*. (Faber) and Stephen Joseph's *New Theatre Forms* (Pitman) are challenging. For those who would like to go deeper into the whole problem of theatre design *The Ideal Theatre – Eight Concepts* published (1965) for the American Federation of Arts by Peter Owen Ltd., London and *Adaptable and Flexible Theatres* (ed. S. Joseph) are also strongly recommended.

Eventually the plunge has to be taken and this is best at the deep end – with theatre in the round. For if you put your actor on an open end-stage first, he will, if he is at all used to proscenium work, retreat to the back wall; and if he comes to the front at all, say on a three-sided platform stage, he will always play straight out in front, erecting his own proscenium frame around him. There is no need for concern that some actors will be facing away from the audience; experience suggests that is no handicap.

OPEN STAGING AND THE CHOICE OF PLAYS

Improvised and other work can be 'presented' on an open stage without difficulty, but the question of the most suitable plays which can be presented on them is a subject about which many contradictory opinions have been voiced. Open staging is generally least satisfactory for grand classical productions (though Racine's *Phaèdre* has been produced magnificently in the round), and most suited to intimately naturalistic plays where the question of the actors' command or domination of the audience is not involved. Shakespeare comes across very well while Chekhov,

Strindberg, O'Neill, Coward, Beckett, Shaw, Ionesco, and Pinter have all been produced on open stages with success; in fact Stephen Joseph has counted over 800 plays which have been produced in theatres in the round in this country and on the continent in the last twenty years. Some perceptive comments on this situation have been made by Henry Miller. They are worth quoting in full:

'Proscenium is a limitation for a hell of a lot of plays . . . you see, the drama has become more and more a first person thing. Even such a really traditional writer as O'Neill started talking biographically as he grew older. There's a subconscious analogy, I think, between the proscenium theatre and the third person; here, the play is pretending to take place without any author; these people are supposed to be really talking to one another, and we are overhearing them. Today, on the other hand, there is a more personal even confidential statement being made; plays are less fictional and more confessional, and consequently the tendency is always to face out to the audience. You see, it's all a question of how much you are pretending this isn't a play, or that this is a play – whether the emphasis is on the author or the actor – presentational or representational. The proscenium favours the latter. There are great works, in verse, in opera, in everything else. But the bread and butter of the tradition is always, more or less, that the guy on the stage is not an elephant or a rhinoceros . . .'

THE OPEN-AIR SETTING

The use of open-air settings in spaces such as gardens, parks, market-squares, castles, courtyards, stable-courts and even the streets has already been referred to. Now is the time to look more closely at the kind of production which can be performed in such settings: the Open-Air School has clung for so long (and through so many downpours) to its Arcadian image that its other possibilities have been overlooked.

In fact far from being a natural home for theatrical enchantment and pastoral idylls, the open-air setting is a place where actors are obliged to exchange delicacy for a declamatory style, and where broad effects are more effective than subtle ones. If there is to be a revival of melodrama, slapstick comedy, masque, symbolic drama and heroic romance, this is the theatre for it. The whole series of mediaeval miracle plays and the

Greek dramas were written to be performed in the open air and these are more likely to be successful than productions of *As you like it* or *A Midsummer Night's Dream* which need the quiet intimacy of an enclosed space to allow their subtleties to come through. Aristophanes' *The Birds* and Punch and Judy have much in common.

Gardens, terraces, the edge of a wood or some other setting of natural beauty are usually used; but there can be no doubt that the architectural background is preferable, both artistically and acoustically (e.g. St Mary's Abbey, York, which is used as a backwall for the setting of the *York Miracle Plays*). Alternatively if a castle or other building is not to hand, a curtained platform stage, rostra and steps amongst the trees can be constructed. Experiments can be made with different forms of staging and seating the audience, either on three sides of the acting area or on all four sides as in theatre in the round. If the acting and spectator areas are on the flat, steps and rostra will have to be used, so as to create as many different levels as possible; unless the audience itself can be raised, or can sit on a hillside overlooking the acting area. Another idea is to situate the stage in front of a mound or bank which not only provides variations of level in acting area but gives a feeling of depth. Exits and entrances, often rather difficult in the open air (because an actor may be noticed behind a bush several minutes before he actually enters) are made more interesting in such a setting.

An actor may suddenly appear running from over the mound, and the appearance of armies, could be handled in the most exciting manner: spectacle and pageantry are best suited to this kind of performance. (Such a permanent setting, constructed of concrete, is used in the Tuileries Theatre, Paris.) As far as the setting is concerned architectural embellishment of any kind is normally more satisfactory than an attempt to compete with natural forms; the settings should be as unrealistic, as 'architectural' as possible. Tall posts can be driven into the ground, and decorated with white ropes and coloured cloths to form 'houses'. Temporary structures can be made out of steel scaffolding covered in with wood and canvas, or a set of arched screens. It is also worth considering the kind of permanent or mansion setting used in France and other countries for the Mediaeval plays (such as the Valenciennes *Passion Play of 1547*) or the large triangular prisms (made out of flats painted on all three sides) which can be turned round by the actors to indicate a change of scene as happened in the Greek theatre.

The Minack Open-Air Theatre. Ed. Averil Demuth (David and Charles)

THE USE OF CARTS

Many of the guild-plays of the Mediaeval Mysteries were performed from carts, a practice that has been revived in recent years for the *York Mystery Cycle* (see plate 12). These movable stages, which can be drawn through the streets by a horse are constructed on a cart, affording an acting area of say, sixteen feet long by six feet wide. The plays are performed in different parts of the city each evening, and several carts can be used as acting areas in a production. Use drums to announce the performance.

THE BOOTH-STAGE

The booth-stage is simply a raised platform at the back of which is a 'room' of curtains (or screens). If you hang a curtain on a cross piece across the entire length of the stage you create two or three entrances – one at each end and one, if necessary, through the middle. Behind the curtain, and between it and the wall against which the booth is set you can store properties, dress, or retire. It is incredibly simple and delightfully practicable for all kinds of out-door work (see plate 8 for a simple form of Booth-stage).

AN INTRODUCTION TO SETTING

So far we have considered staging; we must now consider the setting, a different aspect of the same concern which is to provide an appropriate environment in which the work of the actors, playwright and director can be communicated to an audience with the maximum force.

There are numerous ways of providing the most appropriate environment for a performance. In Visconti's famous Covent Garden production of Verdi's *Don Carlos*, the five Acts included a complete and strictly naturalistic reproduction of the interior of the Monastery at Yuste, a forest near Fontainebleau and the square in front of the Cathedral in Madrid. Some productions, such as Charles Marowitz's of John Herbert's *Fortune and Men's Eyes* at the Open Space Theatre are simpler: four beds on a bare stage. One of these settings is not intrinsically 'better' than the other – each 'play' by its nature determines the setting which suits it best.

There are two traditions which, right from the start, it is as well to distinguish. The simplest concept of a stage is of the unlocalised 'playing place' which represents any place the actors choose to make it, whether it is Duncan's palace, the witches' cave, or a moor. This tradition developed from the very earliest 'theatre', the religious rites of the earliest communities, through Greek Drama, the Mediaeval Liturgical performances, the Elizabethan Theatre, the Commedia dell'Arte to much of our own theatre today. The acting area is usually more or less bare. The properties are either naturalistic objects (4 beds indicate that it is a reformatory dormitory) or symbolic scenic devices evocative of some aspect of the play or scene. In either case they are generally flexible and easily removed.

The alternative tradition, with its roots in the Roman theatre, was developed during the Italian Renaissance, and brought to England by Inigo Jones in the first decade of the seventeenth century. In this the stage becomes a place of illusion – a localised and particular representation of the actual scene in which the drama is taking place: The monastery of Yuste or a Forest near Fontainebleau. To make this illusion complete a new kind of theatre – the proscenium type – was developed, so that the painted backcloths and wings making use of perspective effects could be seen from a central position (the curved auditorium), framed by the proscenium arch itself. This led to the development of a new kind of drama – the English Court Masque, the Spanish Theatre, Molière's theatre in Paris, Grand opera, nineteenth-century melodrama and the naturalistic production of the nineteenth century and of the contemporary stage.

This tradition, though very much with us, is not that with which we are concerned. Such elaborate naturalism is frequently irrelevant to the amateur's creative needs, and often beyond his technical and financial resources. Robert Edmund Jones, the American designer writes: 'The best thing that could happen to our theatre at this moment', he wrote in

1946, 'would be for playwrights and actors and directors to be handed a bare stage on which no scenery could be placed, and there told that they must write and act and direct for this stage. In no time we should have the most exciting theatre in the world.'

This approach is not only expedient but liberating; it frees one from the burden of imitative reconstruction on a shoe-string budget. The environment of the production is created by suggestion, by implication; by communicating an effect rather than by illustrating a fact, by creating an image rather than the imitation of reality.

In the following pages we look at the numerous ways a stage can be developed from the simplest to more elaborate settings. Some groups work as a creative team extemporising their own settings from screens, blocks, curtains, and well-chosen props and furniture carefully lit. Others engage the interest of a specialist designer who takes on the full responsibility of the whole visual aspect. Sometimes the director designs. Each method has a lot to recommend it: we have not tried to lay down any guiding rules, but to make suggestions which may be of value for every kind of production and acting-area alike.

WORK ON A SIMPLE SET

Some of the best settings are developed as rehearsals proceed. There is no specialist designer (though it can be useful to have someone to stand 'outside' in order to make constructive criticisms); the actors add elements as and when they think fit.

There are many ways of constructing such sets. Sometimes a simple permanent setting is used; sometimes even less is necessary, as in a production of John Bowen's *After the Rain*, in which the different parts of the raft on which the action took place were taped out on the floor of the acting area (which was in the round) and labelled accordingly. If the acting is good such simplicity increases the illusion; while if the acting is bad, a full-scale reproduction of the *Lusitania* will not make any difference.

THE DESIGNER'S ROLE WITH A MORE COMPLEX SET

The developed set which consists of something more than a few chairs and a set of rostra, may be put together by a specialist designer, who is responsible for seeing it through every stage of its development. His work resembles an architect's rather than an interior designer's who is called in to smarten a place which is already built. He is there at the beginning, for no design however masterly it looks on paper can exist in a vacuum; it is part of a total production, a total pattern of interpretation. It should be apposite, unpretentious, direct, whether this involves a straight-forward use of blocks, screens and lighting; the complete reconstruction of an historical setting; or a more abstract design such as Svoboda's for *Hamlet* – a giant looking glass hung at an angle above the set in which Hamlet communed with the ghost, his own image reflected, in the darkness above him. For the most disastrous settings are not only those which are technically inadequate but those which draw attention to themselves, or seem to have been designed without thought for the production in hand.

The style of the setting follows from the total concept both director and designer have agreed on. 'It is idle to talk about the distraction of scenery', wrote Gordon Craig, 'because the question here is not how to create some distracting scenery but rather how to create a place which harmonises with the thoughts of the poet.'

Cost, the experience and abilities of back-stage staff and carpenters alike, the size and type of acting area being used, the time allowed for the work, facilities and experience in general, all affect the finished work. This is likely to be approached in the following order:

1. *The Play is read*

Thorough familiarity with the script is essential. It should be read and re-read and also other plays by the same writer or his contemporaries. It is essential to know how to read a play, to absorb its overall atmosphere, its essence. Images of words or lines which crystallise the feeling, even the meaning of the play, can suggest a set. Make notes – the idea of both settings and costumes often consists of an image. Make a scene-plot, too, which is a detailed list of scenes and notes of any special features which the action calls for (the arras behind which Polonius hides in *Hamlet* dictates the pattern of the setting). Discussion, research and further discussion with the director and technicians is essential at this stage which also includes:

2. *Getting to know your Theatre*

The utmost familiarity with the acting area in which the production is to take place is essential before any designs can be formulated. This includes not only a knowledge of its measurements (scale-plan model, sight lines, and fire regulations if applicable) but its overall mood and proportions, as well as seating arrangements, if these are flexible.

3. *The First Ideas*

Preliminary rough sketches are developed after every meeting with the director – usually line drawings with a colour wash. Shape is important. Plans are important too, but the chief need is to know what the set is going to look like and whether you sort this out with line drawings or a scale model does not matter. Try and be simple and direct. Some of the greatest settings are obvious, but carried through with an audacity and conviction that makes them effective. The designer should be in constant touch with the director (and actors) who collaborate over the design.

4. *Preliminary Scale Model*

This can be constructed if necessary quite simply out of scored and folded cardboard and balsa wood and cloth, and then painted to represent the scene. The model represents, in however crude a form, your conception of the final set and is shown to the producer and the actors who like to have an idea of the atmosphere of the setting before they start work on the play. The scale model could be any size but something like 1 : 50 or later 1 : 24 is really essential. In open-staging a model is still worthwhile as it is easier to move things around at this stage and helps you to think visually, and try out lighting effects. Where a group uses a permanent acting area, a small scale model of the area ($\frac{1}{2}''$ to 1 foot) is well worth making.

5. *Execution of Design*

Assuming the model has been completed and then lit and proves acceptable, your next job is to make careful working drawings for the carpenter – a complete ground plan of the set, drawn to scale. Elevations, and large scale drawings (1 : 8) of such details as walls or trees, or even larger drawings (say 1 : 4) for hand props (see pages 214–29 for details on set-construction and painting).

6. *Setting up on the Stage*

Even when the set is up don't consider it finished, it may look awful and need drastic alterations, on the spot. Often some re-painting and correction will be enough.

7. *Lighting*

See Chapter 11.

RECOMMENDED BOOKS – STAGECRAFT

Scene Painting and Design. Stephen Joseph (Pitman)

Immensely practical and full of good advice. Perhaps the best general introduction to the subject there is.

Modern Theatre Practice. H. Heffner, S. Seldon and H. Seldman (Vision Press Ltd)

A Handbook of Play Production. Part III contains a good general account of the purpose, construction, assembling, painting and designing of scenery – very thorough, rather dull.

Designing and Painting Scenery. Harold Melvill (Art Trade Press)

Excellent on the practical side of scene-painting as long as you don't share his taste for what gets painted. Entirely concerned with the processes of getting sets painted for the proscenium-arch theatre.

Designing and Making Stage Scenery. Michael Warre (Studio)

An intelligent and informative introduction. Well illustrated and recommended.

Scene Design and Stage Lighting. W. Parker and H. Smith (Holt, Rinehart & Winston)

An American book concerned with the design and construction of stage scenery. Very detailed instructions on the design of rostra, sets, flats, properties, stairs etc. are given. Hundreds of diagrams. Very practical and thorough indeed. Highly recommended.

Stage Scenery. A. S. Gillette (H. Hamilton)

As above.

Proscenium and Sight Lines. Richard Southern (Faber)

An exhaustive examination of sight lines from the simplest concept of theatre to the most complex. Highly practical, it also deals with the problems of masking, rigging borders, cycloramas and the false systems of flying etc.

Stage Setting. Richard Southern (Faber)
    Fascinating survey of the use of curtain and screen settings. Absolutely
    practical in its outlook. It does not deal with the box set or painted scenery.
Changeable Scenery. Richard Southern (Faber)
    Survey of the scenic theatre in England from its introduction by Inigo Jones
    to the mid-19th century. Fascinating.
World Theatre. Bamber Gascoigne (Ebury Press)
    A survey of different aspects of theatre and scenic presentation. Superb
    illustrations.

Further Developments of a Bare Stage

We have already seen how some well-chosen objects can be used on the
bare acting area of a theatre in the round, on a thrust or proscenium stage
with a curtained or wall background, to suggest a setting without 'rep-
resenting' it: we now consider the development of neutral settings with
screens and other relatively simple adjuncts.

An Upright Screen

In conjunction with a bare area one simple upright screen is a most
manageable setting (say something 8′ high by 12′ long depending on the
scale of the room in which it is set). Such a screen of perfectly smooth
painted hardboard, or covered in cloth, organdie, tinfoil or metal, can
be left plain and simply lit or painted, or used for back-projections, if
required. Properties or furniture can be used to indicate the whereabouts
of a scene and provide the barest necessary representation of locality.
Hanging vertical banners of white linen can be very effective in the right
production too. Lighting, as always, is crucial.

Back-projection

Back-projection – the projection of photographic slides onto a screen, or
cyclorama (see pages 222 and 294) or the floor of the stage itself, offers intriguing possibilities. It is more than a setting in that it abolishes not only
the fixed stage-space, but stage-time and stage-place. An actor speaks but
he can be simultaneously surrounded by images of the past, the present
and the future, or fragments of all three merged together in a fluid visual
mosaic.

Scaffolding

Another basis for a setting not used enough, but eminently practicable, is the use of tubular scaffolding. Scaffold towers and levels, though requiring expert skill in assembly, can provide a permanent framework for the performance and can be used in conjunction with huge screens, ladders, rostra, painted panels, curtains, ropes, flags, tenting etc. Such an arrangement of standard lengths of tubular scaffolding, very lightly constructed, can also provide a variety of levels. Metal scaffolding can be hired from most local building firms but S.G.B. (Scaffolding Great Britain) (see page 232) are specialists in the hire of scaffolding and have branches in most of the larger towns. Certain angled metal pieces used for exhibition purposes (Dexion is a well-known example) can also be adapted for lighter work.

The Simple Screen Setting

For any acting area with or without a proscenium arch, screens are a very suitable and easily adapted form of setting. They can be made in separate sections and assembled in many different combinations, covered with canvas or painted hardboard. They are practical, portable, economical and full of intriguing possibilities. Some (related) types of screen-setting are as follows:

1. The 2-fold or 3-fold *hinged screen* set.
2. The *standing screen* set.
3. The *open arch* set.

1. *The 2-fold or 3-fold hinged screen set*

This, the simplest form of screen setting, provides a background of a 2- or 3-hinged screen to the acting area, either flat (as a back-wall) or hinged to form a shallow three-sided bay. The screens should be at least 12″ or 18″ above the head of the tallest actor or head-dress, and a 3-fold screen 10′ high by 16′ long (in 3 sections, 5′ by 10′, 6′ by 10′, 5′ by 10′) would be a very convenient size for almost any hall or setting. The size, of course, can vary, but as such screens are portable it is worth considering the kind of dimensions which can be accommodated by almost any situation. Once the flats and the two French braces which support this kind of screen are made, they can be either curtained, or canvassed and painted and left plain or finished with a decorative ending. If painted consider painting the floor of the acting area itself as well.

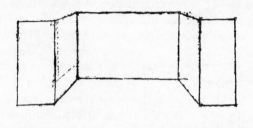

A simple setting can be developed by using a series of screens, either by themselves or backed by a curtain. The screens can be painted on both sides so that a change of scene can be achieved by folding them in new positions (use a loose butt-hinge) in full view of the audience. Used in conjunction with simple but well-chosen properties and rich costumes, the screens can provide a functional and attractive setting, theatrically effective not in spite of but because of its simplicity.

2. *Standing or footed screen set*
A set of 8 or more screens can be used with great effect. These screens need be no larger than 4' by 8', and can be either hung with curtains or canvasses and painted.

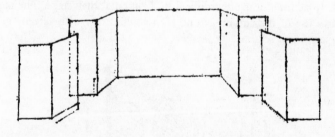

The screens are constructed on the same principle as a hinged screen (see page 227) and are supported by braced stands. Each screen stands separately. They are moved into position before the performance, placed symmetrically or unsymmetrically, boxed in to give the effect of a confined space, or opened out to reveal a painted skycloth. The screens can be pushed forward at the end of a scene to form a flat wall in front of which a scene is acted as new arrangements are prepared behind.

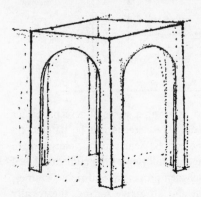

3. *The Open-arch screen set*
Screen settings are capable of endless variation: one of the most useful forms is an open arch (either pointed or round) which can be closed to form a square, opened out into an arcade, or folded into many different combinations suggestive of rooms, studies and cells, in conjunction with curtains, rostra, steps and ladders.

The Curtain setting

A curtain setting has advantages and disadvantages. It provides an unlocalised neutral background which can be used with ground rows, scaffolding, platforms, furniture etc., to provide an unobstrusive background, though the effect of so much pleated material, of a neutral dullish colouring can have a drab, confining, slightly claustrophobic effect. In addition it is often difficult to light on a small stage. The most effective use of the curtain setting is in combination with screens or a semi-permanent set.

The curtains should normally be of a medium or neutral tone, preferably a shade of grey or black. Bolton sheeting or a heavy twilled sheet hangs well, and can be made into curtains of 4′ or 4′6″ width sections.

These are usually hung from a large horizontal frame slung from pulleys in the roof of the stage, and this frame (or fit-up) consists of 4 parts – 2 side battens, a back batten and a border batten – to hide the rigging and stage-ceiling. The square of lashed battens should be made of wood (3″ by 2″) or preferably of tubular steel and should extend beyond the lines of this curtained area, 2′ on either side of the back batten in order to mask entrances.

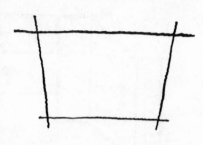

Full particulars are given in Richard Southern's excellent *Stage Setting for Amateurs and Professionals* (Faber) and Frank Napier's *Curtains for Stage Settings* (J. G. Miller).

The simplest curtain background

Assuming that 2 fixtures (in either side wall of the hall) are made, the curtain background can be suspended from a line stretched between them using a wire cable and a wire strainer.

In a larger area, the wire can be pulled right back, by two further wires anchored at points in the back wall. The diagonal curtains are permanent but the curtain on the central wire can be pulled to disclose, if necessary, a further scene (see diagram).

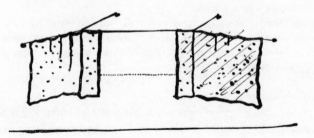

The Arras set

A development of this setting includes the addition of turned-back wings which forms a boxlike acting area, which can be adapted to reveal a central back opening in which a painted backcloth or ground-row (see page 227) can be most effective.

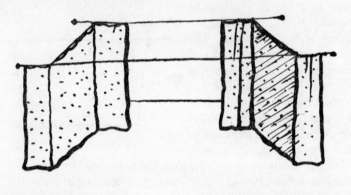

Portable scenery, ground rows etc., in a curtain setting

The very anonymity of a curtain setting makes for quick scene-changes which can be made in many ways – by lighting, making minor adjustments to the arrangement of the curtains, or as follows:

(a) Painted details – small painted details like trees and rocks can be cut out and set among the curtains.
(b) Built details – rostra, steps, ramps, curved screen-walls, ladders, etc.
(c) Built details – columns, or parts of real things, doorways, ramparts, beds, etc.
(d) Real details – furniture etc.
(e) Frame detail – the stage is symmetrically masked on either side with a painted detail of some size which remains permanent throughout the performance, e.g. columns, pavilions, obelisks, statues or some emblem suggestive of the play.

The curtain setting with screens

The use of a built screen against a background of curtains has already been described. The solid screen is used as a background suggestive of something more – say, the corner of a room. The walls are symbolised, rather than being represented, by the folded screen but the room can be furnished as completely as a box set.

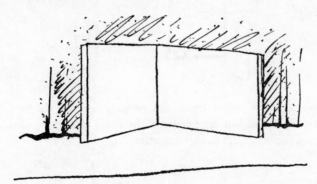

The simple painted backcloth, hung in an opening of the curtains, can be used in several attractive ways. If this backcloth can be placed a foot or so behind the curtains, the opening between them may be filled by a cut-cloth, so that the scene is in two planes:

or similarly a backcloth can be used in conjunction with a small ground-row in front.

Two screens can be used as flats in the wings, framing the stage on either side, while a painted backcloth is set between the opened curtains at the back of the stage:

or more simply a 2-fold screen can be used between the curtains, or screens can be used in conjunction with flats at either side of the stage steps and rostra to form an abstract setting.

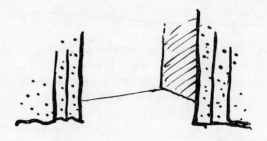

Two screens can be placed to form a 4-sided shape with painted screens which can be turned round or the screens, as described above, can be arches. And this could be related to the use of a series of flats, decoratively painted, on either side of the stage, but by now, there is so 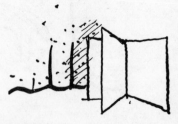 little curtain that we are really describing the semi-permanent set; the subject of the next section.

The semi-permanent and the permanent setting

The semi-permanent and permanent setting provide a framework for the action with the minimum of expense and fuss, which can be altered with the least break of continuity in the performance. The basic structure of a permanent or semi-permanent set needs very careful consideration for it must not only stand as a symbol of the play as a whole but be capable of endless flexibility – a universal setting which becomes, at will a bedroom, a council chamber, castle battlement, a closet, indoors and out-of-doors, a particular place and no place at all – all conjured out of relatively minor adjustments of curtains, backcloth, rostra and screens made in full view of the audience.

Lighting plays a role of exceptional importance. Texture, is important too; one play might need the smooth, polished surfaces of wood, another the clanging hardness of metal.

The simplest semi-permanent or permanent set consists of a series of arches, rostra or columns backed by a painted backcloth, curtains, plaster wall or cyclorama. The wings are masked by curtains or flats.

This set can be adapted by the use of curtains or screens in the arches in the manner already described on page 216.

Instead of the curtained wall, separate structures can be erected either resembling the 'houses' of the Medieval theatre or as a semi-permanent fixture which can become rooms, cells, castles, bedrooms, caverns, or any other enclosed space in which the actors can be seen, or from which they can step forth. These, which can be built on either one or both sides of the stage, can turn round if necessary, and can either be built forward to resemble a compartment with curtains or may be entirely structural, a skeleton of beams or arches against the background of backcloth, cyclorama or curtains, used in conjunction with screens and curtains, rigging or the simplest ground-rows. Such a setting, completely stylised, can be altered to suit the occasion by the addition of decorative features – castellated fortifications, branches, or canopies of cloth.

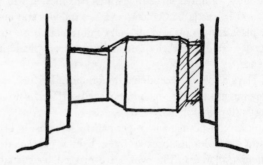

The semi-permanent set can also be combined with rostra, steps and ramps.

Cycloramas (or cycs)

This is the largest single piece of 'scenery' in the theatre and usually consists of a gently curving arc of material which, when lit in the appropriate manner, gives the impression of an infinite void, such as a sky.

In a theatre where space is precious the back wall of the stage can be rendered flat by plastering the two sides and its upper junction with the ceiling and its bottom junction with the floor, brought forward in a gentle curve (about 2′ in radius), which can be painted black, white or a neutral tone.

Alternatively a large piece of material can be fastened to a curved top and bottom batten of piping or wood. The surface of the material, which must present a large uninterrupted smooth surface, on which the light can fall without shadows, is usually a dyed fabric with a surface that takes light well (flannel, poplin, velvet, silk or satin). Cycloramas are not easy to make but the following books do go into the question in some detail.

Proscenium and Sight Lines. R. Southern (Faber)
Modern Stagecraft for the Amateur. G. Lee (Pitman)

Stage Design and Stage Lighting. N. O. Parker and A. K. Smith Noel (Rinehart Winston)

Naturalism and the Box Set

There is also the naturalistic set, consisting of painted flats, doorways, borders, drops, staircases and even a ceiling as well as furnishing, which attempts a complete illusion of reality on the stage. We must mention it; but it is not the concern of this book.

Stage plans in acting editions

Many published plays in acting editions contain stage plans, descriptions and photographs of the original setting, which usually refer to the production in a West End theatre. These can be safely ignored. The descriptions in the text invariably describe the original setting used (as noted by the stage manager) rather than the author's description of the ideal stage requirements. Stephen Joseph makes this very point:[1] 'In the published edition of *The Birthday Party* by Harold Pinter the play begins with the following description of the setting:

> *The living-room of a house in a seaside town. Door leading to hall D.L. Back door and small window U.L. kitchen hatch centre back. Kitchen door U.R. Table and chairs centre. Two ordinary chairs above and left of table, one armchair right of table. Sideboard above small fireplace on right wall. Stool and wooden box for shoe brushes in fireplace –*

'This is quite specific. The synopsis of acts shows that there is no change of setting. After reading the play through you will quickly see that it is a modern play taking place in the present day. However I make an immediate reservation about all this. It is important to know that this is the living-room of a house in a seaside town. We might have gathered as much from the play itself, but it is useful to be told right away.

'There is a door leading to the hall. Yes, it is used in the play and might be expected anyhow. How important is it that this door should be down left? How important are the precise positions indicated for other doors, window, fireplace and furniture? . . .

'It may help if I add that after Harold Pinter produced *The Birthday*

[1] In *Scene Painting and Design* (Pitman).

Party himself for my own theatre-in-the-round company, he used a very different setting from the one described. It was not necessarily a better setting in any way – I designed it – but the conditions under which the production was done demanded something quite different from the original.'

Building rostra, flats, steps etc.

The following notes may be of some use to those who wish to construct the simplest and most basic elements. Detailed instructions and working drawings are available in some of the books listed on page 212.

The construction of a scenic flat

Use selected, well-seasoned timber of some soft wood (pine). For flats more than 8 feet high use 3″ by 1″ timber, otherwise 2″ by 1″. The height

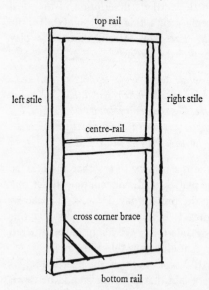

top rail

left stile

right stile

centre-rail

cross corner brace

bottom rail

of flats varies considerably but 12′, 14′ or 18′ are common sizes. The usual width of a flat is 5′9″ but for small stages 4′ is adequate. Flats have to be carefully constructed (see diagram) as they are easily pulled out of the square and warp. An 'open' mortice and tenon joint is far more effective in preventing this than a 'halve' joint. The tenons (or tongue) must always be cut on the stiles and the mortices on the rails (though authorities vary on this) so that the bottom rail should run through from edge to edge of the flat (the corners are usually chamfered a little).

The cross corner brace can now be filled with a 'halve' joint, after the centre, top and bottom rails have been fitted. The 8 joints are joined by glue and by screwing 5 screws into each one. Never use nails, but wooden pegs can be used. Flats should be marked on the back for identification purposes (numbering from down-stage on both sides of the stage).

Canvassing a flat

Scene canvas is usually either 36″ or 72″ in width, and should normally be purchased already fireproofed. Hessian, sometimes used, is unsatisfactory because its surface is too uneven (for stockists see pages 232–3).

The flat is canvassed by tacking (staple-gunning first) the canvas to its structure. Two people are needed – one to tack down the frame and the other to hold it taut. Lay the frame on the floor and place the canvas over it. This should be larger than the frame, but only cut out after it has been tacked on. Begin by tacking in the centre of the top and bottom rails (or alternatively the stiles) pulling the canvas gently, and nailing the tacks 2″ apart. Work towards the corners. The tacks should be on the inner side of the wooden stile. When the ends have been tacked, begin in the centre of the stiles until the corners are reached again. These are split and turned back for gluing. Trim the canvas with a sharp knife and then glue it down. The canvas must not be bent round over the framework. It is now primed with size and whiting, even though the scenic paints may be mixed with P.V.A. (plastic emulsion medium).

Priming and Painting

Priming: Dissolve one pound of size in a gallon of boiling water. In another bucket put a pound of ceiling white or some lump whiting, and cover with cold water. Stir to a creamy consistency and mix half a bucket of size and half a bucket of whiting together. Paint this mixture onto the flats (on the floor) with a large brush and allow to dry for a day or so. The size will tighten the canvas like a drum.

Painting: Scenic colours are bought in powder form. The basic colours are: Burnt Sienna, Raw Sienna, Burnt Umber, Yellow Ochre (which are the cheapest) and Ultramarine, Lemon Chrome, Crimson Lake, Permanent Red, Mid Green, Azure Blue, Drop Black.

There should be a large stock of whiting on hand, as well as brushes of various sizes. All scenic paint must be mixed with size or P.V.A. – Poly

Vinyl Acetate. This plastic emulsion medium is simply thinned with water. If size is prepared (one pound of size to 1½ gallons of hot water) it should not be heated over a direct flame but in a large tin within a bucket (like a double saucepan) containing boiling water. The paint is then mixed up with a little cold water until there are no lumps left. This is then mixed with the size, with an equal proportion of water to size. The thickness of the paint can only be determined by experience, but it is better to start with a fairly thick consistency and gradually water it down.

The wet paint should be applied on a piece of white paper and left to dry because scenic paints dry a much lighter tone than they are when wet. (N.B. The size can be left to set as a thin jelly and warmed up again before use.)

The flats and backcloth are usually laid-in with a smooth coat of their general basic colour, painted with bold vertical strokes. A second coat is then applied more carefully than the first. Old flats should be scrubbed clean, and sized from the back to make them taut again. Backcloths, if they cannot be painted in position (after rehearsals) can be laid out on a floor and painted, and touched up when in position.

Bracing the flats

Flats are joined together edge to edge, but often at different angles to one another, by a method known as 'cleating'. This is done from behind the flats. A thin and very strong rope is attached to the edge of a flat about 18″ from its top. It is brought over a cleat which is screwed to the next flat in an adjacent position. (From behind, the cleat is always attached to the right-hand stile, the rope to the left.) The rope is pulled tight and tied with a slip knot to screws or hooks, one on each flat and about 3′ from the ground.

The flats are braced at intervals, or they will fall over. There are two types of brace in common use, the Extending and French Brace.

The *Extending Brace* is really a prop. It is made of two pieces of wood, joined telescopically by means of an adjustable clamp, so that its length can be changed to suit. One end of the brace has a hook in it, which is passed through a screw-eye in the back of the flat about 6′ from the ground. The other end is either screwed into the floor of the stage through a bent piece of iron which has been attached to the brace, or, if this is impossible, it is supported by an iron brace-weight or a sandbag. Braces and weights are manufactured by the Hall Stage Equipment Ltd., Nova Works, Wynne Road, London s.w.9.

The *French Brace* consists of a triangle of wood hinged to the back of a flat. When the flat is in position, a stage weight or sandbag is placed over the lower rail to counter-balance the weight of the flat. French braces are usually used to support ground-rows (see below).

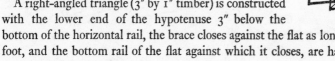

A right-angled triangle (3″ by 1″ timber) is constructed with the lower end of the hypotenuse 3″ below the bottom of the horizontal rail, the brace closes against the flat as long as its foot, and the bottom rail of the flat against which it closes, are halved.

Constructing set pieces or ground-rows

A ground-row is built rather like a flat lying on its edge, with a profile cut out to represent rocks, boulders, hedges, etc. They are usually con-structed out of 3mm. hardboard, oxlene or plywood supported by battens (2″ by 1″ timber) and held upright by small French braces or brackets. The framework onto which the hardboard is nailed always consists of a bottom batten which touches the floor of the stage. The hardboard is painted on the rough side.

Screens

Two or three flats can be hinged together to form a screen which must be assembled (see diagram) for maximum strength. All hinges must be inset, with their flats level with the wood. To prevent the screen from folding as in the diagram, hinge a compensating strip of wood (1″ square) to the edge of the centre flat and hinge the outmost frame to the strip. (The centre flat, in this case, should measure 1″ less if we wish to keep the whole screen exactly as before.) Alternatively use the special 3-part screen-hinge which permits the screen to be folded either way.

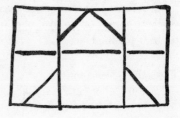

The Base for Standing Screens

A set of large standing screens is not usually supported by the French brace but by the construction of a special base (see *Stage Setting* by R. Southern).

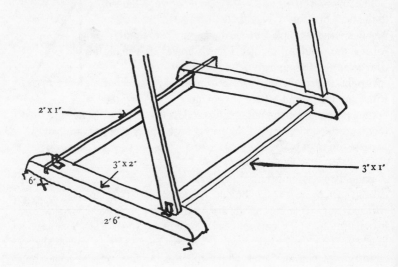

Balconies

A balcony is built exactly the same way as a rostrum though a balcony that projects from a window off the ground will have to be supported by pillars underneath.

Archways and Doors

These can be constructed of hardboard or if a door should look really solid it should be constructed like one with a 'reveal', a piece of 6" by 1" timber running on its edge right round the door. The curved top is made of bent plywood.

Portable Rostrum Units

There are a number of different ways of making collapsible rostra, but the best way for our purposes is what is called the standard parallel, which is very commonly used to build up stage and audience levels. Most big firms which supply stage fittings (see page 232) can provide them without detail drawings, if the overall measurements are given.

Rostra should be interchangeable and modules should be decided so that interchangeability is possible. A good size is 3' by 6' in plan and 7" high. This can be folded and carried without difficulty. Other sizes, say 3' by 3', of the same height may be necessary. They should be solidly constructed so that it neither creaks nor shifts, and 3" by 1" wood for the framework should be sufficient. The top is best made of one piece of plywood. More detailed instructions are available in Stephen Joseph's *Scene Painting and Design*.

Unit-cubes
Four or five unit-cubes like huge hollow children's bricks or cardboard boxes, which can be assembled in various permutations, are worth making out of strengthened 3-ply. They can be any size – a good beginning would be a cube 36" square and 18" high, with handle-holes on two sides. Four by four by one foot is a very good size, too.

Steps
Remember that the risers should be 6" or 7" high and that the treads should be as long as possible (at least 9" to 12" long). All treads and risers should be uniform. It is well worth planning this out on the scale model (or floor plans) as steps, which should be as spacious and dignified as possible, take up a surprising amount of space. Use 6" and 9" floor-boards 1" thick.

Folding Arches or Screens
A triple folding set of arches, like a folding screen, is invaluable. This is made of a plywood framework (3" by 1") with mortice and tenon joints; the curved arches at the top. Two of the arches are hinged together so as to fold face to face; the third is attached by means of a lose-butt hinge, and can be taken out at will. So units of one single arch, a double arch, or a triple arch, standing either flat or in a three-sided bay, can be used with or without curtains.

A SHORT LIST OF MATERIALS FOR SCENIC-CONSTRUCTION
(AND PROPERTIES)
Designers use anything from nylon pot scourers and egg crates to conventional canvas. Read the following notes in conjunction with those
on pages 261–5.

Metals	Bronze, copper, tin sheets, perforated (zinc and aluminium) sheets, wire netting, tubing, scaffolding and sections, brass wire, wrought iron, etc. sheets of aluminium foil
Glass	Mirrors, powdered glass and glue on hessian etc.
Composition Boards	Multiplex, Linex, porous panels, veneers
Synthetic Materials	Polyester foam (latex etc.), Polystyrene, artificial resins and rubbers, formica, Plexiglas, Jablite
Natural Materials	Cork, untanned leather, plaited straw, reeds, rushes, sheepskin, pebbles, wood
Papers	Gold, silver, embossed papers, newspapers, brown packing paper, cellophane, photo-murals, crumpled paper, egg-trays, egg-boxes, cardboard boxes
New Fabrics and Fibres	Plastics, nylon, terylene, gauzes, imitation leather, P.V.C.,

woven glass materials,
artificial jute, net, fur, down,
kitchen cloths, American cloth

Miscellaneous   Netting, hose-pipe, string and ropes,
stove-piping,
sisal-matting

LIST OF STOCKISTS

Aluminium Faced Plywood
Ash and Lacey, Alma Street, Smethwick 40, Staffs.
 A new material coming in various colours at approximately 69/- per sheet.

Fibreglass (see list of stockists on page 262)

Metalwork and Metal Suppliers
Bullanco, 66 Queen's Road, London S.E.15.
 (for expanded aluminium mesh).
Expanded Metal Co., Burwood House, Caxton Street, London S.W.1.

Scenic Paint, Dyes, Brushes, Size, P.V.A., etc.
Brodie and Middleton, 79 Long Acre, London W.C.2.
A. Leete & Co. Ltd, 129–130 London Road, Southwark, London S.E.1.
Metalcote of London Ltd, 28 Leicester Road, New Barnet, Herts.
 (for metal paints).

Plastics
F. J. Bly & Co., 370 Upper Street, London N.1. (perspex sheets etc.).
B. X. Plastics Ltd, Higham Station Avenue, London E.4.
I.C.I. Plastics Division, Welwyn Garden City, Welwyn, Herts.

Resins
Bondaglass Ltd, 55 South End, Croydon, Surrey.
British Resin Products Ltd, Devonshire House, Piccadilly, London W.1.

Vapcolex Metallised Melinex
George M. Whiley Ltd, Victoria Road, South Ruislip, Middlesex.
 (different thicknesses of this material, like tin foil, are available).

Ropes
Mewis Cordage, St Paul's Square, Birmingham 3.
 (for bulk quantities).

Scaffolding
S.G.B. Building Equipment Division. Head Office: Mitcham, Surrey; dozens
   of depots.

Scenic Contractors
Brunskill & Loveday Ltd, 1 Newport Street, London S.E.11.
   (builders of scenery, rostra etc.).
Beck & Windibank Ltd, Clement Street, Birmingham 1.
   (stage equipment and draperies).
Hall & Dixon Ltd, 19 Garrick Street, London W.C.2.
   (stage ironmongery, portable stages for sale only).
Stage Furnishings Ltd, 346 Sauchiehall Street, Glasgow C.2.
   (stage ironmongery for sale).
Watts & Corry Ltd, Jubilee Works, Constable Street, Manchester 18.
   (stage designers and engineers; stage ironmongery and fit-up stages for sale).
Airscrew Co. & Jicwood Ltd, Weighbridge, Surrey.
   (makers of Essex portable stages and rostra).
Byfleet Furniture Ltd, York Road, Byfleet, Surrey.
   (all-purpose and Essex stage equipment, rostra and portable stages).
E. Babbage & Co. Ltd, 1–5 Andrew Place, Cowthorpe Road, London S.W.8.
John Roberts & Associates, 61 Black Bull Lane, Fulwood, Preston.
Stage-Décor Ltd, Browning Hall, Browning Street, London S.E.17.
Theatre Studio Ltd, Neal's Yard, Monmouth Street, London W.C.2.

Scenic and Curtain Materials
Benfield & Sons Ltd, 3 Villiers Road, London N.W.2.
   (canvas for sale).
Brodie & Middleton, 79 Long Acre, London W.C.2.
   (scenic colours, aniline dyes, hessian, fire-proofing material, scene canvas for
   sale).
B. Burnet & Co. Ltd, 22 Garrick Street, London W.C.2.
   (curtain material and curtains made to order for sale).
Cape, 85 Crouch Hill, London N.8.
   (scenery and draperies).
Fosters Ltd, 375 West Dale Lane West, Nottingham.
   (curtains).
Garrick Curtains Ltd, 44 Amhurst Road, Hackney E.8.
   (curtain specialists).
Hall & Dixon Ltd, 19 Garrick Street, London W.C.2.
   (curtain materials and curtains made to order).

John Holliday & Sons Ltd, 12 Little Britain, London E.C.1.
A. Leete & Co. Ltd, 129–130 London Road, S.E.1.
  (scenic colours, dyes, fire-proofing chemicals for sale).
Rex Howard, 12 Connaught Street, W.2.
  (stage draperies for hire and sale).
Russell & Chapple Ltd, 23 Monmouth Street, Shaftesbury Avenue.
  (hessian, canvas, cotton duck, sheeting etc. for sale).
C. J. Reat, 16a Baker Street, London W.C.1.
  (canvas).
Star Scenic Studios, 78 Elms Road, London S.W.4.
  (for second-hand scenic canvas).

Stage Machines
Access Equipment Ltd, Maylands Avenue, Hemel Hempstead, Herts.
  (talloscopes).
Drew, Clarke & Co. Ltd, 562–584 Lea Bridge Road, Leyton, London E.10.
  (ladders and steps).
Hall Stage Equipment Ltd, Nona Works, Wynne Road, London S.W.9.
Lift & Engineering Co. Ltd, 172a Lavender Hill, London S.W.11.
H. C. Slingsby Ltd, 89 Kingsway, London W.C.2.
  (ladders, trolleys etc.).

7 Costumes

One of the greatest difficulties facing an amateur group producing a play is the unavoidable expense and difficulty of costuming it. Even the simplest costume has to be made or hired and either way is necessarily troublesome and costly.

The use of materials and garments that can be borrowed from members of the cast and their friends, and the development of an adaptable wardrobe of basic costumes, provide inexpensive solutions without loss of standards. The use of costumes imaginatively improvised to suit local conditions can be, as John Arden says,[1] 'a hazardous technique – if it goes wrong you can find yourself with a production looking like a badly-hung clothes-line on a March morning, and it is necessary to start with at least a general outline scheme of colours and textures – but it does enable the actors to dress themselves to suit both their own characters and the parts they are playing. They can wear a skeleton of the costume from the beginning of rehearsals, modifying it where it seems best, until it becomes an integral part of their performance. If costumes are hired or even specially made up from a series of designs, they are not likely to be ready until near the opening night; the actors have no time to feel at home in them; and any "amateurishness" in their performance becomes the more pronounced in comparison with the "professionalism" of their clothing . . .

'Thus at Brent Knoll: Herod wore the robes and crown of a mediaeval king over a gold embroidered jacket and black trousers; his Secretary wore a gold high-necked Chinese dressing-gown and a small round black cap; . . . the Shepherds wore pretty much what shepherds wear in Somerset today.'

[1] In the Preface to *The Business of Good Government*, a Christmas play written for and performed by amateurs in the village of Brent Knoll, Somerset (Methuen).

In this way costumes can be devised with imagination, skill and invention which create an illusion without resource to a completely literal representation; an actress in a simple black dress wearing a crown can look more like a Queen than a shoddy substitute of the real thing. As John Bowen says in another introduction – to his own play *The Fall and Redemption of Man*, which was written as an acting exercise for twelve students of the London Academy of Dramatic Art – there is 'doubling, trebling and quadrupling of parts, and the audience sees the actors become each separate character, usually by putting on or bringing on some easily identifiable article of clothing or a property – Pilate, for instance, comes down the steps, goes into the pageant, Right, takes off his toga, comes straight out again, Left, puts on his halo before the mirror, and enters at once as a Disciple. The audience, in my own experience, is never confused, accepts each character as a separate being, and is capable of being very much moved when a young actress in white polo-neck sweater and black skirt with a blue headscarf mourns the death of her son, although they have seen the same actress a few minutes before, in the same costume, but with a black scarf, mocking Jesus with a crown of thorns, and crying "Roll up for the King" (an improvised line).'

There are numerous plays which cannot be presented in such a manner, and even more where it would be unsuitable to do so in a particular production; and for these it may be necessary to consider either the use of a simple adaptable wardrobe, or making and hiring: *Luther*, *A Midsummer Night's Dream* and *When We are Married* fall into this category. For, on the stage, practically everything is a period play, whether it is one of those middle-brow farces where the actors endlessly sip cocktails in a sea of chintz, or *Richard II* or *A School for Scandal* – in every case fastidious attention to historical accuracy or period 'feeling' is important: 1949 is now as much 'period' as 1849. The various solutions to this problem are considered below.

Hiring is also worth serious consideration. It is, however, expensive; this can have the effect of increasing the overall budget for a production which in turn determines the choice of a play which must be a box-office success. The cost of a hired costume can go a long way towards paying for one the group can keep. More groups are therefore making their own costumes as this not only provides pleasure for many who do not wish to act, but enables a producer to impose a stylistic unity on the production where hired costumes, however excellent in themselves, can sometimes seem at odds, not only with each other and the setting, but with the production as a whole.

The following suggestions are therefore made in the hope that every group however small, penniless or ill-equipped will try to make and use their own.

(a) *Simple Costumes*

Children have not forgotten the secret joys of an old box of 'dressing-up clothes' out of which on rainy days they can pretend to become other people, to improvise stories and make their own plays. Every group should have a similar trunk of odds and ends: masks, old clothes, a 19th-century soldier's costume, a Victorian fan, wigs, cloaks and accessories which can be utilized in improvisations unconnected with any text or used as stage costume. Somehow this kind of 'costume' when worn over leotards or old clothes breaks down the selfconsciousness of 'playing period' in 'fancy dress' because the costumes are used with imagination. Chosen by the actors themselves they express the concept of the role where a complete stage costume provided by someone else (especially one first worn only a day or so before the production) can often make an actor feel ill at ease. 'It is infinitely preferable', wrote Komisarjevsky, 'to act a play in some more or less commonplace dress which the audience can accept as a conventionality to be disregarded, than in the most magnificent . . . costumes which have been devised by an artist independent of the idea of the production, and which neither express the meaning of the play nor correspond to the emotions and movements of the actors.'

(b) *Making an Adaptable Wardrobe*

A permanent wardrobe of basic costumes is an invaluable asset. Not only can actors rehearse in costume, but the designer can achieve a unity of style without resource to hiring or the effort of making a complete new set of costumes for every play. Besides which there should be a considerable saving of expense. It is, however, no substitute for accuracy in shape and cutting.

The adaptable wardrobe consists of a series of separate garments, which when put together provide a wide variety of costumes of different periods. These basic units are skirts and trousers, tights and sleeves, jackets and waistcoats etc. The addition of such accessories as garters, aprons, neckerchiefs, epaulettes, sashes, belts, jewellery and the right sort of footwear and headgear provides an enormous variety of costume.

These units should be made in various sizes and of the best material not only because they will have to stand up to very hard wear but because they should look attractive in themselves. Beautiful colours and textures: wool, leather, good cotton, velvet are essential as well as an adequate supply of hooks and eyes, press-studs etc. Hems should be exaggerated so that the lengths and tucks can be effected.

WOMEN

Skirts

Several full ground-length circular skirts may be made in a variety of heavy materials, which could be lined so that they not only hang well but can be reversed.

Skirts made from rectangular pieces (say two widths of 54″) gathered on to a length of elastic down one long length of the piece, make good gathered skirts which can be worn over a hip roll (for the Elizabethan period), looped back (for the Restoration) or over a crinoline (for the Victorian). Worn with an underskirt, either singly or several at a time they can be utilised in an amazing variety of forms. Calico petticoats will help fullness.

The Blouse and Bodice

A fitted cloth jacket or buttoned wool cardigan with long sleeves is very adaptable, while commercial blouse patterns cut oversize can be used to make a basic blouse with elastic around a wide neck and at the end of the sleeves. Fullness in cutting is important so that the basic shape can be readily adapted by using press-studs, ribbons, or pinning.

Bodices extending to the hips and fitted to the waist with darts can be used as a bodice or a rustic jerkin. The front can be either laced, buttoned or fastened with press-studs. Alternatively the front of the bodice can be lengthened, stiffened down the front and shaped into the familiar V-point of the Elizabethan costume. White choir ruffs can be obtained from Mowbray's, 28 Margaret Street, London W1.

A variety of sleeves should be made: wide and full, darted, close-fitting and with or without elastic at the wrists and so on.

MEN

Usually the basic costume for male actors consists of wool tights or trousers (see below) and a buttoned wool cardigan with sleeves or waistcoat (or leather jerkin). These can with the addition of shirts (see below), cloaks, coats, ruffs, belts, hats and so on be adapted almost endlessly.

Trousers and Shirts

Knee breeches should be reasonably tight fitting and buttoned below the knee. These can be worn for Jacobean and early Georgian costumes. Tights can be obtained from Burnet's. Shirts can be adapted from patterns, and varied by the use of a different neck opening and sleeves.

Motley's *Designing and Making Stage Costumes* and Conway's *Amateur Drama on a Small Income* both give further practical suggestions for an adaptable wardrobe.

Shoes and Boots

Attention to detail cannot be overdone, all accessories should be very carefully made and styled (and stored). If the actors are wearing tights, it may be necessary for them to wear shoes. On a carpeted stage these can be adapted from a pair of black or dark brown stockings worn over the tights or over dancing pumps and rolled down as far as the ankle. Foam rubber can be stuck, using Copydex on the soles. It is even possible, using old plimsolls or dancing pumps, to build up a fair copy of a mediaeval flat-heeled shoe, using felt and hessian, stiffened with size. When heels are worn it is far more difficult, and the home-made shoe is not really a practical proposition. It is worth hiring it from a costumier. However, reasonably successful shoes can be made using ordinary shoes with heels, disguised with a buckle or rosette (for 18th-century) or with a narrow shaped strip (for 17th-century shoes). Boots and shoes can be hired from:

Anello and Davide, 30 Drury Lane, London WC2.
Gamba Ltd, 46 Dean Street, London W1.

(c) *Making Period Costumes*

Unless the director designs or chooses all the costumes himself someone else will have to do this for him, and ideally this person should be responsible not only for the costumes, but the setting, lighting and properties. The trouble with hiring is that a set of hired costumes can create an atmosphere at odds with the production as a whole. If the hired costumes have been chosen by the designer and producer together, this discrepancy can to some extent be avoided; but if they have been ordered by post, there is no certainty that the costumes will not create an atmosphere which is alien to the general spirit or style of the play. Designer and producer should ideally be the same person but where this is not possible they should collaborate and share the same imaginative vision, continually meeting and discussing every aspect of the production, even exchanging roles.

The making of costumes falls into various stages which will be dealt with separately as follows:

1. Making the design
2. Materials to use
3. Making the costume

1. *Making the Design*

Begin by studying and re-studying the play until you are familiar, not simply with its plot, but its meaning and atmosphere (see pages 106–7). Attend rehearsals; try to imagine the look and the feel of the play in your mind's eye. Make sketches. Maybe some memory of an engraving or painting will be the basis of these (see pages 243–4). At the same time read memoirs, biographies, histories and everything you can lay hands on about the period in which the play is set. And this is as important for a play which is set, say, in 1967 as 1637.

Too many pictures can somehow blunt one's imaginative response, but memoirs can provide the kind of internal evidence which enables the designer so truly to sense the mood of his period that he can recreate it, not so much by means of an exactly literal or scrupulous copy based on evidence, as by a leap of imaginative understanding.

Once you have found a starting point for the style of the whole production discuss this with the producer and show him your first very rough sketches, which will probably include suggestions for the setting as well as the costumes. These first suggestions will no doubt be revised; they will, however, show the colour scheme you favour and the style and mood of the whole.

Bertolt Brecht's description of the genesis of *Galileo*,[1] with his first working ideas, is a particularly interesting description of the approach that can be made.

'First we had to look through works on costume and also old pictures showing costume in order to find costumes that were free of any element of fancy dress. . . . We sighed with relief when we found a small 16th-century panel that showed long trousers. Then we had to distinguish the classes. There the elder Breughel was of great service. Finally we had to work out the colour scheme. Each scene had to have its basic tone: the first, e.g., a delicate morning one of white, yellow and grey. But the entire sequence of scenes had to have its development in terms of colour. In the first scene a deep and distinguished blue made its entrance with Ludovico Marsili, and this deep blue remained, set apart, in the second scene with the upper bourgeoisie, in their grey-green coats made of felt and leather.

'Galileo's social ascent could be followed by means of colour. The silver and pearly-grey of the fourth (court) scene led into a nocturne in brown and black (where Galileo is jeered at by the monks of the Collegium Romanum), then on to the slight, the cardinals' ball, with delicate and fantastic individual masks moving among the cardinals' crimson figures.

'That was a burst of colour, but it still had to be fully unleashed, and this occurred in the ninth scene, the carnival. After the nobility and the cardinals the poor people too had their masked ball. Then came the descent into dull and sombre colours. The difficulty of such a plan of course lies in the fact that the costumes and their wearers wander through several scenes; they always have to fit in, and to help build up the colour schemes of the scenes that follow.'

Once the general ideas have been approved, and designer and producer are on the same wave-length it is then, and only then, that more developed drawings should be produced (though it is often useless to make over careful drawings because the people who are going to make the costumes

[1] *Brecht on Theatre*. Trans. by J. Willet (Methuen).

Left :
THE ELIZABETHAN
THEATRE
'The Knight of the Burning
Pestle' in a reconstructed
Elizabethan Theatre at
Bretton Hall, Wakefield

Below :
A MEDIAEVAL MYSTERY
RESTAGED
The Noah Play from the
Cornish Cycle at Piran
Round, Perranporth

Top THEATRE IN THE ROUND
  'The Disguises of Arlecchino' in Scarborough Library

Bottom THEATRE FROM A CART
  The Noah Play in York, 1966

probably won't be able to understand your intentions). Do not begin with rigid ideas but produce fairly general and evocative sketches indicating workroom instructions of construction and accessories, as well as a more detailed individual drawing for any part which requires special explanation.

SOURCES OF REFERENCE. A note on historic costumes from contemporary painting
It is an advantage to be acquainted with the works of art of the period in which your play is written. A knowledge of out-of-the-way sources is even more valuable and, although it is impossible to deal with this in detail, a list of suitable references will be found below.

There is no more authentic source of reference to period costumes than in painting. Always refer to this rather than to books on costume with modern illustrations. From painting you will discover the feel or atmosphere of a period.

Obviously certain works will be more valuable than others: but while Hogarth and Brueghel, for instance, could be of more use in designing costumes than El Greco or Blake, some imaginative stroke of theirs, some combination of colours, may suggest a valuable basic idea which can be developed into the design of the entire play.

The Use of Costume Books for Designing Costumes
Stage costumes can either be historical reconstructions of a certain period or imaginative and fanciful. Gordon Craig in *On the Art of the Theatre* gives excellent advice about the use of costume books as a source of reference: 'Do not trouble about the costume books. When in a great difficulty refer to one to see how little it will help you out of your difficulty, but your best plan is never to let yourself become complicated with these things. Remain clear and fresh. . . . The coloured costumes are the worst and you must take great care with these and be utterly independent when you come to think about what you have been looking at. Doubt and mistrust them entirely. . . . Keep continually designing imaginative costumes.'

On the other hand actual historical costumes are of value and the following suggestions may be useful.

Museums with Original Costume Collections

Bath	Assembly Rooms (Mrs Langley Moore collection)
Belfast	Vester Museum
Birmingham	City Museum and Art Gallery
Bristol	Bristol City Museum
	Blaise Castle Folk Museum
Cardiff	National Museum of Wales
Cheltenham	Near Cheltenham: Snowshill Manor (National Trust)
Doncaster	City Art Gallery and Museum
Edinburgh	Royal Scottish Museum
	National Museum of Antiquities of Scotland
Exeter	Royal Albert Memorial Museum
Glasgow	Art Gallery and Museum
Hereford	Hereford City Museum and Art Gallery
Ipswich	Christchurch Mansion
Leeds	City Art Gallery
Leicester	Leicester Museum and Art Gallery
London	Victoria and Albert Museum
	London Museum
	Bethnal Green Museum
	Geffrye Museum
	Forest Gate Museum
Malton, Yorks.	Castle Howard, near Malton
Manchester	The Gallery of English Costume
	Platt Hall
Norwich	Castle Museum
Nottingham	Castle Museum
Taunton	Somerset County Museum
York	Castle Museum

In addition the National Portrait, the National Gallery and Tate Gallery should certainly be visited. Also galleries in Edinburgh, Oxford, Liverpool, Reading, Birmingham and so on. It is well worth making a personal collection of postcards, photographs, reproductions, illustrations etc. and filing them in a systematic way.

SOURCES OF REFERENCE: Paintings, engravings etc.

Classical
An obvious source of reference for classical costumes are the paintings on the Greek vases of all periods. Terracotta figurines. See also Mantegna, David, Ingres.

Mediaeval Plays
Illuminated manuscripts, bibles, psalters, Books of Hours (N.B. that of the Duc de Berry), stone figures from the cathedrals (e.g. Rheims), carvings from pew-ends, misericords, embroidery, stained glass etc.

Mediaeval
Paintings by Breughel, Van Eyck, Rogier Van der Weyden, Memlinc, Dirk Bouts, Piero della Francesca.

Renaissance
Benozzo Gozzoli, Botticelli, Pisanello, Uccello, Piero della Francesca, Pintoricchio, Crivelli, Carpaccio, Bellini, Titian, Veronese.

Tudor, Elizabethan and Jacobean
Holbein, Nicholas Hilliard, Isaac Oliver (and other miniaturists). Church brasses. Early engravings.

Restoration
Van Dyck, Lely, Kneller, Wenceslas Hollar.

Molière and 18th-century English Dramatists
Watteau, Lancret, Pater, Pietro Longhi, Nattier, La Tour, Fragonard, Boucher, Chardin, Hogarth, Gainsborough, Reynolds and Rowlandson Pottery Figures. Numerous engravings and cartoons.

New Directions

19th Century
(France) Ingres, Guys, the Impressionists, and Ladies' Fashion Prints
and magazines. (*La Belle Assemblée, Le Beau Monde,* etc.)
(England) Frith, Pre-Raphaelites, early photographs, costume-prints.
Charles Keene and *Punch* drawings; also *The Gallery of Fashion.*

Early 20th Century
Photographs. *The Illustrated London News. Punch.*

In London, the Victoria and Albert Museum, the British Museum, the
National Gallery, the Tate Gallery and the National Portrait Gallery will
be of great use. Also the Radio Times Hulton Picture Library, 35 Maryle-
bone High Street, London w 1, for the largest collect of suitable material
for reference. Outside London the Kirk Museum, York, is invaluable.
Local art galleries can be consulted, but reproductions are easily obtained.
Art Schools often contain good libraries which can be consulted. The
British Drama League Reference Library is unequalled.

A good designer will soak himself in prints, engravings, paintings and
the architecture of the period, studying them with such thoroughness that
he will not need to copy certain costumes but will be able to re-create the
feeling of the period almost at will.

SOURCES OF REFERENCE: Books with illustrations of historical costume
and useful engravings, photographs, etc.

Costume of the Western World edited by James Laver (Harrap)
   Early Tudor by James Laver
   Elizabethan and Jacobean by G. Reynolds
   Early Bourbon by André Blum
   The Dominande of Spain by B. Reade
The Gallery of English Costumes (1760 to the present day)
(A series of books published by the Manchester Art Gallery)
Costume Illustrations from the Victoria and Albert Museum
   The 17th and 18th century costumes (edited by J. Laver, H.M.S.O.)
   19th century costumes
The Fashionable Lady in the 19th Century (Charles H. Gibbs-Smith)
(H.M.S.O.)
Fashions and Fashion Plates (1800–1900) edited by James Laver (King
Penguin)

Illustrated Social History of England. G. M. Trevelyan (Longmans)
 Volume 1. Chaucer's England and Early Tudors
 Volume 2. Shakespeare and the Stuart Period
 Volume 3. 18th century
 Volume 4. 19th century
The Book of Costume. Millia Davenport (Crown Publishers, New York)
 Volume 1. Costumes of Europe and America up to the 15th century
 Volume 2. Costumes from 1600 up to the 19th century
                (an excellent text and hundreds of reproductions of drawings
                and paintings)
Victorian Costume and Costume Accessories. Anne M. Buck (Herbert Jenkins, 1962)
Fashion and Reality 1840–1914. A. Gernsheim
The History of Photography. H. and A. Gernsheim (Thames & Hudson)
A Country Calender. G. Winter (Country Life)
Costume in the Theatre. James Laver (Harrap)
Modes and Manners. Max von Boehr (Harrap)
Life and Work of the People of England. Dorothy Hartley and Margaret Elliot (Batsford)

SOURCES OF REFERENCE: Modern Drawings of Historical Costumes

Handbook of English Mediaeval Costume. C. Willett and P. Cunnington (Faber)
Handbook of English Costume in the 16th century. C. Willett and P. Cunnington (Faber)
Handbook of English Costume in the 17th century. C. Willett and P. Cunnington (Faber)
Handbook of English Costume in the 18th century. C. Willett and P. Cunnington (Faber)
Handbook of English Costume in the 19th century. C. Willett and P. Cunnington (Faber)
English Women's Clothing in the 19th century. C. Willett and P. Cunnington (Faber)
English Women's Clothing in the Present Century. C. Willett and P. Cunnington (Faber)
The History of Underclothes. C. Willett and P. Cunnington (Michael Joseph)
Occupational Costume in England. P. Cunnington and Catherine Lucas (Black)

Excellent texts with a scholarly approach, these books are amongst the best of their kind.

Costume Cavalcade. Harold Hansen (Methuen)
A Short History of English Costume and Armour. 1066–1800. F. M. Kelly and R. Schabe (Batsford)
Shakespearean Costume for Stage and Screen. F. M. Kelly (Black)
Period Costumes and Settings for the Small Stage. J. M. Cunningham Green (Harrap)
English Costume. D. Calthrop (Black)
Historic Costume for the Stage. L. Barton (Black)
The Mode in Footwear. R. Turner Wilcox (Scribner)
The Mode in Hats and Headdresses. R. Turner Wilcox (Scribner)
Greek, Roman and Byzantine Costume. M. G. Houston (Black)
Assyrian, Persian and Babylonian Costume. M. G. Houston (Black)
Peasant Costume in Europe. K. Mann (Black)
Biblical Costume. M. L. Wright (S.P.C.K.)
Costumes in Elizabethan Drama. M. Chenning Lincthicum (University of London Press)
See also Bibliography compiled by the Costume Society (c/o Victoria and Albert Museum, South Kensington, London)

2. *Materials to use*

The actual fabric out of which a stage costume is fashioned is as important as the design and cut, and there is no substitute for wise spending. Every sacrifice should be made to get only the best. Out of rough wools, tweeds, and even hessian, unbleached calico, and Bolton sheeting, something very close to the reality of old materials can be achieved at very little expense. This is infinitely preferable to the use of soft machine materials and artificial fabrics – nylon, rayon, dacron, orlon, chiffon, as well as soft machine-made satins and velvets, rayon taffetas and brocades, which give no feeling of period, and always contrive to make any costume out of which they are made look like fancy-dress. The way such materials can be treated is discussed below. Furnishing fabrics and household linens are generally much more effective for period costumes and cheaper than ordinary dress materials, as these are usually too flimsy and too contemporary in design. Avoid shiny satins at all costs. Plain, firm-textured materials such as woollen and heavy cotton, Bolton sheeting, furnishing damask, rayons and furnishing velvets are all effective on the stage. Try to buy materials with weight so that they will hang well. Do not use materials that run counter to the whole spirit of the play. Do not try to economise in this case. Use pure colours, and buy that which has the weight and substance of real clothes. Substitutes have to be found for the most expensive materials, and there is no alternative to continual improvisation – bottle tops, bath plugs, rope, heavy braiding, electric flex, pot scourers, and so on can be utilised, and the costume designer and maker have to have a magpie's acquisitiveness for cheap scrap that becomes rich and strange. The list of materials and suggestions in the chapter on stage settings (pages 230–31) should be consulted here. Heavy felt (floor felt) stiffened with thick size is a very adaptable material for headwear, and with its surface treated all over with moist yellow soap which is then painted, sprayed and broken down, it can be made to look like heavy leather most effectively.

NOTES ON THE MOST APPROPRIATE MATERIALS FOR STAGE USE
Wool Jersey
But for its cost this would be ideal – it is light, tough, drapes and folds beautifully, comes in a wide variety of colours, and surface textures, and can be made to fit any size or shape of body. Comes in 52-inch widths.

Rayon Jersey
Probably the most acceptable cheaper substitute for wool jersey. Very practical.

Hessian
Should be washed first to remove the dressing and then dyed (though it is now manufactured in many colours), and stencilled. Excellent, a very adaptable material.

Velvet
The cost of velvet has often proved prohibitive, but it looks well on the stage and falls superbly because of its weight. Velveteen (lined with tailor's canvas etc.) is a good substitute. Though sold in a wide variety of colours it dyes well and reacts splendidly to light.

Upholstery Materials
Furnishing damask etc. Excellent for use in period costumes these materials come in an enormously wide selection of colours and designs.

Filter Cloth

This little-known material (it is used as a filter in certain dairy-farming processes) has a marvellous soft and fleecy appearance something like velvet at a distance. It dyes well, but as it tends to cling and is not particularly strong, it should be lined. (Obtainable from Clare's, Wells, Somerset.)

Satin

No suitable substitute has yet been found for real satin, though the cotton-backed satin is satisfactory.

Cotton

Heavyweight cottons such as Bolton sheeting, sail-cloth, unbleached calico, twilled sheeting and winceyette blanketing are practical, dye well and are extremely useful; lightweight cotton tends to crease, but is useful for such things as scarves and head-dresses.

Silk Taffeta

Admirably suited for simulating eighteenth-century silk.

Nylon, rayon, dacron, orlon, chiffon etc. are not recommended for stage wear.

Where to obtain materials

Most of the above materials are obtainable from good drapers' shops or open markets. (Always try the markets first.) Certain stores specialise in materials which they buy straight from the mills, off-cuts up to about eight yards in length which are sold at about half-price (or write directly and state your requests to the mills). Watch sales and all ex-army stores for paratroop silk, arctic underwear, etc. Search *Exchange and Mart* and the theatrical magazines continually. Advertise for old costumes too.

STOCKISTS OF MATERIALS

Fabrics and other Materials

Emil Adler, 46 Mortimer Street, London W1.
Bradley Textiles, 15 Stott Street, Nelson, Lancashire.
  (Cheap cotton, winceyette, nylon, etc.)

Brodie & Middleton, 7–9 Long Acre, London WC2.
  (Hessian, Bolton sheeting, butter muslin, calico sheeting, etc.)
B. Brown, 32 Greville Street, London WC2.
  (Felts and hessians.)
B. Burnett & Co. Ltd, 22 Garrick Street, London WC2.
  (All types of theatrical textiles, and tights.)
Clare's, Wells, Somerset.
  (Filter cloth, cheese greys and other dairy textiles.)
Empee Silk Fabrics Ltd, 39 Brick Lane, London E1.
  (Tarlatans, velveteens, cottons.)
Hamilton & Hargreaves Ltd, Walton's Buildings, 5 New Brown Street, Manchester 4.
  (Unbleached calico and twill.)
Jove Household Products, 12 Neasden Lane, London NW10.
  (Unbleached cotton sheeting.)
Leff & Jason, Soho Street, London W1.
  (Cheap theatrical fabrics.)
John Lewis, Oxford Street, London W1.
  (Fabrics.)
Limericks, Hamlet Court Road, Westcliff-on-Sea.
  (Sheeting of all kinds.)
Victor Laurence, 62–4 Hampstead Road, London NW1.
  (Government surplus clothing.)
McCulloch & Wallis, 25 Dering Street, London W1.
  (Haberdashery.)
Pontings, Kensington High Street, London W8.
  (Cheap fabrics.)
Walter Seiler Ltd, 9 Stratford Place, London W1.
  (Elastic fabrics.)
Theatreland, 51 Middlesex Street, London E1 and 14 Soho Square, London W1.
  (Tarlatans, laces, net, etc.)

Other Suppliers
Ellis & Farrier, 5 Princes Street, London W1.
  (Beads.)
Frederick Freed, 94 St Martin's Lane, London WC2.
  (Tights and leotards.)
Fishers, Albany Street, London NW1.
  (Theatrical cleaners.)

A. H. Isles, 77 Gresham Street, London EC2.
   (Bast and straw fabrics.)
Macadam, 5 Lloyds Avenue, London EC4.
   (Liquid latex.)
Taylors, Brewer Street, London W1.
   (Buttons and button covering service.)

PAINTING AND DYEING MATERIALS

The limited budgets at the disposal of most groups will inevitably reduce the amount of velvet, wool jersey and say, furnishing damask, they are likely to buy. But even the most seemingly hopeless budget can be surmounted by skill and hard work. There is a wide variety of relatively cheap materials suitable for costume making including hessian, Bolton sheeting and unbleached calico all of which can be suitably dyed, painted and trimmed with more expensive fabrics.

Dyeing

Commercial dyes are good for cottons, sheeting, and cheese cloth, but of poor intensity. The more powerful aniline dyes should be added for strength, and these are obtainable in a wide range of colours from Brodie and Middleton, 79 Long Acre, London WC2. (an ounce of each is sufficient). Dylon dyes can be obtained in 1 lb tins from Mayborn Products Ltd, 139–147 Sydenham Road, London SE26. These are mixed together to make subtle shades ($\frac{1}{2}$ teaspoonful to a dye bath). Aniline dyes can also be painted on to fabrics, particularly the heavier ones like hessian which can be made to look like tapestry, brocade, or an embroidered material by painting a rich, all-over pattern with bold but broken paint strokes on to hessian laid flat on a table. One ounce of Glauber salts to every pint of dye will prevent the pattern from rubbing off. Gold or silver metallic paint (also obtainable from Brodie and Middleton) can enrich the material when it is dragged on or sprayed. Designs can be adapted from prints of innumerable fabrics in the paintings of many painters.

Painting

Patterns can also be painted on to the material (or printed on by using a lino-cut pattern, or stencils can be cut out of cardboard or strong brown paper and then sprayed with dye or metallic paint. Cotton or Bolton sheeting can be painted with oil stencil colour (which can be dry-cleaned) or poster paint (which can be washed out and used again). All-over patterns are first marked out within a square or diagonal framework, using charcoal. An even better emulsion-based material, Printex Printing Inks, is manufactured by Windsor and Newton Ltd. These have clearer colours and are more versatile than oil-based inks.

The great advantage of making your own materials (besides the considerable saving in money) is that you can use patterns. You can rarely buy a patterned material which has a genuine period character, but by using a design derived from some textile of the period in which the play is set, and painting it into calico or sheeting, you can give exactly the right feeling.

3. *Making the Costume*

Because we are dealing with an amateur production it is not enough to present the dressmaker, whoever she may be, with a design, the materials that have been bought, the pattern, some measurements and advice. It will be necessary to watch the costumes at every stage of their manufacture, for the execution of the designs is perhaps the most arduous part of the designer's whole job. It is essential that he does his own shopping or supervises the preparation of the materials which are to be used, for this is part of the overall control which is the designer's most important function.

The designer, in fact, will need to supervise every stage of each costume's manufacture, for constant supervision and encouragement will be necessary not only in the earliest stages, but during fittings, and in the purchase or making of hats, wigs, gloves, jewellery, shoes and other costume props.

Fitting and Cutting of Period Costumes

The very unmistakable silhouette and character of a period costume can only be achieved by understanding design and by padding, corseting and particularly the correct cut.

Perhaps the cutting of period costumes is one of the most difficult problems a designer can face. For even if you are fortunate enough to acquire the services of a professional cutter she may be reluctant to follow authentic period cut, having been conditioned by contemporary convention. However, it is an important part of every designer's job to woo and win a cutter, so that there can be a real collaboration between them over the designs.

Several books contain diagrams (to scale) for the cutting of male and female costumes of every period and these should be consulted.

Costume Design and Making. Mary Fernald and Eileen Shenton (A. & C. Black)
  Good cutting diagrams of every period and contemporary illustrations of dress. Excellent.
Dress Design. Talbot Hughes (John Hogg)
  An account of costume for Artists and Dressmakers. Contains diagrams.
The Cut of Men's Clothes, 1600–1900. Norah Waugh (Faber)
The Cut of Women's Clothes, 1600–1930. Norah Waugh (Faber)
  Contains a sequence of diagrams, accurately scaled down, from patterns of actual garments, also contemporary prints etc.
The History of Costume. Carl Kohler (Dover Paperback)
  Shows cut of a wide variety of costumes of all periods.
Designing and Making Stage Costumes. Motley (Studio Vista)
  Useful, but rather sketchy illustrations explaining the cutting of some typical period costumes.
Costume and Fashion. H. Norris (Dent). Five volumes.
Costume in Detail. Nancy Bradfield (Harrap)
  Women's dress from 1730 to 1930 described through 300 full-page drawings of dresses, accessories and underwear.
Mediaeval Costume and Life. Doris Hartley (Batsford)
Patterns of Fashion. Janet Arnold (Wace)
Corsets and Crinolines. Norah Waugh (Faber)
Mediaeval Theatre Costume. Iris Brooke (Black)

As a rule cut the garment first in a cheap material such as unbleached calico and try this on the actor, leaving the cutting of the more expensive material until you are quite sure about the correct shape, style and seams. Watch that the cut is right and follow the fabric's grain. Don't skimp material. Most fitted bodices should be lined with good calico in order to keep a firm shape. Linings and material are made up together as one cloth and should be firmly fastened together before seams are stitched.

Padding and corsets are important too, for the right shape under the figure is the key to period style. It is not simply a question of using padding corsets and petticoats to indicate character, age, social position and occupation, important as this certainly is; but of using it as the indispensable framework of the costume. Most period costumes have much more sloping shoulders than we are used to and the chest is usually more rounded; a genuine period costume can look quite indifferent on the wrong-shaped body. Padding (cotton-wadding usually, or foam rubber) is stitched layer upon layer on a foundation of a well-fitting calico garment. Before this is finally covered with a soft butter muslin or similar material, the costume should be tried on over and over again, and the padding developed and adjusted, and many fittings are usually essential before the dress parade itself.

Petticoats and corsets – consult Norah Waugh's excellent *Corsets and Crinolines* (Faber) – and the right placing of seams (consult contemporary paintings and engravings) are likewise essential if authenticity is to be achieved.

Some Useful Books on Making Costumes

Wardrobe of adaptable garments. N. Lambourne (British Drama League)
Chart of adaptable garments. N. Lambourne (British Drama League)
Dressing the Play. N. Lambourne (Studio)
Making stage costumes for Amateurs. A. V. White (Routledge)
Planning the stage wardrobe. J. C. Green (Nelson)
Historic costume for the Amateur Theatre and how to make it. H. Melville (Barrie and Rockliff)
Historic Costuming. N. Truman (Pitman)
Manners and Movement in Costume Plays. Chisman and Hart (Deane)
Designing and making Stage Costumes. Motley (Studio)
Simple Stage Costumes and how to make them. S. Jackson (Studio)

Wearing the Costumes

Throughout rehearsals actors should be dressed in the equivalent of what they will wear in the performance, particularly when it is something to which they are unaccustomed (e.g. a long dress). This is where the basic wardrobe is particularly useful. There cannot, in theory, be too much rehearsal in costume, and the lack of it is behind the awkward appearance of many plays.

Costumes must be made and designed so that they do not restrict or embarrass the actors who should learn to make the most of their possibilities. Wearing costume is as much a part of acting as anything else. Irving used to wear his a considerable time before the date of performance and grew into it so that the clothes took on, as it were, not only the shape of his body, but some aspects of his character in that part. All actors should have the experience of their costumes well before the show, and should be able to wear them for long periods at a time and not merely on the stage. 'The costume has as important a function on the stage as the actor's face. . . . Costume either accentuates the transmission of the actor's emotions to the audience, or neutralises, or even destroys them. . . . Even the best actor in a costume which does not fulfil its requirements is like a statue by a good sculptor on which some passer-by has put his overcoat, leaving the head alone uncovered.' (Komisarjevsky.)

If you are attempting to make your own costumes these will probably be finished at different times, but you should have a dead-line well before the play is actually performed. If, on the other hand, your costumes have been hired they will arrive a few days before the performance, when they must be checked, hung upon racks and tried on for minor adjustments. No actor can give a good performance in a costume which feels uncomfortable.

At the technical dress-rehearsal the producer, the designer, and dress-makers should, if possible, all attend. Make notes of everything which needs altering and if there is time alter it at once. Be scrupulous over details: rings, shoes, hair, partings, buckles, belts, swords, socks, wigs and head-dresses. Look for watches, hair styles, socks. It is best if this dress parade should take place in a large changing room, or if necessary, on the stage itself. Ruth Green's *The Wearing of Costume* (Pitman) is certainly worth consulting (for fuller details of the Stage Manager's responsibilities see pages 296–320).

During the performance the actors should be in the care of a dresser. Needles, cottons, safety pins and elastic should be at hand.

(d) *Hiring*
Uncomplicated but very expensive. The money can be better spent on buying materials and paying a dressmaker, but hiring is sometimes

necessary when the director has neither a designer nor anyone to make the costumes, or in the following cases:

1. Elizabethan, Restoration and 18th century costumes. (These require considerable skills to make)
2. special costumes that are unlikely to be used in another production.
3. elaborate armour (see page 267)
4. wigs (see page 287)

A list of firms which specialise in hiring stage costumes is given below and these will provide detailed information regarding cost, period of hire etc.

Get an estimate of the cost before any definite orders are given. It is wiser to send very detailed specifications, accompanied with coloured sketches rather than a general order for the costumes of a certain play. Always hire the best costumes. Economy is disastrous.

Costumiers in London
Morris Angel & Son Ltd, 119 Shaftesbury Avenue, WC2.
M. Berman Ltd, 18 Irving Street, Leicester Square, WC2.
C. H. Fox Ltd, 25 Shelton Street, WC2.
C. & W. May Ltd, 41–3 King Street, WC2.
L. & H. Nathan Ltd, 143 Drury Lane, WC2.

Outside London
Charles Alty, 57 Aughton Street, Ormskirk, Lancs.
Arena Theatre Studios, Marston Road, Sutton Coldfield.
Avoncroft Arts Society, Bromsgrove, Worcs.
Black Lion Costumes, 25 Summerville Road, Bristol 7.
Bristol Old Vic Wardrobe Dept., Colston House, Colston Street, Bristol 1.
Canterbury Festival Costumes, Festival Manager, Marlowe Theatre, Canterbury, Kent.
Trevor Cresswell, facing Drill Hall, Bury, Lancs.
John Dibley, 1 Osborne Road, Lee-on-Solent, Hants.
'Dickie' (Richard Lancaster), 28 Crompton Road, Birmingham 20.
Eltham Little Theatre, Wythfield Road, SE9.
W. A. Homburg Ltd, 31 Call Lane, Leeds.
Lyndon Costume Hire Service, 16–20 Hamlet Court Road, Westcliff-on-Sea, Essex.

Masque Costumes, 72 Tenbury Road, Birmingham 14.
William Mutrie & Son Ltd, Proscenium House, Broughton Street, Edinburgh 1.
Louise Newell, 3 Ryehill Grove, Preston Road, Hull, Yorks.
B. & J. Price, 20 Montpelier Place, Brighton.
Royal Shakespeare Co., Stratford-upon-Avon.
Sign of Four, 20 Goldsmith Street, Nottingham.
Nellie Smith, 190 Mansfield Road, Nottingham.
Stage Furnishings Ltd, 346 Sauchiehall Street, Glasgow C2.
S. B. Watts & Co., 18–20 New Brown Street, Manchester 4.
Wilmslow Guild, 1 Bourne Street, Wilmslow, Cheshire.

Special Costumes and Accessories for hire
Morris Angel & Son Ltd, 119 Shaftesbury Avenue, WC2 (uniforms).
George Cook, 45 Longfellow Road, Coventry (fans).
A. & L. Corne Ltd, 3 Tanner Street, SE1 (headdresses).
R. Dendy & Associates, 2 Aultone Yard, Carshalton, Surrey (armour).
English & French Embroidery Co., 57 Neal Street, WC2 (embroidery).
Alan Gale, 62 Croydon Road, Beckenham (panto costume).
Kensington Carnival Co. Ltd, 123 Ifield Road, SW10.
Moss Brothers & Co. Ltd, 20 King Street, WC2 (modern costumes).
Pantomime House, Oozells Street, Birmingham 1.
M. Prager Ltd, 6 St Cuthbert's Road, NW2 (furs).
B. & J. Price, 20 Montpelier Place, Brighton (sequinned and beaded dresses).
F. Stuart, 3 Medway Court, Leigh Street, WC1 (animal skins).
Theatre Zoo, 28 New Road, St Martin's Lane, WC2 (animal costumes, masks).
Tropical Shells Co. Ltd, 16 Clapham Junction, Station Approach, SW11
    (shell jewellery and hula skirts).

Top CARNIVAL ENTERTAINMENT
Giant, masked figures in the Nice Carnival

Bottom TRANSVERSE STAGING
'Sweeney Todd' in Torrington Town Hall

Top ENTERTAINMENT WITH A DRINK
An illustration of an early Music Hall. The Grampion: 1874

Bottom MEDIAEVAL STREET THEATRE
The Mummers' Play at Marshfield, Gloucestershire.

8 Properties and Furniture

There are few rules about properties, and the best one is that hardly any are essential; most can be cut out.

Those that remain play a part of unusual importance; status, class, income, period and occupation are all expressed through properties: Polly Peachum's garter is not Lady Windermere's. The bric-à-brac of everyday existence with which we, and our ancestors, have surrounded ourselves, can be reduced to a bare minimum on the stage, so long as both actors and the audience remain convinced of its reality.

The second rule is that the props should correspond to the mood and meaning of the theme of the play. This is not simply a question of historical accuracy for genuine objects can seem out of place in a production. A crown, for example, might need to look:

Cardboardy; painted in circus colours of red and gold; cartoon-like.

Regal: an exaggerated Byzantine mood in a production emphasising epic or hieratic qualities; made of iron or pewter; archaic, very heavy.

A genuine reconstruction of a fourteenth-century crown in the Armoury; jewelled, gold.

The Madonna's crown; mystical, star-lit, elegant.

The third rule is that properties must be attractive objects in their own right. They must look as if they are really used, as if they belong. Unless the actors can obtain a sensual pleasure from the handling of their properties, they will never be able to act naturally with them. Texture is important, and so is weight.

Properties in Medieval and Elizabethan Plays

That the actors were often richly dressed in 'gorgeous and sumptious apparell' we know from many sources; and properties were treated with a similar importance. It is a mistake to believe that productions of this period were austere or visually unattractive. Henslowe's inventories (1598) list innumerable properties that were used on the Elizabethan stage –

i rock, i cage, i Hell mouth, i globe and i golden sceptre; iii clubs, Iris head, and rainbow, i little altar, iii Imperial crowns; i plain crown, i boars head, i tree of golden apples etc.

Choose props carefully and make them well, but unless they are really essential they should never be introduced. Sturdiness is essential.

Properties in Restoration and 18th Century Plays

Sets and props for such plays are very difficult. Try to base your work on contemporary sources – Hogarth's engravings, Bewick's wood engravings, Rowlandson's water colours etc. Try to borrow objects which will fit in, and avoid 'reproduction' furniture. Make rooms look as though they are lived in, and have been lived in for years.

Properties in 19th Century and Early 20th Century Plays

Again stylistic accuracy is important. Never make do with objects of a later or earlier period. Detail is very important. Properties of these periods are fairly easily obtained, but they need careful selection. Beware of silly anachronisms. Search museums, books, old copies of *Punch*, the *Illustrated London News* etc. Watch changes of fashion, class, season and so on.

Organisation

This is the Stage Manager's job; he hires, buys, borrows props and furniture, after first making a careful list of what is needed. Always try borrowing first. List Personal Props (fans, swords, etc.), On Stage Props (those to be set on stage before the action starts) and Off Stage Props (which are taken on during the action of the play). View and book props you intend to hire as soon as possible. Start making other props immediately.

Such preparations will go on in close consultation with both the Director and Designer. Problems will crop up; a piece of furniture may be too heavy to handle easily in a quick change, or a costume may encumber an actor. In such cases the Director will ultimately have to decide.

See that properties are ready for use in early rehearsals. Properties are *used*, and their use makes an extraordinary difference to the way an actor works, moves, speaks. Further information about the organisation of props in performance are given on pages 304 and 307.

A LIST OF MATERIALS FOR MAKING PROPERTIES

No list of materials would ever be complete. There are no hard and fast rules governing the making of stage properties, and human ingenuity is the largest factor involved. The following list suggests sources of materials which can be used, but a careful scrutiny of old junk shops, Woolworths, ex-army supply stores, street-markets, advertisements in theatrical magazines and *Exchange and Mart* can be very fruitful.

A Note on the Use of Samco

Samco is a modern invention that is ideally suited to the construction of properties and it is a wonderfully light, adaptable material which is as hard as iron once it is dry. It comes in several thicknesses and when saturated with a solution can be used to simulate anything. Solution and Samco (which is rather like thin felt) are obtainable from the manufacturers: Samco Strong Ltd, 12 York Way, London N1. Though rather expensive (though not so much as fibreglass) it is certainly worth it. One usually uses Samco, wringing wet, over elaborately modelled clay or plasticine moulds. (Clay sold as 'Plastelena' is excellent.) These moulds are prepared first and then covered with oil, vaseline or a parting agent (sold by the retailers). Aluminium foil is then applied over this and carefully pressed into every part of the modelled relief before the Samco itself, thoroughly saturated in the solution, is pressed over the foil and left to dry. It dries fast and comes away like a shell of hard papier-mâché but much thinner, more durable and very light. Very small properties (ear-rings for example) are not suited to the medium but it is invaluable for larger things. It takes paint and metallic sprays extremely well.

A Note on the Use of Papier-mâché

Papier-mâché is used extensively in the theatre, though less so since the development of Samco, fibreglass and other recent materials which have been introduced since the war. It is suitable for all kinds of theatrical work, including masks, breast-plates, statuary, jewellery, and small moulded properties of every kind.

The usual procedure, which closely resembles the use of Samco, is to build up a shell of papier-mâché over a modelled form of clay, plasticine, etc. This is made of several layers of paper, torn into small lengths, and glued one above the other, until a sufficient thickness has been achieved. Once dry, the paper sets hard and light. Sometimes the properties are not modelled first. The larger ones particularly are constructed upon a wire armature and strips of paper are pasted all over. The model is built up, layer by layer, from these rather crude beginnings with lengths of rope, bits of felt, and so on, incorporated as necessary.

More often a mould is prepared. This is coated with vaseline and then very carefully covered with a layer of tissue paper soaked in cellulose paste (Polycell) etc. Use a brush to poke the wet paper into the crevices of the mould. Small bits should overlap each other. When the whole surface is covered, repeat the process, stick another layer of paper of another type (e.g. newspaper) so that by using two colours you can see to make the different layers fairly even. (For tougher work use blue and grey sugar-paper instead of tissue and newsprint.) Next add a layer of small pieces of tarlatan or butter muslin, repeat the process with paper, then more paper, finishing off with another of muslin – six layers in all though more can be stuck down if a very strong mould is desired. Leave the model for two or three days until it is thoroughly dry, and then ease the papier-mâché shell away from its mould. Cut and trim the edges with scissors and stick bandages of paper or muslin over them for strengthening. The surface can be rubbed down with sandpaper and painted with shellac to act as a filler and then painted as required.

In the case of a solid object the papier-mâché shell will have to be cut open in two in order to release the mould. This can be done with scissors and the two halves are then joined with a bandage of muslin and paper.

Using Metallic Paints
Use metallic paint for painting on hard surfaces, hessian, felt, wood, metal and so on in order to simulate the appearance of metal.

Properties, scenic flats etc. once prepared, may be improved by some kind of texturing or wearing down. These paints are bought in powder form (as silver, gold and brass) and mixed with a clear hard varnish in a little tin. Shake the powder into the varnish but do not use more than you will require at one time. (Always remember to clean the brushes – turps, Polyclens or acetate – or leave them in water.)

The metal paint is painted or dragged over a surface undercoat of poster-paint a tone darker than the metal used – e.g. dark grey for silver and a dark reddish brown for gold or brass. Allow some of the undercoat to show through to give a heavy quality, and paint highlights with discretion.

Other Paints

Oil paint has, of course, innumerable uses, especially where careful colour mixing is required. It is obtainable at most artists' stockists or, for cheaper but larger quantities, at Brodie and Middleton, 79 Long Acre, London WC2 and Mayfield Bros., Sculcoates, Hull (small tins only). Thos. Parsons & Sons Ltd, The Manor House, London Road, Mitcham, Surrey, supply a flat finish, oil based paint (Unicote) and stainers.

For painting suitable textures on properties, and depending on the finish required, celosil and french enamel varnishes will give a semi-matt silky appearance.

Metalcote and Ardenbrite are very hard wearing metal paints for shields, armour etc. The address is: Metalcote of London Ltd, 28 Leicester Road, New Barnet, Hertfordshire.

Scenic Textures

Properties, scenic flats etc. once prepared may be improved by some kind of texturing or wearing-down. This can be provided in innumerable ways but the following mixtures are all useful for producing varying degrees of texture on timber, hessian, Samco, papier-mâché and so on. Metallic and other paints can be used on top, too.

1. Sand and glue*
2. Micafil, plaster and glue*
3. Sawdust and glue*
4. Sawdust, cement and glue*
5. Freshtex, sawdust and glue*

* Scotch granular glue and hot water.

Freshtex is obtainable from George Hull Ltd, 28 Horsefair, Birmingham 1.

Fibreglass
Extraordinarily adaptable and well suited for all forms of sculptural property – helmets, armour, shields etc. More expensive than the traditional paper-mâché. Obtainable from:

Bondaglass Ltd, 158–164 Ravenscroft Road, Beckenham, Kent (also supply resin etc.).
Fibreglass Ltd, 34 Dover Street, London W1.
Tiranti Bookshop, 72 Charlotte Street, London W1.

The last named can supply materials as follows:

25 yd. roll of fibreglass tissue, £1 11s. 6d.
50 lb. drum of polyester resin, £6 10s. 0d.
Liquid hardener at 3s. 6d. for 2 oz.
Liquid accelerator at 1s. 0d. an oz.

Felt and Hessian
Many properties (particularly costume properties which require a moulded shape, such as headdresses, helmets, shields, breast-plates etc.) can be made out of felt (or buckram and hessian). This can be cut, shaped and sown when soft and then soaked in a very concentrated solution of size and left to dry after careful moulding. It can then be painted or finished with Samco. The Bury Felt Manufacturing Co. Ltd, P.O. Box 14, Hudcar Mills, Bury, supply quantities. Hessian, soaked in a concentrated solution of size, can be moulded in the same way, and is invaluable.

Wood
Has very limited use because it splinters and breaks so easily – and is remarkably heavy on a large scale. It also has the maddening tendency to look like painted wood however you try to make it look like anything else. For lances, pike-staffs, poles and staves and as an armature for other properties it is ideal.

Aluminium tubing is thinner in proportion to its length than wood. Wood, of course, is obtainable through any local dealer but for large quantities of materials like Douglas Fir, Plywood, Birchwood, or Gaboon Block Board, one of the largest importers in the country is Marshall Knott and Barker, Grimsby, Lincs.

Foam Rubber

This is a useful material which can be carved up as desired, either to build up on hard surfaces for detail or into large pieces of decoration. It can be built up on a firm foundation of felt or canvas and covered with scrim, Samco etc.

Metal mesh, metal foils and veneers

Experiments are being made with all forms of metal mesh which can be used rather like felt, and metal foils and veneers. Contact the Expanded Metal Company, Burwood House, Caxton Street, London SW1 (metal mesh) and for expanded aluminium mesh – Bullanco, 66 Queens Road, London SE15. Veneers are obtainable from some local timber stockists of metal foil, or Bingham Gilbert & Son Ltd, 89 Abbey Road, London NW8.

Expanded Polystyrene (Jablite)

Obtainable from local timber merchants, is rather expensive but very useful. It can be carved either with a sharp knife (a Stanley Knife) or with a red hot knife, knitting needle or soldering iron. It can be rubbed down with sandpaper and is as light as a feather, though rather easily broken. It is best carved or modelled first, then stuck to some base as a foundation (never use quick drying glues such as Evostick with expanded polystyrene), sandpapered and then covered with scrim or butter muslin before being painted. If the shape is elaborate cut the scrim into small pieces and press well into all shapes. It is also obtainable from Shell Chemicals Co. Ltd, 15 Great Marlborough Street, London W1.

Other Essential Materials for Making Properties

Concentrated size (half pound packets) from hardware stores
Iron wire (as an armature) from hardware stores
Chicken wire, millinery wire, pipe cleaners, from hardware stores
Aluminium sheeting
Perforated zinc

Metal foil and tin foil
Fibreglass
Expanded aluminium mesh

Adhesives
Bostick*
Copydex* (for sticking materials etc. of all kinds)
Evostick
P.V.A.
Sellotape
(a staple gun is invaluable)

Paints

Metallic powders (gold, bronze, silver and copper for use with varnish)	Brodie and Middleton, 79 Long Acre, London WC2.
Clear hard varnish	Hardware stores.
Aniline dyes	Brodie and Middleton.
Cellulose lacquer, automobile cellulose celosil, french enamel varnish.	A Leete & Co. Ltd, 129 London Road, London SE1
Metalcote, Ardenbrite, metal paints (and all normal scenic paints)	
Celosil and other paints	W. H. Palmer, 'Chief Works', 44–46 Garman Road, Tottenham, London N17
Timonox (fireproof)	Tirantis,
Graphite (black powder)	Charlotte Street, London W1
Paint sprays, especially dark tones of grey, khaki and brown	Woolworths

and, of course, scenic powder paints (see page 231).

Papers

Coloured Cellophane	E. J. Arnold, Butterley Street, Leeds 10
Tissue, gold, silver and all fancy papers, also cardboard	F. G. Kettle, 23 New Oxford Street, London WC1
Corrugated card	Russell & Chapple, 23 Monmouth Street, Shaftesbury Ave., London WC2 (in rolls)
Cardboard of different thicknesses	most printers' or artists' suppliers

* really essential

Cord and Rope

Mewis Cordage, St Paul's Square, Birmingham 3, for bulk quantities.
Paper ropes and braids ($\frac{3}{8}''$, $\frac{1}{2}''$, $1''$) of varying thicknesses are supplied by
Somic Ltd, P.O. Box No. 8, Alliance Works, Preston. They are called
Somrib 'D' Section Formers, are very cheap and though strong are
invaluable in property making.

Miscellaneous
metal snipping shears
metallic cloth
braids of all kinds
buttons
corks
curtain-rings
beads
sequins
simulated pearls
bottle tops etc.
electric flex (plastic covered as a braid)
feathers
plasticine
modelling clay
plaster of paris (dental plaster only)
Vandyke crystals
fine and course scrim
tailor's canvas

   B. Burnet & Co. Ltd, 22 Garrick Street, London W C 2, supply hessian
and all theatrical fabrics, braids, artificial glass jewels etc.

Hiring Properties and Furniture
So far we have dealt with the problems of making properties, furniture
and scenery, but there may be occasions where you would rather hire
because there are properties or furniture you cannot borrow or make. The
firms which specialise in prop making are as follows:

Cape of Chiswick (large props)
85 Crouch Hill, London N 8

Elizabeth Hethrington Ltd,
20 Colebrooke Row, London N 1
(props, making and finding)

Enterprise Metal Company,
87a Newington Causeway,
London SE1

Star Scenic Studios,
78 Elms Road,
London SW4

Stage Decor Ltd,
Browning Hall, Browning Street,
London SE17

Drama Props,
54 Aldermans Hill, London N13

Stage Properties Ltd,
12 Orange Street, London WC2

B. M. Ventures Ltd
(glass fibre props),
10 Netherwood Road, London W14

Robinson's
76 Neal Street,
London WC2

Furniture can also be hired (see list below) but the cost of transport from warehouse to theatre and back must be added to the hire cost. Ask for a quotation when you state your requirements, and look for advertisements in *The Stage*, *Drama* and *Amateur Stage*.

Theatre Directory published by Stacey Publications, 1 Hawthornedene Road, Hayes, Bromley, Kent, price 3s. od., also contains a most useful list of names and addresses of theatrical suppliers and organisations and should certainly be consulted. Spotlight *Contacts* published, price 3s. od., twice yearly by The Spotlight Ltd, 43 Cranbourn Street, London WC2, also contains a very full list.

Hiring furniture in or near London is comparatively easy but further afield this becomes a real problem. Consult your nearest Theatre for advice.

When furniture is chosen, the stage designer should take with him not only a length of measuring tape but an accurate ground plan of the sets where the furniture is going to be used. Even the finest furniture must not be allowed to clutter your acting area.

Stuffed animals, animal skins and masks etc.

Edward Gerrard & Sons, 85 Royal College Street, London NW1
  (stuffed animals, birds, reptiles)
Theatre Zoo, 28 New Row, St Martin's Lane, London WC2
  (masks)
Walls Carnival Stores, 161 Caversham Road, Reading
  (masks and animal costumes)

Furniture for hire

Old Times Furnishing Company, 135 Lower Richmond Road, London SW15
(furniture for hire)
Gimberts Ltd, Victoria Mill, Manchester Road, Droylsden, Nr. Manchester
(modern and period furniture for hire)
Bristol Old Vic., Theatre Royal, King Street, Bristol 1
(furniture for hire)

Other specialised hire firms are as follows:

Artificial Flowers, Fruit and Food

Floral Decor Ltd, 53a Brewer Street, London W1
A. J. Miller, 56 Half Moon Lane, London SE24 (plastic flowers)
Pytam Ltd, Central Avenue, West Moseley, Surrey (fruit, food etc.)
R. Windram Ltd, 12 Cecil Court, Charing Cross Road, London WC2

Armour and Swords

Bapty & Company, 9 Macklin Street, London WC2 (weapons, armour etc.)
The Stage Armoury, Hounds Road, Chipping Sodbury, Bristol (armour)
Robert White & Sons, 57–59 Neal Street, London WC2 (armour and jewellery)
Tudor Armoury, Tudor Lodge, Annesley, Woodhouse, Notts. (weapons, etc.)

Unusual Metal Props

Enterprise Metal Company, 87a Newington Causeway, London SE21

Ornaments, Painting and Sculpture

Charles de Temple Designs Ltd, Studio Three, 98 Jermyn Street, London
SW1

Statue-maker

Len Fowler Ltd, 78a Neal Street, London WC2

Antique Musical Instruments

J. Morley, 4 Belmont Hill, London SE13

New Directions

List of Recommended Books
You cannot really learn to make properties from reading books but the
following are valuable:

General Bibliography

Stage Properties and How to Make Them. Warren Kenton (Pitman)
  An indispensable handbook and as invaluable to the property-master as
  Frank Napier's *Noises Off* is to the sound-technician. Demonstrates how to
  make innumerable properties.
Small Stage Properties and Furniture. K. N. Cookson (Allen & Unwin)
Costumes and Fashion. H. Norris (Dent)
  For jewellery, wigs, accessories.
  Vol. 1. Evolution of European Dress through the Earlier Centuries.
  Vol. 2. Senlac to Bosworth (1066–1485).
  Vol. 3. Tudor Period (1485–1603).
  Vol. 4. The Nineteenth Century.

Armour, Hats, Crowns

Making Stage Costumes for Amateurs. A. V. White (Routledge)

Jewellery

Designing and Making Stage Costumes. Motley (Studio Vista)
Dressing the Play. N. Lambourne (Studio Vista)
  Both contain good chapters on jewellery, crowns etc.

Weapons

Weapons in the Theatre. Arthur Wise (Longmans)

Furniture

English Furniture Styles 1500–1830. R. Fastnedge (Penguin)
A Picture History of Furniture. Frank Davis (Hulton)
An Illustrated History of Interior Decoration. M. Praz (Thames & Hudson)

9 Music and Sound

Sound – which includes the use of song and instrumental music, sound-effects, and the spoken word itself – is one of the most important aspects of any production. In some work, such as documentaries and improvisations, the music has great immediacy and emotional impact. Even in a naturalistic production the sensitive use of sound can have a powerful effect: so also in films, puppet-shows, mixed-media presentations etc. Making a sound-ballad (see pages 92–101) as well as listening to radio-productions of all kinds can help towards this increased awareness of the use of sound textures in the theatre.

Although the LP and the tape-recorder have revolutionised our attitude to sound, in the theatre their place, though valuable, is only a substitute for 'real' music or live sound-effects which offer vastly greater possibilities. Seek out people who play the piano, the guitar, the drums, or accordion and who are accustomed to improvising their own music. In the first production of *The Royal Pardon* a polygonal cage of dowels (see plate 4) at the side of the stage, and in full view of the audience, provided a light scaffolding on which to hang a richly varied collection of musical instruments. These included various drums, cymbals and bells, xylophones, whistles, home-made pottery cups (each tuned to a different pitch) a banjo, guitar etc. which were in reach of the two musicians (Boris and Russell Haworth) who sat inside the cage throughout the performance, improvising a kind of musical counterpoint to the action of the drama. This had been developed during rehearsals, for it is a good idea that invited musicians should work with a group right from the start. Live music, whether sung or played, in or out of sight of the audience, strikes a listener often more forcibly than recorded music, and its textures can be woven into the play's action and words.

The sound in each production has to be considered afresh; the simplest sound-effect, such as a closing door, has to be carefully studied. For the way it is closed, the weight of the door, the acoustics of the room, and the door's distance from the actors all affect the sound, just as much as the kind of production in which the effect is heard. A door the Porter opens in *Macbeth* might need to sound different from one in Chekhov: it is no good leaving a list of sounds with a tape-recording 'expert' and then hoping for the best.

In a naturalistic production very close attention to detail is required. Train noises or street noises, for example, are not all alike. We can distinguish steam trains, diesels, trains moving up hills or down gradients. Similarly we can compare street noises in the Thirties with those of today: these would sound different in a basement to the open windows of a house in Audley Street, in rain to fine weather, on a Saturday afternoon to a Sunday morning. Careful listening is important: the sound-detail can suggest time and place and period and status more vividly than anything else.

Obviously there are limits. We would not expect to have to get a Russian recording of a 19th century steam train for *The Cherry Orchard*, but we should aim at being as true as we can in a naturalistic production, where the train in the night can suggest the infinite spaces beyond the house and its orchard.

In a symbolic or ritualistic production (of a Shakespearean play, for instance) sound effects can be treated differently. There are no rules here. The sounds become extensions of the images in the work. The thunder in *Lear*, for example, is no ordinary storm, but must suggest the chaos of both the human and the natural worlds. The knocking at the gate may have an equally ominous sound in *Macbeth*. In *The Merchant of Venice* the sounds and music which accompany the ceremony of choosing the caskets can reflect their various qualities, gold, silver, lead. Just as the music of the words seem to suggest to Bassanio the right choice, so can the music we use.

In short, 'sound' in a production means much more than we usually imagine. We must listen not just to the words in isolation, nor to the effects in isolation, but to the completed pattern of everything in our productions from the music at the opening to the moment when everything dies into silence at the end.

MUSIC IN THE THEATRE

(a) *Recorded Music*

It is difficult to lay down rules about the use of taped music in a production though excessive use of recorded music is always to be avoided. In improvisations or spontaneous work, the use of recorded music can act as a spur to invention; the music providing the germ of the idea on which an improvisation is based. But in general nineteenth-century orchestral music (such as a Brahms Symphony) is less suitable than 'programme music' (which already has a literary basis), electronic music, or the work of contemporary composers. Folk-songs, brass bands, street-cries etc. can also be used. In a set production recorded music can indeed provide atmosphere and charm; but always try to make your own.

Recordings of Music. Apart from the well-known manufacturers, such as Decca, HMV etc., Messrs. Felix de Woolf of 80–82 Wardour Street, London W1 have a large selection of recorded music for the theatre. Guy Woolfenden's music for a number of productions by the Royal Shakespeare Company is now available on record from Abbey Records, All Saints Passage, Cambridge.

(b) *Live Music*

Drums, recorders, flutes, bells, trumpets, strings, cymbals and other percussion can be used, as well as songs, chanted speech and vocal noises (such as the chorus Brek-kek-kek-kek-coax-coax in Aristophanes' *The Frogs*) to tremendous effect.

In Documentaries where the Ballad-type songs need an instrumental accompaniment; in mixed-media shows where music intermingles with mime, readings, back-projections and fictional dialogue; as well as in straight plays and improvisations where the musical element can play an important part, the music should be as much a part of the live performance as the actor's contribution, and should be played and sung, wherever possible, by the actors themselves.

In mime, for example, two instrumentalists – a flautist and a pianist – can not only enhance the mood but, in a dialogue without words between the actor and musicians, contribute to the drama itself. Even a singer accompanied by a guitar can create an atmosphere, while a much larger group makes as brilliant an effect as was the case in Peter Brook's production of the *Marat/Sade*, where marvellous songs were accompanied by musicians in the theatre boxes.

Period plays frequently need music and though there is no need to be historically accurate, the music should always be chosen in concord with the play. Fanfares and martial music should be produced live though useful records do exist (e.g. HMV 7FX21), besides the work of innumerable composers.

DIFFERENT TYPES OF SOUND EFFECT
There are two distinct but closely related uses of stage sounds:

1. *Essential Sounds*
E.g. the firing of a gun, banging doors, the ringings of bells etc. These can either be made by the actors on the stage, or produced by amplifying sounds from recordings on discs and tapes. Such sounds are the essential ones marked or recorded in the plot.

2. *Atmospheric Sounds*
These are not necessarily marked in a script, but may seem useful if not essential. For example, you might want to suggest mood or heighten tension by the use of music, drum rhythms etc. Care and restraint are necessary; it is easy to overdo the use of atmospheric sounds.

General Principles
Think out what sounds you need in your production. Think out their relative importance. Knowing exactly what you want, try to produce it by any method possible; record, tape, live instruments etc. Spend as much time over the production of the sound as over choosing it, i.e. see that it is very well amplified, very well played. Experiment carefully to dovetail sounds and action. Let your actors work with needed sounds, and be ready to change balance, volume etc. Be careful how you mix real sounds with taped sounds and those produced by effects. Whatever effects you choose let them be right for your production; they should fit with the total idea you have.

HOW SOUNDS ARE PRODUCED
Stage sound effects are made in three different ways, by purchasing records, by hand-produced methods or by taping the sounds (see page 274).

1. *By Purchasing Records (or tape)*

This is the most reliable method but should only be used for special effects. All kinds of sound are available on record. A list of addresses where these records can be obtained is given below. In every case write for particulars and prices from the firms concerned.

Effects Records

HMV Effects records: 7" 45 rpm. (standard records). These records may be re-recorded for private purposes, and may be used without licence fee for public performances by private individual and by amateur dramatic societies. The series, which is far too long to list here includes car effects (door slam and depart, reverse, approach and stop, door slam, crash etc.), church bells, dogs, horses, sea effects, thunderstorm, rains, wind, birds, street noises, aeroplanes, demolition, glass crashes and hammering, space-ships, ghosts etc. Other effects can be obtained on record or tape from:

Bishop Sound and Electrical Co. Ltd, 48 Monmouth Street, London WC2
  (Sound effects records for sale).
E.M.I. Studios (Special Recordings Dept.), 20 Manchester Square, London W1
  (Sound effects records for sale).
Stage Sound Ltd, 11 King Street, Covent Garden, London WC2
  (Sound effects records for sale, also sound equipment for hire).
K.L.P. Film Services Ltd, 3 Queen's Crescent, Richmond, Surrey
  (Sound effects on tape).
Theatre Projects Ltd, 10 Long Acre, London WC2
  (Sound effects).
Micro Sound, 70 Nursery Road, Cheadle Hulme, Cheshire

A complete list of sound recording services is given in *Spotlight Contacts*, published by The Spotlight Ltd, 43 Cranbourn Street, London WC2, price 3s.

For the amateur who feels that recording and editing is beyond his powers, the recorded effects of most West End productions can be obtained on disc or tape from:

Stage Sound, 11–12 King Street, Covent Garden, London WC2.

2. *By hand-produced methods*

In a book of this scope it is not possible to give instructions for making more than a few fundamental stage sounds. Those needing more detailed instructions should consult the following books:

Noises Off. A handbook of Sound Effects. Frank Napier (Garnet Miller)
Stage Effects. A. Rose (Routledge)

L. W. Hunt Drum Co., 10–11 Archer Street, London W1 sell and hire effects machines.

Wind. (a) An electric motor which has lengths of drain-cane fixed to radiate from its fly wheel. This is housed in a box having one side open (save for a screen of wire netting). The machine is controlled by a dimmer.
(b) A wooden drum composed of two circles of wood connected by laths is mounted to rotate on a wooden stand, a strip of sailcloth is stretched over it.

Rain. A closed box (6′ × 6″) has nails thickly driven into the bottom of the box. A shovelful of dried peas is put inside and the effect is produced by letting them rattle in and out of the nails. Two boxes are better than one.

Thunder. On record, or better still by using a thunder sheet. (A fairly heavy gauge sheet of sheet iron (6′ × 3′) suspended and shaken by a handle riveted to its bottom edge. A bass-drum, slackened off to kill its musical quality, can be used in conjunction with the sheet.)

Sea. (a) On record. (b) Gong – drum and peas (two pints or more). The drum is tilted, one side resting on the floor, the other on some object a foot high. The peas are worked by hand, pushing them round the side of the drum to make the sound of a wave coming shorewards, and releasing them at the top, so that running down across the skin they sound like it breaking. Experiment.

3. *By Taping*

The use of pre-recorded effects (with all cues in sequence) is probably the most important method of making sound.

Sound effects and music (if recorded) should be in the charge of a reliable person. He should attend rehearsals at the beginning so that the actors may get accustomed to being interrupted by sounds and the volume of sound can be exactly controlled (see page 308).

MUSIC AND ITS COPYRIGHT

All music used in a play, either 'live' or recorded (including interval music) must be covered by a licence from the Performing Right Society, and, if need be, the Phonographic Performance Ltd. (see page 327).

Gramophone Records

Apply to the Phonographic Performance Ltd, Evelyn House, 62 Oxford Street, London W 1 for particulars of licence. Give full details of the nature of your society, number of productions etc.

Played Music

The Performing Right Society Ltd, 29–33 Berners Street, London W 1 is the national organisation for the collection of royalties on copyright music. It states that, as far as the copyright law is concerned, a performance is public unless within the home-life of the audience. Royalties are, therefore, payable to this society when any music is performed either 'live' or on a gramophone record. Some halls and educational premises may have a general licence. Certain exceptions are granted.

10 Masks and Make-up

The use of make-up is the culmination of a process that begins when a child of four puts on a hat and pretends to be a grown woman. The child, for the moment, *is* the grown woman and the hat is useful not only because it helps her imaginings, but because it helps us to believe that she is no longer a child but her own mother.

The idea, the emotion and the imaginative projection of what one is doing comes first *and* last. Make-up, or the simplest bits and pieces of suggestive costume which are part of the make-up, are solely and simply 'the process of assisting subtly and surely the expression from within'.

The words are Ellen Terry's who is commenting upon Henry Irving. They are worth quoting in full. 'Make-up was, indeed, always his servant, not his master. He knew its uselessness from his Dubosc because of the way he held his shoulders, because of his expression. . . . He used to come on the stage looking precisely like the Van Dyck portraits (of Charles I) but not because he had been building up his face with wig paste and similar atrocities. His make-up in this, as in other parts, was the process of assisting subtly and surely the expression from within'.

A performance, then, is built up from within. This complex process begins at the first rehearsal and goes through innumerable developments as rehearsals progress, until it is made manifest in an appearance that has been fully and imaginatively conceived not only in terms of the actual character portrayed, but in terms of the context of the production. For the style of one production may be quite different from the style of another and appropriateness of appearance differs in each case.

Make-up, costume, accessories, posture, shape, voice, movement, gesture are indivisible; they communicate the external appearance of an internal reality. To apply make-up as a mask at the dress-rehearsal, or worse still to rely on another person applying it, is a complete denial of everything we mean by acting. It shows an abuse of its function.

Some people, Joan Littlewood for example, consider make-up has been abused as it is. She writes:

'I never let anyone use make-up on the stage – at least not unless it's stylised. You use three-dimensional lighting instead. Make up's for gas lighting. If you want to look like a pretty girl you use everyday make-up but the men are never allowed to use anything'.

Such an attitude is refreshingly valid for it is not only a fact that some of the greatest actors and actresses of the past, Eleonora Duse, for instance, eschewed its aid altogether, but that the development of make-up on the stage was the direct result of the building of larger theatres and the introduction of gas lighting.

There is no positive evidence that the boy-actors who used to play girl parts on the Elizabethan stage used make-up at all, while ghosts and murderers simply made up their faces with chalk, and Moors used blacking. It was only in the nineteenth century that it became a common practice on the stage.

In our day with the tendency for smaller theatres and for seating the audience as close as possible to the stage, when plays, anyway, are so varied, our whole attitude to make-up needs re-thinking.

Where naturalism is required an exact, subtle and loving care for detail is essential and no pains should be spared to secure exact effects which are in keeping with the whole style of the production. But once we move away from naturalism in the theatre how should make-up be approached? How should the make-up be designed for the following plays:

The Medea	Euripides
A Midsummer Night's Dream	Shakespeare
Peer Gynt	Ibsen
The Insect Play	Capek
The Caucasian Chalk Circle	Brecht
Play	Beckett

No final answer can be given without reference to the costume, the setting, the theatre and the whole style of the production, but one thing is certain: that naturalistic make-up is out of place. In such plays make-up is an extension of the costume; it may be a mask.

Some Notes on Naturalistic Make-up

Some books suggest that there are two kinds of make-up; straight and character. The truth is that there is no such thing as a straight make-up since all parts, however subtly developed, are in character. We very rarely play ourselves in a play unless it has been written for us or is an improvisation, in which case make-up probably isn't being used.

Make-up is the art of knowing how to use your own face to the best advantage. Experience is really absolutely essential. Try to watch actors at work, practice on yourself continually, mixing colours, trying new methods, and practising on others. There are many good books on the subject (see below) but experience is more important still. *Observation* and ceaseless experiment are essential. Study photographs and the living faces that you meet. No one would try to paint a portrait a few hours before the painting was due for exhibition, yet many are prepared to do their make-up just before the performance. It is time to think of study in those fallow months when there is no production. Clubs should establish small groups who specialise entirely in make-up, and can engage make-up experts to teach the actors how to apply it for themselves (see below).

NOTES ON HOW TO MAKE-UP

(a) *What to buy*. Every actor should purchase his own materials and do his own make-up. A basic set (obtainable from most chemists or from the stockists listed on page 287) would include most of the following though this is largely a personal choice. Buy the minimum.

Removing cream used for cleansing the skin and removing grease-paint after the performance.

Grease-paints, Standard Sticks. Sticks are used for covering large areas and only a few are really required, but skill in mixing is all important. Sticks Nos. $2\frac{1}{2}$, 3, $3\frac{1}{2}$, $4\frac{1}{2}$, 5, 6 and 16 are ideal for ordinary purposes but sticks Nos. $1\frac{1}{2}$, 8, 8b, 9, 20 and peach dark and green 2 No. 335 are valuable. Leichner stage make-up can be recommended. Also Max Factor products, e.g. Pancake, Panstick for basic make-up.

Liners. These are thin pencils of grease paint used for finer work. In the darker colours they are used for shadows and for making up the eyes. Lake No. 25, Brown No. 28, Dark Grey No. 32, Black No. 42, Dark Blue No. 326 and Carmine No. 322 are fairly basic.

Blending Powder. This is dusted over the finished make-up to set it, and, being transparent, does not essentially alter make-up colours. Used with a lambswool powder puff or large piece of cotton-wool and a neutral tin of blending powder.

Crêpe Hair. A medium brown, medium grey, white and black are basic colours but hair would normally be bought to match an existing colour. It is applied with spirit gum and a brush and removed with surgical spirit.

Hair Powders. White, black, grey, brown, blond and red powders can be dusted into the hair for minor changes.

Nose Putty. Nose putty comes in sticks and is moulded directly on to the face. Like everything else use economically.

Sundries. A good supply of cotton-wool, a sponge, some soap, hot water and towels, a large cloth to drape over the shoulders and a well-lit mirror are essential. A make-up brush for fine details (e.g. wrinkles) is important too.

(b) *Procedure*. It is impossible to give more than the briefest description but many books (see below) can be consulted.

1. Always standardise as far as possible the conditions in which you make-up. In a normal dressing room you usually have a table or shelf attached to the wall with a mirror behind. This should always be lit with lights around or above it. When making up away from a theatre, try to simulate similar conditions, e.g. use a wash-basin with a board placed over it, and having a mirror behind with a light above. Distance from the mirror and lighting can strongly affect the finished make-up.

2. The make-up is applied before the player completes dressing. Make sure you don't have to take any clothes off afterwards over the head because this can easily remove some of the make-up. Wear an old dressing-gown and spread a towel over your knees to catch loose powder.

3. The face should be washed and dried. A very thin coat of removing cream is stretched over the face. Then wipe off any greasy patch, and smooth over again with the fingers. The skin should not be oily. (Use astringent lotion if the skin tends to be greasy.)

4. *The foundation or basic face colour* is applied.

   There are several worthwhile methods, e.g. Max Factor Satin Smooth Panchromatic (useful because it is a standard colour, easily blended with other shades); Leichner Spotlite Klear: Max Factor Pancake (quickest and easiest), and Panstick. For these see *Practical Stage Make-up* by Phillipe Perrottet, pages 13–16.

The classical method and probably the most flexible is with Leichner greasepaint. For this either dot or streak the face with the required colours or mix them on the palm or back of one hand where they will soften. Then work them into the face with the fingertips of the other hand. The paint must be smoothly blended and not streaky. The base colour will usually be a blend of several colours (see the Leichner chart). For 'straight' make-up some of these will be needed:

Male – 3½, 5, 9 and 16.

Female – 2, 2½ or peach dark foundation.

The ears need only light brushing over with the fingers but the neck should be covered to about halfway down (depending obviously on the costume being worn) where it fades away into the natural colour. Often just use powder on the hands – make-up on them easily spoils clothes. Avoid also rubbing make-up into the roots of the hair.

5. *Highlights and Shadow.* The golden rule for the application of make-up is an understanding of highlight and shadow. Careful observation of bone structure under strong light will show where the natural highlights and shadows occur. Make-up should be built up round these, the features highlighted to bring out the desired contours of the face. A light colour applied to the face will make that part more prominent, while a darker or shadow colour will make that part recede or appear sunken. Cheekbones can be made more prominent by applying a lighter shade (No. 5 normally) than the base to those parts, while a darker one (a touch of No. 16, blended with lake) is applied to the hollows below the cheeks to make them appear sunken or thin. These tones must be carefully and subtly blended into one another. Wherever there is a shadow there must be a highlight as well, and in age these become more pronounced.

6. *Eyes.* The lids should first be shadowed with a tone slightly darker than the base coat, fading up to meet the eyebrows. Unshaded lids can look unnatural with overhead lighting, but there is also a tendency when applying colour to the lids to deepen the eye socket unnecessarily. This needs care. To make the eye appear older or sunken, Lake may be applied below and above, blending into a highlight. Wrinkles

may be applied with a highlight line between each one. Take care with the drawing in of the eye, because a continuous line tends to harden rather than emphasise, and this may produce an effect you do not want.

7. *Mouth.* For men Leichner No. 8 and for women No. 9 greasepaint produce a natural-looking mouth, i.e. one without lipstick. Take care to make-up only the actual area of the lips, keeping the colour edge firm, unless it is your intention to change a mouth shape. Use just one or two light dabs of carmine 3 on the upper lip and of carmine 2 on the lower lip and then spread carefully. Remember that a mouth which is lighter than the colour of the skin makes a character look ill.

8. *Nose.* Usually a nose needs no extra emphasis for a straight make-up on a well-lit stage. Noses can be shaped by shading along the side and highlighting the centre, but far too often tramlines are painted down either side which only spoil the shape and add nothing.

9. *Wrinkles.* These are often badly painted because badly observed. Wrinkles are not mere lines but actual indentations in the face, so that lines of No. 5 greasepaint will not do. Wrinkles need preparing carefully. Wherever possible follow the natural line of wrinkles of your own face. Shade an area about ¼″ wide with lake and work this in with the fingertip. Then draw along the centre of this 'fold area' a narrow line (No. 16 plus lake); fade this in but not quite so much. Use a square-tipped make-up brush or cherry stick. Powder and apply a smaller area of highlight of No. 5 close to the wrinkle but without touching it. By using a wrinkle you can at times effectively disguise a wig join.

9. *Finishing off.* Make-up needs powder to set it and to give a matt finish to an otherwise greasy appearance. Dust liberally with powder, and then use cotton-wool to remove the excess.

10. *To remove greasepaint.* Grease the face all over with face cream after removing the wig (from the back forwards) and costume. Plenty of cream should be used and it should be applied evenly over face and neck. Then wipe it off with an old cloth or cotton-wool (slightly damped) which can then be thrown away. Finally wash in plenty of warm, soapy water, finishing with cold.

11. *The problem of hair and wigs.* Hair is vitally important, and plays a

much greater part than make-up. If the play is a period piece wigs are almost essential, and though these can be rented from costumiers (see page 287) they are expensive. Producers are strongly urged to consider the possibility of acting the entire play without them. Wigs are a convention, and once you start to use them on a few characters it will be necessary to be consistent and to use them for the entire cast. This can prove very expensive indeed. When ordering wigs it is important to send exact head measurements and carefully detailed requirements of colour and style.

Beards and moustaches, mounted on gauze, can be hired (from costumiers) and can be stuck on to the face with spirit gum (gum will not stick to make-up and must be applied first). Alternatively with great care, beards can be made out of crêpe hair, combed and pressed under a damp cloth, and stuck on, in small sections, with spirit gum. A full beard requires about six pieces, which overlap each other. Crêpe hair beards etc. should be prepared in advance, and stitched on to a sheet of paper ready for use. Crêpe hair is removed by applying rubbing alcohol. Beards should only be attempted with great care. They become unnatural and rather melodramatic. The best ones, after all, are real. Wigs and hair pieces are now available in nylon as well as crêpe hair.

GENERAL RULES CONCERNING THE APPLICATION OF MAKE-UP

1. Be careful not to over-exaggerate unless special effects are required. It is better to err on the side of being under-made-up.
2. Economy of application is essential. Do not use too much make-up. It is the depth of colour and the amount of light and shade applied, not the amount of make-up put on, that is important.
3. The size and lighting conditions of the theatre determine how much make-up ought to be used. Use less in a small hall, more in a large. Remember that in most amateur theatres the lighting is far less intense than on the professional stage and that there should consequently be a corresponding reduction in the amount of make-up. Always try and carry out your make-up practice under conditions as similar to the stage illumination as possible; this means that it should be done under a fairly strong light. It should be seen by the producer

on the stage so that he can make suggestions if he wants to. If it is not possible to do make-up under such lighting conditions then at least have it checked under the stage lighting before the final powdering.

4. Leave ample time before the performance to complete make-up; *at least* a full hour may be needed.

5. Just as every painter uses paint individually (compare Van Dyck and Matisse) so, in spite of the how-to-do-it books, every user of grease paint must teach himself, and no two people will use it in the same way. Some, for example, do all the lines before powdering, (when they may be blurred) others do them after powdering. (when they are usually clearer and can be over-powdered if too emphatic). The method is all a question of personal taste.

6. Meticulous attention to detail is essential. The whole body (back of the neck, ears, hands, wrists) has to be made up consistently. No detail of appearance is too small for attention.

Stylised Make-up

So far we have only dealt with the use of make-up in a naturalistic or relatively naturalistic production, but its use in the presentation of a more stylised drama is even more important. Make-up is the only way – or the most convenient way – of stylising the human face or body.

Occasionally the playwright himself will suggest the use of a strongly stylised form of make-up, and it is instructive in such cases to see how closely he conceives of the make-up in relation to the style of the play. Samuel Beckett describes the face of his old man in *Krapp's Last Tape*: 'White face. Purple Nose.' The obvious clown-like effect that is being sought here tells us a lot about the antecedents of this character, and the style of acting that Beckett envisages. One of the first things Krapp does is to slip on a banana skin.

General advice is impossible to give because every production will present new problems and need a fresh approach, when make-up is an extension of the function of costume.

Masks

Masks have been used all over the world from time immemorial as part of religious dramatic ceremonies and ritual. The growth of naturalism in the theatre led to their decline, and their recent revival has coincided with the growth of the new theatre. John Arden, Alun Owen, Benjamin Britten have all used them in order to achieve more formalised effects.

For amateurs, the use of masks can have exciting possibilities, especially in improvised work. The self-consciousness which plagues so many amateur efforts can miraculously disappear when the actor puts on even the crudest of masks. The influential French director Jacques Copeau explains what happens:

'The actor who performs under a mask, receives from this papier-mâché object the reality of his part. He is controlled by it and has to obey it unreservedly. Hardly has he put it on when he feels a new being flowing into himself, a being the existence of which he had before never even suspected. It is not only his face that has changed, it is all his personality, it is the very nature of his reactions, so that he experiences emotions he could neither have felt nor feigned without its aid. If he is a dancer, the whole style of his dance, if he is an actor, the very tones of his voice, will be dictated by this mask – the Latin 'persona' – a being, without life till he adopts it, which comes from without to seize upon him and proceeds to substitute itself for him.'

Masks used in early religious drama, Greek and Roman tragedy and comedy, tended to be full face. But the Italian Commedia dell'Arte tradition developed the half-face mask, which had the advantage of not muffling the voice, and of relating the head more naturally to the rest of the body.

The Commedia dell'Arte exploited masks for dynamic effects. Clearly, the modern actor would be foolish not to experience at some time or other their liberating effect.

Some Simple Masks

1. *Using bags and card.* Mask-making, particularly for children, should never become an activity in its own right (even though, perhaps, it is one) but a means to an end. Simple masks can be made with large paper bags, inverted carrier-bags, cones of cardboard, or by cutting out a rectangle of thin card and tying it to the head above the ears with string or tape. Such masks are superbly effective and should be used as beginnings – as a kind of introductory play for all kinds of mime, improvisation and work with masks, before more elaborate masks are

made. Simple masks, for their very lack of precision, help ideas to grow. There are also half and full masks which are usually about the same size as the head they cover, and then really giant full masks.

2. *Using chicken-wire mesh as a frame.* Choose some small wire-mesh and cut and fold this into place. Overlap the joins and tie with wire, or simply crush the bits together, until the head is modelled, with the wire pressed into shape. Cover with tissue or newspaper-strips, using cellulose paste (e.g. Polycell). Use handkerchief tissues or pieces of foam rubber if you want to build up details on the features. Naturally the inside of the head may need a couple of layers of paper if this is not going to scratch. The mask can be painted when dry and can be elaborated with strips of cloth, raffia, tin-foil, cord, corks and so on.

3. *Using thin card, wire or cane.* Using strips (say 1″ × 6″) of thin card (from a cornflake packet) pin these together to form the armature of the mask. Ordinary wire paper-clips are satisfactory and the strips should be pinned on the head of the person who is actually going to wear the mask. The first strip should be placed round the head, across the forehead and above the ears, to form a band right round the head. The second strip, pinned to the first above the ears, should go across the crown of the head. The third strip should be attached to the first above the nose and so across the crown of the head to the centre of the back. Over this skeleton drape a piece of butter muslin and secure with more clips. Tear brown gummed strips into small irregular pieces and start to cover the muslin. (Dip the strip in a saucer of water to avoid licking.) Shape the mask as you continue building up layer by layer of gummed paper, but scribble over each layer in turn so that you will be able to tell when you have completed a covering. Make the nose or any raised portion with screwed up, wet paper handkerchiefs. Ideally each layer (and about five or so are usually necessary) should be left to dry before adding another. Helmets and other headgear, crowns, portions of armour can be made in this way, as well as masks.

4. *Masks built upon a mould, papier-mâché or Samco.* First make the mould. This should be modelled with clay or plasticine, either solid, or over a brick or plaster base. Modelling should be generous and slightly exaggerated. Coat this mould with vaseline and then apply a piece of

butter muslin, large enough to cover the whole mould. Apply five or six layers of torn paper, using cellulose paste. These should be allowed to dry, before a further layer is added. The mask should come away from its mould quite easily. Cut eyes and mouth in the mask with scissors and paint (full details of this method are given on page 260, alternatively Samco can be used instead of papier-mâché, see page 259), and is particularly suited for the half mask. Samco is ideal for mask making as it is light and very strong.

5. *Masks built up with cardboard.* Use thin sheets of corrugated cardboard (obtainable from Quarmby's, Britannia Rd., Milnsbridge, Huddersfield, and elsewhere). This, though reasonably firm, can be cut, bent, pinned and generally moulded into shape and is particularly suitable for large animal masks. Brass paper fasteners are needed. The mask can be painted as it is or covered with cloth, imitation fur etc. This method is particularly suited for making large animal masks.

RECOMMENDED STOCKISTS, SERVICES AND BOOKS

Max Factor, 16 Old Bond Street, London W1 will give demonstrations for individuals or groups by appointment. They also provide a full postal advisory service including charts.

Leichner, 44 Cranbourn Street, London WC2, like Max Factor give free advisory service on all problems of make-up to individuals and management by appointment or by post.

Books cannot hope to replace experience but the following can be recommended:

Practical make-up for the Stage. T. W. Bamford (Pitman)
Stage make-up. H. Sequeira (Jenkins)
The Art of Make-up. Serge Strenkovsky (Muller)
Practical Stage Make-up. Philippe Perrottet (Studio Vista)
Fashions in Hair. Richard Corson (Peter Owen)
Historic Hairdressing. Joyce Assev (Pitman)
Historic costume for the stage. Lucy Barton (Black)

Visits to galleries (as well as observation in the streets and all public places) are essential. (*The English Face* by David Piper, Thames and

Hudson 1957, a study of the development of the face through portraits, is recommended.)

Stockists – *Make-up*

Timothy Whites and Taylors (Frizell's), 1 Cranbourn Street, London WC2
L. Leichner Ltd, 44a Cranbourn Street, London WC2
Max Factor Salon, 28 Old Bond Street, London SW1
Nathan Wigs, 143 Drury Lane, London WC2

Most large local chemists, including Boots, sell limited supplies of make-up. The address of your nearest Leichner stockist can be obtained from L. Leichner (London) Ltd, Administration Division, 436 Essex Road, London N1.

Stockists – *Wigs*

'Bert', 46 Portnall Road, London W9
Nathan Wigs, 143 Drury Lane, London WC2
Wig Creations Ltd, 25 Portman Close, Baker Street, London W1
Charles Fox Ltd, 25 Shelton Street, London WC2
O'Brien, 6 Belvoir Street, Leicester
William Mutrie & Son Ltd, Proscenium House, Broughton Street, Edinburgh
W. A. Hume & Sons, 88–94 Oxford Street, Manchester 1
Wrathbaron & Company, Ravenshill, Sutton, Keighley, Yorkshire
Boots', Woolworth's and large department stores stock nylon wigs, hair pieces etc.

11 Lighting

There are three ways of lighting a stage: by undifferentiated white light throughout the performance; by the atmospheric recreation of naturalistic lighting effects; and by the rather stylised use of following spots which belong to the Music Hall. Each production by its nature determines the kind of lighting that suits it best.

The main consideration for most amateur groups, who necessarily have a limited amount of lighting equipment, is to make sure that the actors are adequately lit. This need not mean a loss of atmosphere or excitement. For a production in a church hall in Cambridge, the Open Space Theatre put the audience round them in a circle, a couple of flood lights on stands, and the three actors, in jeans and sweat shirts, had only the script and their talent with which to work. The effect was totally riveting. Variety and colour came from the frequent changes of mood and the absolutely convincing and accomplished performances. The result was theatrical in the best possible sense. This only confirms the experience of the great Polish director, Jerzy Grotowski, which he describes in an article called *Plea for a poor theatre*.[1]

'Wishing to seize more clearly the heart of theatre, we have gradually eliminated from our performance everything we could get rid of; lighting effects, make-up, costumes, decorations, sound-effects, even the stage itself. By trial and error we have found out that theatre, stripped of all these trappings, can still continue to exist. But it stops existing as soon as one loses the dialogue between actor and spectator, their direct, living, palpable transaction.'

The most honest way to light a stage is to flood it with blank white light. All it seeks to do is to reveal the actors as clearly as possible, to concentrate

[1] In *Flourish*, Autumn 1966.

the attention of the audience upon the acting area. The best creative work is done because of limitations which free one to think deeply about what it is wished to achieve.

Subtle lighting can, however, be an enormous help in the creation of the visual and emotional atmosphere, while blank light can be totally inappropriate with a naturalistic set. Lighting itself can be used to provide a setting. So long as the lighting designer works within his resources and remembers that his first task is to let the audience see the actors, he can greatly aid the mood and feeling of the play. As with all parts of a production, the lighting should be related to the total style; in the hands of a sensitive technician who works alongside the actors and the director from the beginning.

The Lighting Designer

The Lighting Designer in the professional theatre is part of a team that may include a designer for costumes and another for the setting; but over complication in responsibility – and lighting – should be avoided where the technical resources are more restricted. Do not suppose it necessary to take the lights up and down unless it is helpful to the actors and the play, and you have the technical resources to do it efficiently.

The lighting, like the setting, should be regarded as another 'actor' whose contribution is evolving from the first rehearsal – and before. Its operation should be in the hands of a competent electrician whose concern is equally divided between technical efficiency, unobstrusive operation and absolute dedication to the needs of the production in hand.

Stage Lighting

The notes in this chapter are the briefest outline of a complicated subject beyond the scope of this book; the following are recommended to those who wish to study in more depth.

Lighting the Stage. Frederick Bentham (Pitman)
The Art of Stage Lighting. Frederick Bentham (Pitman)
  Both books are indispensable; clear, thorough and practical.
A Method of Lighting the Stage. Stanley McCandless (Theatre Art Books)
Theatre in the Round. Stephen Joseph (Barrie & Rockliff)
  Deals with the problems of lighting in the round.

Other useful guides (issued free by Strand Electric) are their *Colour Mixing Guide, Further Advice on Stage Lighting*, and *Lighting on a Shoestring*.

Basic Equipment

Stage lighting is ineffective without a bare minimum of equipment. But the position or placing of this equipment is more important than its quantity; every light cast on the acting area should be under the strictest control. Dimming equipment is, therefore, essential, and is probably more important than anything else. At least ten dimmers of about 1,000 watts plus or minus one third capacity, so that they can take 750, 1,000 or 1,250 watt loads on each dimmer, are necessary.

Between eight to fifteen spotlights (following the total capacity of the dimming equipment) are necessary – though obviously everything depends on the size of the room. Alternatively use something like ten 500-watt spotlights (five of them soft edge, five hard) for general illumination. With a limited budget these spotlights will be far more useful than floodlights, for a soft-edge spot will perform many of the functions of a floodlight e.g. backings of doors, windows etc.

This could be the minimum equipment for a conventional amateur stage not more than 15' deep, 20' across the proscenium opening, and 10' high. Lighting for a comparable sized theatre in the round or open stage would also come from spotlights; floodlights and battens have virtually no application but 250-watt lamps in Pattern 123 spotlights could be used in the corners of the room. More ambitious lighting schemes might involve six, eight, or ten spotlights. In an acting area of 18' x 21' up to thirty or even forty spots can be used.

The Switchboard

Complete flexibility can be realised with a switchboard with dimmers. A Junior Switchboard with eight or twelve circuits is excellent. The switchboard should be placed so that the electrician has a full view of the stage (on a balcony above the stage). It need not be a permanent fixture.

Dimmers – the Control of Intensity

Dimmers are used for controlling the amount of light by gradual and almost imperceptible changes. Each circuit needs a separate dimmer; the usual type is a wire-wound resistance. Probably, the most useful for the small stage is the Junior Slider Dimmer or the General Purpose Slider Dimmer. The dimmer controls the intensity of light by resisting or checking the flow of the electric current; thus fades, cross-fades (when part of the stage becomes lighter as another part goes dark) and blackouts all require the use of a dimmer.

Spotlights

The major part of any lighting for the stage comes from a series of spotlights, mounted so that their beams reach the acting area at an angle of about 45° from the horizontal; a minimum of two spotlights is needed to illuminate the human face without flattening out the features. These lanterns are probably best placed to the front and to each side of the actor, about 45° above his eye-line and 45° to each side of him, in fact 90° apart. This is called Front of House (FOH) lighting because for Proscenium stage work a fair proportion of the lighting should be positioned on either side, and also from the centre of the auditorium (on a balcony perhaps) where the lanterns are bracketed to the wall and therefore accessible by ladder.

There are two basic kinds of spotlight. Mirror (profile) spots which project a hard-edged beam of light, the profile of which is determined by the shape of the mask inserted in the gate between the reflector system and the lens. And Fresnel spots which give a soft beam of light without a definite edge, so that there is a gentle transition of lighting levels from one area to another; the beam is variable from a narrow intense spot to a medium angle flood. These qualities make the Fresnel the most useful and flexible lantern for lighting the acting area from the stage itself. The Mirror spot is more frequently used from the Front of House, or wherever stray light cannot be tolerated as, for example, close to a cyclorama, or for theatre in the round. A Mirror or profile spot can act as a soft-edge spotlight with the addition of a diffusing glass or change of lens. Different lens combinations are, in fact, available. Nearly all spotlights can be focused down or opened up as required.

The main spots on sale are the Strand Pattern 123, 250/500-watt Baby Fresnel Spot and the Mirror Spot Pattern 23 250/550-watt Baby Mirror Spot, both of which give tremendous power of illumination. Photometric data on different spotlights is clearly set out in Strand Electric's Catalogue (available free).

Battens

For general purpose lighting of open-stage work battens are now obsolete; although they are still essential for lighting cloths, cycloramas, door and window backings or other areas in a proscenium setting, where the light from FOH or stage spots cannot reach. They are either flown or placed on the stage floor from where they provide a wide angle evenly-distributed beam which makes them quite unsuited to open stage work on account of spill. Battens are generally supplied in 6' sections of three or four circuits, with a set of metal colour frames with each batten consisting of about eight 60, 100 or 150-watt bulbs.

Colour

Colour is not essential. Some people do use strong colours but others either prefer to use the subtlest and palest of colours, or like Sir Tyrone Guthrie, to develop a system of stage lighting that does without colour entirely. Obviously the way you use colour will depend not only on your production and your stage, but also on your understanding of its value.

As a rule use colour *very* sparingly indeed and beware of the use of strong colours from the charts (deep reds, ambers, blues) except for special effects. These colours are better reserved for colouring your backing. For lighting actors use the lightest tones of reds, blues and ambers according to the time of day. The dimming of 'white' light of course changes its colour value. When special effects are required a wide range of coloured Cinemoid is obtainable.

The Proscenium Theatre

The proscenium stage is lit by spots, whose beams reach the floor at an angle of about 45°. These are attached to the walls or balconies of the auditorium (for lighting the front half of the stage), and on the so-called No. 1 Bar – a long bar running parallel to the proscenium wall behind the curtain and above the proscenium (for the back half of the stage).

Floodlights and battens for illuminating the cloths are also fixed to flown bars while battens are also placed on the stage itself (behind ground-rows etc.).

This is a basic pattern for lighting the proscenium stage and the basis of all further improvements; more unusual visual effects can be arranged as required.

Theatre in the Round

So far we have considered the proscenium stage; in open stage work and theatre in the round the lighting will normally come from spotlights. Floodlights and battens have virtually no place. The most suitable lantern is a soft edge spotlight with a Fresnel lens and a beam that can be adjusted with the approximate limits of 15° and 45° and using a 500-watt lamp: the Strand pattern 123 Baby Fresnel Spot is ideal. In small theatres a 250-watt lamp is sufficient, in larger ones a Strand pattern 223 with a 1,000-watt lamp may be preferred. We have already discussed the quantity of lanterns which might be needed.

These spotlights should be placed so that their beams are no more than about 45° to the horizontal; special effects may dictate something different but if it is much less than 25°, difficulty may be experienced in keeping direct light out of the eyes of the audience. The throw of these spotlights, in the sort of theatre we are discussing, will be about twenty feet so that they will not be directly over the acting area but outside it, over the seating rows, and preferably fixed on a guide fixed to the ceiling.

Stephen Joseph devotes a chapter to Lighting in his excellent book, and Walden Boyle's *Central and Flexible Staging* is also good on open stage lighting. *Planning for New Forms of Theatre* (from Strand Electric) discusses lighting for the open stage in some detail, as does an essay in *Tabs*, Vol. 23, No. 2.

Planning the Lighting

The actual business of lighting a play depends on the approach preferred by each director. Perhaps the best method is to start from the systematic illumination of the entire stage so that there is a basis of good illumination to start with. The equipment needed for this is best worked out, as far as possible, on paper beforehand.

Proper lighting rehearsals are an essential part of the development of the production. At the technical dress-rehearsal the lighting – with actors and set in place – is gone through from beginning to end (see pages 305 and 308). A sample lighting plot is shown on pages 317 and 318.

Scenic and Effects Projection

Projected effects have been effective tools in the hands of the designer for some time. During recent years considerable advances have been made and the projection of scenery or effects have been successfully demonstrated in many productions, notably by Svoboda whose sets depend a lot on optical projection, as for example his *Die Frau ohne Schatten* at Covent Garden, and *The Storm* at the National Theatre. Projected slides have also been used, more simply, in productions like *The Promise* and in innumerable Documentaries.

Pictorial projection of this kind needs a reasonably deep stage where film or photographic slides can be thrown on to a seamless linen drop. The normal 35 mm slide projector is adequate.

Effects projection equipment is expensive to hire but such firms as Strand Electric or Theatre Projects will give advice, for each problem needs careful consideration. The slides can be made to suit any projector and these are invariably predistorted to counteract the angle of the projection beam, which is rarely at right angles to the screen.

All kinds of optical effects – fleecy clouds to dissolving colours – are also best dealt with by the firms listed below but it is worth considering the Linnebach projector for simple and inexpensive effects.

Lighting the open-air production after dark

Open-air productions after dark can be lit by spotlights or floodlights (on stands) or flares.

Spotlights and floodlights of various kinds are available from the main stage lighting consultants listed below. Their advice should certainly be sought.

Flares can also be effective in certain out-of-door productions. These can be burnt, on a sand foundation, in decorative stands or tins. A quarter portion of Napthalene (obtainable from Agricultural Suppliers) is mixed with three quarter portions of Hexamine, then lit. (Hexamine is obtainable from Brothertons & Co. Ltd, Westgate, Wakefield, Yorks.) Other effects on the same lines are obtainable from:

Richard Dendy, 46 Sutton Lane, Banstead, Surrey (smoke, fog, mist)
Donmar Productions Office, New Theatre, St Martins Lane, London WC2
  (CO_2 smoke guns, etc.)

Advice and help will be given by any of the following firms, specialising in lighting: contact them direct with all your problems.

Strand Electric and Engineering Co. Ltd, 29 King Street, London WC2
Equipment available for sale or hire from branches in Bristol, Glasgow, Manchester and Dublin. They also hold lectures on lighting at their demonstration theatre in London, and provide many other services on application.

Theatre Projects Lighting Ltd, 10 Long Acre, London WC2
Provide an advisory service. Equipment for sale or hire.

W. J. Furse & Co. Ltd, 20 Traffic Street, Nottingham
Also have offices in London, Salford, Glasgow and Dublin. Equipment for sale or hire.
20 Mount Street, Manchester and 9 Carteret Street, London SW1.

12 Stage Management

Stage Management is concerned with the technical organisation of any kind of production from the arrangement of the first rehearsal right through until the last curtain call. There are no set rules – only certain methods which have been proved to be the most efficient over the years. And though techniques of staging change all the time and the production may be anything from *Krapp's Last Tape* to a full-scale staging of *Carousel* with chorus and orchestra, these methods still remain of use.

The Stage Management can consist of one harassed and overworked dogsbody or a staff of thirty; one thing only is important – to avoid confusion and inefficiency – the final decision for everything must be in the hands of one person.

The Stage Manager. The Stage Manager is the technical equivalent of the Director. His job is to translate the ideas of the director and his designer into practical reality. He must be sympathetic to the aims of the director and constructive in his approach to any problems – not obstructive. On the other hand, if in his opinion certain effects or scene changes are impossible to achieve it is his job to say so and to suggest practical alternatives.

He controls the different departments – the Property Department, Lighting, Master Carpenter's Department, the Wardrobe, and keeps them in touch with developments and changes in the production. He supervises the work of his assistants – the Deputy Stage Manager and the Assistant Stage Managers, if these are necessary.

The Stage Manager's job is one of organisation and preparation, and he must be aware of every eventuality in the production and allow for it. He must have the special ability to take sudden changes in his carefully laid plans with equanimity and to be able to make important decisions quickly. The more efficiently he uses the rehearsal period of the production to perfect the separate parts of the jigsaw puzzle that is a production, the easier his job will be when it comes to fitting the jigsaw together at the Technical and Dress rehearsals. He supervises the smooth running of the performance. The remaining duties are shared between the Deputy Stage Manager and the Assistant Stage Managers according to the needs of the production.

The Deputy Stage Manager. The Deputy Stage Manager has special responsibility for rehearsals and for making out and looking after the Prompt Book – the Bible of a production. In it are contained all the script changes and moves used in the production and all the cues, calls etc. needed to run the performance.

The Deputy Stage Manager usually makes out the cue sheets and plots needed to direct the staff. He has the important job of giving all the cues and prompting during the performance – he runs the prompt corner – under the direction of the Stage Manager. This job can be shared with the Assistant Stage Managers.

The Assistant Stage Managers. Assist anybody, at any time, in any way. Assistant Stage Managers are responsible for the properties and effects. They help run the prompt corner, if necessary. They make tea.

The Stage Staff. If there are plenty of helpers available, as in a school or youth club, these can be divided up into the different departments of the stage staff. This is a good way of interesting a wider range of children or adults than would normally be involved in a production.

The Stage – The Master Carpenter. The Master Carpenter and his assistants build the sets and put them up for a production. He supervises the set scene changes.

The Property Department – The Property Master. The Property Master makes props. During the performance he is responsible, with the Assistant Stage Manager, for all the props. This includes the furniture.

The Electrical Department – The Chief Electrician. The Chief Electrician and his assistants are in charge of all the lighting and electrical equipment during the setting up of the production and during the performance. He also works the lighting board.

The Wardrobe – The Wardrobe Mistress. The Wardrobe Mistress makes, mends and maintains costumes. She looks after the wigs. She helps the cast to dress during the performance, if need be.

297

The Call Boy. He calls the actors, staff etc. and is directed by the Deputy Stage Manager from the Prompt Corner.

The Stage Management work falls into two separate parts: the rehearsal period and the actual performance of the play.

Part 1 – The Rehearsal Period

The Stage Manager's job starts before rehearsals begin. Before the first rehearsal all the major technical details of the production will in all probability have been decided, e.g. the place of production, the form of staging to be used, the points in the action where any major scene changes are to take place. The designer will already have supplied a ground plan, drawn to the scale of the set. Copies will have been made and given to the Director, the Deputy Stage Manager and the Master Carpenter. The names of the cast will be known.

If any auditions are to be held the Stage Manager arranges them. He comes to the first rehearsal with a fairly clear idea of the production – technically, though a lot can happen before the rehearsals are over.

It is the Stage Management's job to find a suitable room or stage for the rehearsals and to inform the members of the cast when the first rehearsals will take place. If any music is involved in the production a rehearsal pianist will be needed and obviously a piano. Enough scripts must be bought or hired for the cast (and understudies, if any) plus one for the Director, one for the Stage Manager and one to make up into the Prompt Book. There must be enough chairs and tables in the rehearsal room. Ash-trays are very important if adults are involved. This is especially so if any of the rehearsals are to take place in a theatre where there are very stringent fire regulations.

It is most important to write down the names, addresses and telephone numbers of everyone involved in the production. It is also a good idea to write down any times that an actor cannot be present at rehearsals so that the Director can arrange accordingly. Obviously the cast have to be present at each performance of the play but it is also important that all the stage staff right down to the stage hands understand that if they agree to help with the production they must guarantee to attend all the performances.

If possible the Director must be persuaded to arrange a Rehearsal

Schedule; although waiting is a known occupational hazard of the theatre, a schedule does save a lot of frustration and time. It is the Deputy Stage Manager's job to post up the schedule and to make sure that everyone knows its contents.

The ground plan of the set should be shown to the actors and also, if possible, a coloured model of the set, made to scale. The actors will then be aware, even before the rehearsals start, of the physical and visual aspects of the production.

The Deputy Stage Manager attends every rehearsal. He sits beside the Director facing the actors. He is going to be sitting there for a long time so it is best to make himself comfortable. He provides himself with a table and plenty of pencils and rubbers. The pencils are for himself and to lend to the cast when they start writing their moves into their scripts. Pencils only, not biros nor pens, may be used to mark hired scripts, so that marks can be easily rubbed out when scripts are returned. Most Deputy Stage Managers have a board on to which they clip their notes. Deputy Stage Managers are great note-takers – they write notes on anything and everything that they think could possibly be of interest to the Stage Manager.

It is very useful for the actors and the Director if a copy of the ground plan is marked out on the floor of the rehearsal area. This should be done even if the set consists of one rostrum in the centre of the acting-area. Chalk can be used for marking – especially if the marks can be left permanently in place. But if, as is most usual, the rehearsal space has to be cleared after rehearsals the best method to use is tapes. The tape is measured to size and marked, e.g. Down L. Return Flat. Fireplace Right. Gaps are left for doors and windows. Indicate whether they are double or single and which way they open. The tapes are fixed to the floor with drawing pins. It saves a lot of time if a few drawing pins can be left in the floor between rehearsals to mark strategic points and angles.

Stand-in furniture is provided and placed accurately. It is important to represent the space of the actual furniture that will be used for the production. Its position is marked on the ground plan. Later on in the rehearsals when all the lines have been learnt and the scripts set aside stand-in props are also provided. They should approximate as near as possible, at least in size, to the actual props that will be used during the performance. The Assistant Stage Managers usually find and set these props during rehearsals.

The Deputy Stage Manager during rehearsals records each script change and plots each move made into the Prompt Book. He stands in for every effect – stamps his foot for every door slam or pistol shot and goes Brr, brr . . . brr, brr for every telephone bell. He prompts.

Prompting is an art which can be only acquired by practice, concentration and a very thorough knowledge of the production. It is important that the person who prompts during the later part of the rehearsals should be the one who prompts for the performance – otherwise the actors lose confidence. Therefore if an Assistant Stage Manager is to prompt part of the play he must take over during rehearsals and not just at the dress rehearsal or actual performance.

If the method of production used is theatre in the round it is probably best to dispense with the prompter altogether. The actors must know of this early in the rehearsals.

A great number of lists will have to be drawn up during the early rehearsals; lists of props, furniture, wigs, effects and lighting equipment that may be needed for the production.

A rough lighting plot is obtained from the Director showing the main areas of light and the sources – lamps and light through windows. Also the colour that will be needed, e.g. night scenes or tropical sunlight, and any special lighting effects, e.g. back projection or cloud effects. This is used as a guide by the Electrician in deciding what extra lighting equipment he needs to order.

The Assistant Stage Managers acquire any props or furniture they can beg, borrow or steal. It is amazing how many expensive props can be obtained by merely asking for them. It is always best to get in touch with the Managing Director rather than the sales girl in a shop. A complimentary seat or a credit note in the programme often works wonders.

It is best for the Director to see, hear and approve every detail of effects and props well before the dress rehearsal to allow time to find substitutes.

The Stage Manager accompanies the Director and the Designer when any furniture is hired. He must have a working knowledge of historical styles. He takes the ground plan with him and is very careful to check all measurements. He also makes quite sure that when the Director decides on a fragile 18th-century table he has remembered that the hero climbs on to it during Scene Three and jumps up and down on it six times to prove his virility.

It must be remembered that dressing will be needed for the set – in other words extra furniture, props etc. not specifically needed in the production but used to give atmosphere, e.g. in a writer's study, bookcases and books; in a down-and-out's shelter piles of old newspapers and empty tin cans. It is far better to get too much than too little.

A good idea is to make a list of each article or piece of equipment used in a production with beside it a note of where it came from, when it will arrive and – if it has to be collected – a convenient date for collection. If possible it is best for furniture, props, effects that are closely involved in the action of the play to be obtained at an earlier date than the rest so that the actors have the opportunity of rehearsing with them.

The Prompt Book (see page 312). The Deputy Stage Manager is responsible for making out the Prompt Book. He must look after it most carefully, never lend it to anyone, never let it out of his sight if he can help it.

Unpublished plays are ideal for the purpose of a Prompt Book as they are duplicated on one side of the page only, leaving a blank page opposite each dialogue page for columns of moves and cues. But as the fashion nowadays is to publish plays even before they have been produced it is most likely that the prompt script will be in book form. It is then necessary to take the book to pieces to make the prompt copy and to interleave each page of script with sheets of plain paper before assembling it all in a loose leaf file. Another method is to stick each page of script on to a separate sheet of plain paper but this requires two scripts and is rather an extravagant method. Scripts used for the Prompt Book must be bought and not hired. The interleaved sheet of paper is divided into two columns; moves are recorded in one column, cues in the other. The cues column should be further subdivided into columns for Elex, Effects, Curtains, etc. Make as many columns as are needed. It should not often be necessary for calling to be done during the action of the play, but if it should be found useful calling would come under the cues column.

Recording Moves. The object of the Prompt Book is to have a complete record of every move made during the play's action. Pauses are also marked. A form of shorthand is frequently used for speed. It is always better to draw a diagram for a complicated movement rather than attempt to write it out in words. Diagrams can also be used for furniture and any parts of the set that affect the action such as doors and windows. Here are some of the symbols which will be found most useful. They are, like everything else in stage management, mostly a matter of common sense, but it is important that the Prompt Book should be immediately understandable to anyone and these are the signs that are most commonly used. All directions are written from the actor's point of view, e.g. Stage R is the actor's right when he faces the audience.

Door opening outwards – hinged on the left.
Door opening inwards – hinged on the right.
Double doors. French windows.
Square table.
Round table.
Chair.
Armchair.
Cross to.
Circle round.
Pause.
Down stage.
Up stage.
Right.
Left.
Centre.

A Plan of a Stage (see diagram on next page)
From this plan of a stage and with the symbol X or an arrow any move can be charted. If there is furniture on the set it is often helpful to use this as well – so instead of writing, Gertrude crosses from the bottom right hand corner of the stage to in front of the throne in the middle of the stage – all that is needed is Gert. X D.S. $\bigcap$ C. – or alternatively

Gert $\longrightarrow$.

Diagrams are particularly useful when more than one character is involved in a move.

When marking the moves in the script a number is put beside the exact

302

point that the move takes place. The move is then written in detail opposite the corresponding number in the moves column. This can be seen clearly in the sample page of Prompt Book on page 312. Pauses are marked on the script itself. It is very important to mark pauses accurately as there is nothing more infuriating for an actor than to be prompted in the middle of a most dramatic pause.

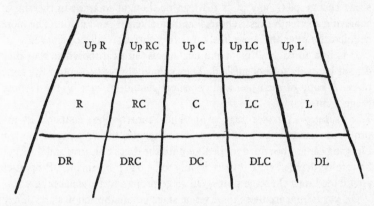

Up R	Up RC	Up C	Up LC	Up L
R	RC	C	LC	L
DR	DRC	DC	DLC	DL

Marking Cues. The cues are not marked in until late in the rehearsal and should be written in pencil to start with as there are sure to be alterations. Then, when everything is finally decided, which may not be until the Technical Dress Rehearsal, the cues are marked in different colours so that they can be quickly distinguished from each other. It is usual to give a 'warning' cue and a 'go' cue. The 'warning' is given at least a minute and a half before the 'go' so as to give the staff concerned time to prepare for the cue. One page of script in most acting editions is roughly one and a half minutes. There are many different methods of marking cues; all that is important is that the cue is easily seen and distinguished. One of the clearest methods can be seen in the sample page of Prompt Book. It is also quite useful to mark the top corner of the page of script whenever a cue is about to occur. This is particularly valuable if the cues are few and far between as it is quite easy to miss cues even when they are properly marked when concentrating on the prompting.

Calls are marked at the side of the script as numbers. No warning need be given. Then the names of the actors to be called are written under the number in the appropriate cues column. It must be remembered that it is not only the actors who may need to be called; there is the orchestra, the audience (who need warning that the play is about to start) and the stage staff.

Plots and Cue Sheets. Plots are made for each department to assist with the smooth running of the actual production. Property plots, effects plots, scene change plots, any plots that can be thought to assist in the aim of achieving a smooth dress rehearsal and an efficient production. The more detailed the plots the more likely it is that this aim will be achieved.

It is best to back all plots and cue sheets with cardboard so that they cannot be easily torn or mislaid. They should always be kept in the same place. A copy of each plot and cue sheet should be kept by the Deputy Stage Manager.

The Property Plot (see page 316). The Property Plot contains all the properties used in the production. This includes the dressing of the set. Dressing cannot be added to the Plot until the dress rehearsal and does not have to be detailed at all if there is only to be one performance. Properties are divided into On stage props, Off stage props and Personal props.

On stage Props are those to be set on stage before the action starts. They should be written down in order, e.g. D.R. to D.L.

Off stage Props are those properties which are set off stage, either right, left or centre depending on the set and the production and are taken on stage during the action of the play.

Personal Props are props which the actor carries on himself and for which he is responsible, e.g. a cigarette packet, a sword.

Each scene change is divided into two parts – strike and set.

Strike includes all the props to be taken off the set during the scene change. Under *Set* are all the props to be taken on the set during the change.

It is a good idea to add to the property plot anything needed for off-stage effects.

Furniture Plot (see page 314). Furniture plots are usually drawn in diagram form. A sketch is made of the ground plan with all the furniture in position. If the plot is very complicated it is best to number the pieces of furniture for clarity and add a key underneath the diagram. A diagram is needed for each new set. If there is little change from one scene to the next it is only necessary to write the alteration in the plot, no diagram is needed.

Effects Cue Sheet. The effects cue sheet shows the various effects cues, dividing them into acts and scenes. The length of time of the cue, in seconds, and the volume is also given, e.g.

> Act 1 Scene 1. Cue No. 1. Door slam.
> Cue No. 2. Thunder. Loud. 5 secs.

It is often necessary to make out a special cue sheet for the taped effects. The cue sheet should give details of the name of the effect, the tape setting, the volume setting and the amplifier used, e.g.

Act 1 Scene 1. Cue No. 1. Distant Crowd. 0001. Vol. 3. Amplifier R.

Scene Change Cue Sheet. It may be useful to make a cue sheet for the set scene changes. One sheet for each side of the stage should be made giving details of the various changes under Strike and Set and putting the name of a stage hand by each particular job, e.g.

> *Scene Change Cue Sheet. R. side*
> Act 1 Scene 2 *Strike*
>   Rostrum C.   Steven Taylor.
>   John Burton.
>   *Set*
>   Canopy Up.L.   Michael Groom.

D.S.M. Check Plot. It is a good idea for the Deputy Stage Manager to write down a list of all the special points he must check just before curtain up on each scene. This plot can obviously only be completed at the dress rehearsal, e.g.

> Act 2 Scene 1.   Door L. open.   Pageant On.
>   Back projection of map on.
>   Beginners.   Ann Lawson.
>   Susan Wright.

Lighting Plot and Cue Sheet (see page 317 and page 318). A lighting plot and cue sheet will be worked out at the dress rehearsal. It will note the positions of the equipment used and will plot the opening lighting for each scene and detail every cue.

Now the first part of the Stage Management's job is over – the actors are ready, the set is built and painted, the props, costumes and furniture are waiting to be unpacked. The work of preparation is complete and the second part of the Stage Management's work, which is concerned with the actual performance of the production, is about to begin.

Part 2 – *The Performance*

The methods of staging being used for the production – theatre in the round, end-staging, proscenium arch – have a considerable influence on this part of the work, as does the actual place where the play is to be performed – school, well-equipped theatre or village hall. Some general notes only can be suggested which would apply wherever or however the production is staged.

The Set-up – The Stage

1. Make a plan of the work to be done.
2. The ideal start to a set-up is a bare acting area, newly swept, a ground plan of the set to be built, plenty of helpers and plenty of time.
3. Lay the stage cloth first (if one is used).
4. Fly next. This includes everything that is hung above the stage, cloths, ceilings, hung screens, any electrical equipment that has to be rigged.
5. Reverse the Acts and Scenes in the order of setting, i.e. First set up the last scene of the play including furniture and lighting and then work backwards so that the correct set is in position to start the dress rehearsal.
6. Remember to mark the positions of the flats, screens, curtains etc. before they are struck. Also mark the flats themselves, e.g. D.R.No. 1. Up C. Rostrum No. 4. Use a different coloured paint to mark each act. If paint cannot be used, coloured Sellotape will do, though this is not as satisfactory as paint. Brass studs can be used for the stage-marking, using a different grouping of studs for each Act, e.g. One stud for Act 1. Two studs for Act 2.
7. Organise the striking as carefully as the setting. Remember always to stack the flats in the right order, with the flat to be set first at the top of the pack.

8. Check all sight lines. Check that all the cloths are hung correctly; take especial care of any sky cloths, as any crease on these will show when lit and ruin the effect. Make sure there are sufficient braces to hold the set steady – one each side of a door, one at each corner of the set (see page 226).

9. If at all possible rehearse the scene changes. This is very important if the stage hands are inexperienced.

10. Useful objects for the stage management to have at a set-up: clear Sellotape, coloured Sellotape, coloured paints, safety pins, chalk, needles, black and white thread, duster, Copydex, tape splicer and tape adhesive.

Properties and Furniture

1. Unpack. A list will have been sent with any hired props etc. Check.

2. It is best to hang curtains up as soon as possible otherwise they will look very creased and sad. Mirrors and very shiny objects sometimes need dulling in case they reflect the lights too brightly and make hot spots on the set. China has to be washed or dirtied. Furniture needs polishing or blackening, silver cleaning or tarnishing – according to need.

3. As soon as the first set is up – set the furniture, props, etc. Make sure that everything is made as easy as possible for the actors, e.g. set matches sticking up out of a box so that they are easily found. Mark the positions of the furniture on the set. Decide with the producer on what dressing is needed. Add the extra furniture and props used as dressing to the Furniture and Property Plots.

4. Organise a place where the furniture is to be struck to and stored.

5. Set up tables for Off stage Props at convenient places. Set Off stage Props. Take Personal Props to the dressing rooms.

6. Supply containers for setting and striking props, if necessary. Wicker clothes baskets are useful as they are both light and virtually unbreakable.

Effects

1. Set up and rehearse effects for the producer to decide on the volume etc. required. Mark volumes on to Effects Cue Sheet.

Lighting

1. The Electrician knows from his rough lighting plot (a) where the main areas of light are to be concentrated and (b) the sources of light. He sets up his equipment accordingly.
2. A Lighting Rehearsal is held. One of the stage management is needed on stage while the lighting is being set so that the spots can be focused on his face as required in the production – in a sitting or standing position.
3. As each spot is set it is a good idea to make a note of where it is being focused, the amount of spread used and the colour, e.g. Spot 1 D.L. On rostrum C, standing, ½ spread, 54 cinemoid. (Note if cinemoid or gelatine media are being used as the shades vary considerably.)
4. All off stage lighting positions should be marked with paint on the stage, as well as a note made of the direction of the light.
5. Each scene is now lit and each lighting cue worked out. Time must always be allowed for the Electrician to plot down the settings for each cue. The exact place in the script where the cue is to take place must be marked in the Prompt Book. The length of time in seconds to be allowed for each cue must also be noted, e.g. Fade down for five seconds. Dead black-out – D.B.O. on switch.

Music Call

If any live music is involved in the production a convenient time must be arranged before the dress rehearsal for the musicians to rehearse. Chairs and music stands must be organised for them.

Costumes

1. Costumes must be unpacked and checked against the lists sent by the costumiers (if hired).
2. They must be ironed, and hung in the appropriate dressing rooms.
3. It is a good idea to arrange a final costume parade before the dress rehearsal. If possible this should be held on the stage where the production is to take place and should be adequately lit.
4. Lists should be made of all the alterations that have to be made. Of course if the costumes have been designed and made especially for the production this can all be done well in advance of the dress rehearsal.

It is only with hired costumes that everything has to be left to the last minute.

Dressing Rooms

1. Arrange for the dressing rooms or room to be as near to the stage as possible and also near wash basins and lavatories.
2. Tables, chairs, mirrors – one full-length one – should be organised.
3. Quick changes are sometimes required in a production – a place must be provided where these can take place if the dressing rooms are any distance from the stage. A mirror hooked to the back of a flat and a hook for a coathanger would be better than nothing.

Cueing

1. All methods of cueing must be worked out before the Dress Rehearsal so that everybody concerned is quite clear on the method of cueing to be used, e.g. cue lights, hand signals, a buzzer etc. If a hand signal is to be used it must obviously be clearly visible and not obscured at the crucial moment by an army of soldiers charging off stage.

Calling

1. Calling can be done by a call boy or girl who stands near the Deputy Stage Manager in the corner and is directed by him when to call.
2. If the play is to be performed for any length of time it may be worth while to make out a Call Book which would enable the Call Boy to be responsible for his own cues. He will still need to be directed from the corner for the first few performances, until he has had time to learn the calls. A Call Book is a notebook with all the calls to be made throughout the play written in beside an easily recognisable line of dialogue, e.g. Call 10. 'Bang, bang. My God, he's dead. You've shot him'. . . . Call John Armstrong.
3. A system of calling usually only met in theatres is the 'cue call' system. This is an automatic system of calling with a microphone in the prompt corner and a loudspeaker in each dressing room.
4. A useful small system that could very easily be fitted up is the Triang Tri-onic Baby Alarm – or any other of the small baby alarms on the market. This alarm could also be used for cueing.

5. As well as the calls that are cued into the Prompt Book there are also the general calls, half an hour, a quarter of an hour, and five minutes before the curtain is due to rise. These calls are always given five minutes early, so that the half is actually called thirty-five minutes before curtain up. Beginners – those actors needed on stage for the beginning of the play – are called five minutes before curtain up. The orchestra used to play the overture at this time – when every theatre had its own orchestra – and the call is still 'Overture and Beginners, please'.

The Dress Rehearsals

If at all possible there should be two dress rehearsals. The first – the Technical Dress Rehearsal – with its emphasis on the technical side of the production will be slow and full of stops to perfect this or that lighting cue or tape effect. The second, the Dress Rehearsal, should resemble a performance in as many respects as possible.

The Stage Manager should watch both rehearsals from the auditorium and should take notes of everything that needs changing. He must make sure that the actors know their positions for the curtain calls, and that the calls have been rehearsed if they are at all complicated. A note should be taken of the time taken for each scene.

Notes for the Performance

Keep calm. Arrange with the front of house when the curtain is to go up. Five minutes licence is sometimes allowed for latecomers. This is not a good idea as the audience merely gets used to the new late time – and arrives even later. It is far better to have a reputation for strict timekeeping and a punctual audience.

Sweep the stage.

Re-set the first set. Set the furniture. Check. Dust furniture.

Check effects, buzzers, tape-recorders, amplifiers, cueing systems.

Call the half hour and check that all the actors are in their dressing rooms.

Set onstage and offstage props. (If the production is open stage, theatre in the round, traverse etc. it may be necessary to set and check all onstage furniture, props and scenery before the audience arrives.)

Check Personal props.

Call the quarter of an hour.

Check that all the stage staff know their duties.

Call five minutes.

Check anything that hasn't been checked before.

Call Beginners. Cue orchestra for Overture.

Warn the audience. It is usual to give the audience warning three, two and one minute before the play is due to begin.

Set the lighting for the opening. (Remember that front of house lights will have to fade in as the curtain rises.) Check the Deputy Stage Manager's List. Check Beginners.

Warn Curtain up. This applies even if there is no curtain to go up as it is also a general warning to all the different departments and to the actors to stand by.

Fade House Lights.

Curtain up.

During the performance while the Deputy Stage Manager runs the corner the Stage Manager should be available at all times in case of an emergency. If he leaves the stage he must give directions where he can be found.

Quiet during the performance

There must be absolute quiet backstage during the performance. If there are a lot of children involved it is a good idea to have someone in charge of them all the time they are off stage. It is very exciting taking part in a production and very difficult to remember to keep quiet all the time. Runners of carpet could be laid down the side of the stage from the exits to reduce the noise from footsteps. It is a good idea if all the stage staff wear rubber-soled shoes.

Intervals and scene changes

Warn the electrician and the stage staff to stand by.

It is also a good idea to warn the bar or the coffee makers that the interval rush is about to begin.

Have ready any music you may be playing during the interval at scene change.

The electrician will need to know when the curtain 'go' is given if he

Sample Page of Prompt Book (Scene from 'The Changeling'
by Middleton)

LOLLIO   We have but two sorts of people in the house,
and both under the whip – that's fools and
madmen; the one has not wit enough to be knaves,
and the other not knavery enough to be fools.

ALIBIUS   Ay, those are all my patients, Lollio,
I do profess the cure of either sort:
My trade, my living 'tis, I thrive by it:
The daily visitants that come to see
My brainsick patients, I would not have
To see my wife: gallants I do observe
Of quick enticing eyes, rich in habits,
Of stature and proportion very comely –
These are most shrewd temptations, Lollio.

LOLLIO   They may be easily answered, sir; if they come
to see the fools and madmen, you and I may
serve the turn and let my mistress alone – she's
of neither sort.

ALIBIUS   'Tis a good ward; indeed, come they to see
Our madmen or our fools, let 'em see no more
Than what they come for: by that consequent
They must not see her: I'm sure she's no fool.

LOLLIO   And I'm sure she's no madman.

ALIBIUS   Hold that buckler fast, Lollio, my trust
Is on thee, and I account it firm and strong.
What hour is't, Lollio?

LOLLIO   Towards belly hour, sir.

ALIBIUS   Dinner time? Thou mean'st twelve o'clock.

LOLLIO   Yes, sir, for every part has his hour: we wake
at six and look about us, that's eye-hour; at
seven we should pray, that's knee-hour; at eight
walk, that's leg-hour; at nine gather flowers
and pluck a rose, that's nose-hour; at ten we
drink, that's mouth-hour; at eleven lay about
us for victuals, that's hand-hour; at twelve
go to dinner, that's belly-hour.

FFECTS	ELEXS	CURTAIN	CALLS	MOVES
				① Lol.sits R of steps L.C.
				② A X R. Lol.
				③ A↓ ∠Lol.
	GO ELEX [CUE 10] WARN ELEX CUE 11 12]			④ Quick turn to Lol.
			⑭ MICK OTTO JOHN ANGEL	
				⑤ A. Turn D.S.
EFFECTS CUE 23]				⑥ A. X Lol. ⑦ Lol. up to. D.S. steps. Lol. A. ⑧ Hand on shoulder.
WARN EFFECTS CUE 24].				⑨ Lol. A X D.S tog. Hand on shoulder. Lol.A ⑨
				⑩ O ⑩ Lol. A Lol X R.

THE EFFECTS CUES ARE IN GREEN.
THE ELEX. CUES IN BLUE.
THE CURTAINS AND CALLS IN RED.

SAMPLE FURNITURE PLOT

PLOT 1. (For Theatre-in-the-Round)

ACT 1.

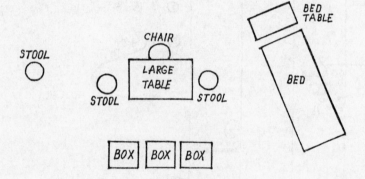

ACT 2.

STRIKE   Table C.
             2 Stools at C.
             Chair.

SET   Packing case to C.
             3 Boxes to Act 3 positions.

SAMPLE FURNITURE PLOT 2.   (PLOT WITH KEY)

<u>ACT 1.</u>

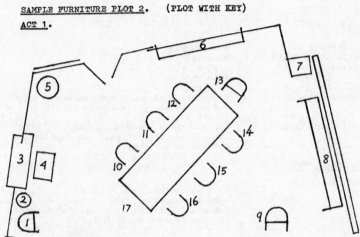

1. Blue armchair.
2. Small round table.
3. Fender.
4. Square footstool.
5. 3-tiered round table.
6. Sideboard.
7. Jardiniere.
8. Garden seat.
9. Upright chair with arm.
10, 11, 12, 14, 15, 16 Upright chairs.
13. Upright chair with arms.
17. Dining table.

SAMPLE PROPERTY PLOT- (1 ACT)

ACT 1. SCENE 1.

ONSTAGE PROPS
SET

Armchair D.R.	Blue cushion
Table above chair	Book with marker
Tiered table Up R.	Bowl of roses
1st shelf	Nuts in dish
3rd shelf	Nut cracker
Sideboard Up C.	8 knives. 8 forks. 8 soup spoons
	8 fish knives. 8 fish forks
in drawer	6 napkins
Jardiniere Up L.	Aspidistra in brass container
L. stat.	Crochet bag with crochet and keys on chair
Table C.	Tablecloth (folded)

ACT 1. SCENE 2.

STRIKE

Book and marker from armchair D.R.Plates, cutlery, napkins, nuts in dish, nutcrackers tablecloth from table C. Crochet bag and crochet from armchair D.R.

SET

Tiered table Up R.	Cigar piercer
Table C.	Bible
Sideboard Up C.	Tray with jug of water and 6 tumblers

OFFSTAGE PROPS.

OFF UP R.

ACT 1. SCENE 1.

    2 Napkins
Tray with soup tureen with soup.Soup ladle
8 soup bowls
8 plates
Key

ACT 1. SCENE 2.

    Ashtray

PERSONAL PROPS.

Sam	Handkerchief with black edge
	Prayer book
Reverend Smythe	Cigar. Matches. Pen.
Rosie	Letter. Ring on string

SAMPLE LIGHTING PLOT

POSITIONS OF SPOTS

NO.1	Arch Up R.C. (standing)	$\frac{3}{4}$ spread	54 cinemoid
NO.2	Top steps L.C. (standing)	$\frac{1}{2}$	52
NO.3	Stool L. of rostrum C. (sitting)	$\frac{1}{4}$	9
NO.4	3 ft. L. of bench C. (standing)	$\frac{1}{4}$+	17
NO.5	5 ft. D.S. steps R.C. (De Flores position)	$\frac{1}{4}$	36
NO.6	Arch Up R.C. (standing)	$\frac{3}{4}$	54

PERCHES

R.TOP	2 ft. D.S. steps R.C. (standing)	$\frac{3}{4}$	52
R.BOTTOM	3 ft. L. of C. (kneeling)	$\frac{1}{2}$–	36
L.TOP	Stool D.L. (sitting)	$\frac{1}{4}$	17
L.BOTTOM	2 ft. D.S. steps L.C. (standing)	$\frac{3}{4}$	52

F.O.H. SPOTS

NO.1	Steps L.C.	$\frac{3}{4}$+	36
NO.2	Rostrum C. (standing)	$\frac{3}{4}$+	54
NO.3	Stool D.C. (sitting)	$\frac{1}{2}$–	7
NO.4	C.	$\frac{3}{4}$+	52
NO.5	Steps R.C.	$\frac{3}{4}$+	36
NO.6	4 ft. D.S. R.C. (standing)	$\frac{3}{4}$+	52

OFF STAGE LIGHTING

4 Floods U.S. to light cloth. 2 R. 2. L.

1 Pageant through Arch Up R.C.

1 Pageant through Arch Up L.C.

SAMPLE LIGHTING PLOT - (ONE SCENE)

ACT 1. SCENE 1.

BATTEN 1.   Red at full.
SPOTS $\frac{7}{1}$ $\frac{6}{2}$ $\frac{5}{3}$ $\frac{5}{4}$ $\frac{7}{6}$

PERCHES R.TOP   7
        R.BOTTOM   8
        L.BOTTOM   6

F.O.H. $\frac{7}{1}$ $\frac{8}{2}$ $\frac{6}{4}$ $\frac{3}{5}$ $\frac{7}{6}$

DIPS   D.S.R. Red at full.
                       D.S.L. White at full.

CUE 1.   Fade out in 30 seconds. Spots 1, 2, 6.
                                            F.O.H.1, 2, 5.

CUE 2.   Fade all to out in 5 seconds.
CUE 3.   Fade in for 5 seconds. F.O.H. 3.
CUE 4.   D.B.O.

cannot see for himself so that he can fade F.O.H. lighting as the curtain falls.

Don't forget to put the house lights up for the interval. . . .

Scene changes should be effected as quietly as possible. Quick scene changes must have been very carefully rehearsed as the continuity of the play often depends on their speed.

Theatre in the round or any form of open staging obviously presents certain problems which must be solved beforehand. Strike props and furniture first.

Curtain Calls
As a general rule it is far better to take one curtain call too few than one too many.

Clearing-up
This is the last job of all that the Stage Management has to do, and it must be done well. It is a very good idea to organise helpers to clear up, otherwise everyone will rush off the moment the last curtain falls, leaving all the work to be done by one or two.

Any properties, costumes, wigs, equipment or scripts that have been hired must be checked and properly packed up before being sent back to the hire firms. All marks in hired scripts must first be rubbed out. Everything that has been borrowed must be promptly returned – with thanks. All the scenery must be stored away; cloths must be tightly rolled and secured. Costumes belonging to the company must be cleaned before they are packed away. Polythene bags are very useful for storing costumes. Props must be packed away in boxes or baskets. Write a list of contents and fix it to the top of the basket.

The Stage Management must make up an account of all they have spent, if this is necessary, and give it to whoever is responsible.

The Stage Management and the stage staff of a company should always aim at doing a thorough job, even under difficult conditions. There is no reason at all why their work should not be of the very highest standards.

When any part of their work is being decided it is best to aim for a simple solution that can be perfected – rather than a badly bodged elaboration.

New Directions

There are many books written on the subject of Stage Management for those who wish to pursue it further.

Stage Management. Hal. D. Stewart (Pitman)
Stage Management and Theatrecraft. H. Baker (Garnet Miller)

13 Organising the Performance

The Audience and the Play

Every detail of the production has been considered by the Director – nothing left to chance; now it is the turn of the audience, an indispensable part of every theatrical occasion. Audiences need a good deal more attention than they normally get. They should be welcomed in a natural, unembarrassing way. Serve food and drinks. Let musicians make music; the theatre should be an easy, relaxed and friendly place. All front of house arrangements should be modest, classless, unpanicky, efficient. There should not be queues of people in gangways or at the entrance. There should be someone unobstrusively in charge in case of difficulties. The play *must* start at the advertised time. The only way to build up good audiences is to choose good plays and give good performances in an attractive building. These do the work for you; but look after the audience that comes.

The Programme

Programmes might be free, good to look at, and well produced. Make them essentially informative; give details of the play, its author and his work, its date, its sources, perhaps also a note on the historical background, the characters and the music. Make it an *interesting* programme; a source-book of the play and the production rather than a list of actors and advertisements.

It is not always necessary to list the cast in order of appearance for a full list of all those who have contributed to the success of the play (including actors and stage assistants) can be given with the names in alphabetical order. The latter method has the advantage of anonymity – everyone works towards a single end, and every contribution, however small, is valuable. This helps to get away from the commercial star system which there is no need to introduce. No single contribution is all-important. Perhaps there is no need for names at all?

Take pains with the design or typographical layout of the programme and of all publicity. When the programme is typed on to stencils and then run off on a duplicating machine, the design is more limited than if it is printed. But in this case there is no reason why the outside cover should not be beautiful. The Roneo Company (17 Southampton Row, London WC1 with branches in all large provincial towns) makes stencils of photographs or engravings which can be used on the cover. Title pages of the early quartos or old engravings and photographs can be used to the greatest effect.

If you have your programmes and other publicity material printed, then control is more complicated. Most local printers (with exceptions) are incapable of designing good work. Search among acquaintances for a typographer or for someone who can sketch out the design (the Graphic Department at your local Art School). The printing can then be done by any small, local printer a good fortnight or three weeks in advance, but the proofs should not be passed for printing until the last possible moment in case of unexpected changes in the cast. The type should be left standing until the last performance in case a further supply of programmes is required. If there is an offset-litho press in your area you can design all the programmes direct, using an electric typewriter.

The design of publicity material and tickets is important, and once a suitable style has been established it is worth keeping to this for everything so that posters, showcards and programmes are instantly recognisable. The general standard is really very low and there is vast scope for improvement.

Ticket Sales

If the performance is free of charge, there is obviously no need to consider these problems, but most groups do charge not only to cover expenses but to build up a fund for expansion.

The Business (or Bookings) Manager should organise the sale of tickets very carefully. There should be a central box-office at a local shop and members of the society should also sell tickets. A receipt should be signed for each lot of tickets taken and there should be a definite date for return of unsold tickets.

A seating plan (for each night) should be kept, and marked up as each ticket is sold. Different markings can be entered for different types of sale (e.g. complimentary and half-price tickets etc.). It is often better to arrange the seating with two side gangways rather than one central one. If the tickets are numbered, the seats must also be numbered; tickets should indicate date, time and place of performance, price of seat etc. A constant check must be kept on ticket-sellers to make sure that they are actually selling tickets. If a member is unsuccessful his tickets should be recalled without delay and given to someone else. Ushers should be carefully instructed before the play regarding the seating plan, complimentary seats etc.

Publicity

The Business Manager (unless there is a Publicity Manager) must see that the society's activities are adequately advertised. Information about current productions should be given to the public by all possible means; personal contact is invaluable. Publicity should start about a month in advance of the first night and should build up during the following weeks.

There has been little research on the best possible means of advertising theatrical productions so no-one is really sure about the most effective methods, although the best recommendation are the societies' previous productions. The following sources of publicity are also important:

Newspaper advertisement.
Indoor advertisement – in shops, clubs, libraries etc. (hanging-cards).
Outdoor posters – bill-boards, shop-windows (shops do not take larger than crown). Building Societies etc. take window displays.
The Society's Mailing list.
Programme notes – mention in earlier programmes.
Car-stickers.
Cinema advertisement.
The local Press. Criticism, news-items, photographs.

A free mailing list service is of the greatest value as it keeps a potential audience regularly informed of future productions and can be used to keep the general public interested in the society's activities, aims and achievements. The local press should be invited to attend dress-rehearsals and may be ready to print items of interest about the society and its productions from time to time. Photographs of the production for the press are useful. Complimentary tickets should be sent out in good time.

Once the Play Has Begun

1. All refreshments should be served outside the auditorium (watch the noise of clinking cups etc. in intervals), preferably at the end of the performance.
2. A well-publicised system of bells or other signs should indicate the end of the interval, so that the audience can get back to their seats in time. Intervals should last exactly the advertised time. Does the play need an interval?
3. All front-of-house workers should remain quiet and attentive during the performance even if they have seen the play numerous times before.
4. Curtains if used should be pulled carefully and no light allowed to enter the auditorium. Extraneous sounds should also be carefully shielded. Are curtains essential?
5. Late-comers should either be shown to their seats put aside for them near the door, or if possible, should not be allowed to enter the auditorium until the end of the scene.
6. Fire regulations (e.g. use of exit signs) should be obeyed.

Performances

Although the Director leaves the running of the show in the hands of the Stage Manager, his responsibility does not end when the curtain rises on the first performance. He should take notes of anything that can be improved, and should call more rehearsals if required.

A group of actors has a responsibility to its audience; and its aim, rightly enough, is to please. But as John Allen writes: 'An audience has a strange way of developing its unspoken will. It sometimes happens that a certain performer becomes a favourite. He is the funny man, perhaps. The audience laughs and wants to laugh more. The player senses that he is a success and pulls faces a little bit funnier than he did at rehearsals. The audience laughs louder; the faces become exaggerated. Then something goes wrong. A performance that was rehearsed as a comedy has turned into a farce; or a play that was rehearsed as a drama has become melo-drama. The play has lost its style, its sincerity, almost its credibility. The player will justify himself by saying that the audience seemed to enjoy it and went home thoroughly entertained. But that is questionable. During the war I used to laugh loudly at the vulgar comedians in ENSA concert parties but underneath my laughter I loathed and despised the whole performance. Sometimes we feel that if the play had been a little less funny or dramatic, and a little more sincere, we would have enjoyed ourselves more.'

Yet everything we do in the theatre ultimately depends on the audience. In subtle ways the actors must be prepared to adapt their performance to the spirit of each audience – quickening a scene here, pausing for laughter there.

The most vigorous theatre has always drawn its strength from its ability to entertain and satisfy its audience, whether it was Greek Classical drama, Elizabethan plays or 19th-century Music Hall.

In this book, we have suggested that the amateur theatre can afford to experiment because it does not depend upon box-office returns. But this does not mean that it can afford to ignore its audience. The danger of amateurs relying less upon play scripts and more upon their own invention is that the resulting production will be a cosy narcissistic theatre of self-indulgence. The audience is in fact a necessary touchstone to the success of any group's work. Performing should be a humble activity which continually strives to make itself understood, and when it fails, asks why.

John Bowen makes this point in his introduction to the *Fall and Redemption of Man*, written for group work at an acting school:

'At a time when more and more attention is being given in schools to what is called "contact acting" – that is the necessary and important process of working with other actors, getting and giving to create some-thing shared, a situation or a scene, something which is worked out in action together – sometimes too little attention is given to another aspect of acting which is also necessary and important, and which is contact with the audience.'

This does not mean a constant and fearful backward glance at the supposed tastes of a mythical public. It means faith in one's own judge-ment, and a concern for what one is doing. Charles Chaplin once wrote:

'I prefer my own taste as a truer expression of what the public wants . . . I have heard directors, scenario writers and others argue under the shadow of this great fear of the public. . . . It is difficult to consider the public secondarily, but unless the person making the picture can achieve that state, there will be no originality in his work.'

Business and Legal Matters

Though dull and tiresome these have to be attended to. Failure to observe official regulations can result in serious difficulties, even though many school societies and amateur clubs break the law in some way or other. The following is a summary of official ruling.

Further particulars are available in:

The Law of the Amateur Stage. S. Page (Pitman)

Organising an Amateur Society. Mason & Gibson (Lovat Dickson)

A Handbook of the Amateur Theatre. P. Cotes (Oldbourne)

Show Business and the Law. E. R. Hardy Ivamy (Stevens)

The Business Side of the Amateur Theatre. A. Nelson-Smith (McDonald & Evans)

The Play and its Copyright. All modern plays are copyright. Copyright exists during the lifetime of any author and for fifty years after his death when it expires. If a play is performed posthumously, copyright exists for fifty years after the date of the first performance. Adaptations and translations may also be copyright. Permission in these cases must be sought from the author's agents or the owners of the copyright. This must be obtained before the play is put into rehearsal because it is not always given.

Licensing of Plays. New plays being performed for the first time in public are no longer required to be licenced by the Lord Chamberlain. The Theatre Act 1968 repeals the Theatres Act of 1843 and abolishes the power of the Lord Chamberlain to censor stage plays. It provides instead for it to be a criminal offence to present or direct an obscene performance in public or in private. Obscenity is defined in terms of the likelihood of the performance as a whole to deprave and corrupt persons who will be likely, having regard to all relevant circumstances, to attend it. It is obligatory for a copy of the script on which the public performance of any

new play is based to be delivered to the Trustees of the British Museum –
free of charge – within one month of the performance. It should be
addressed to Keeper of MSS., British Museum, Bloomsbury, London WC1.

Licence of Buildings. All buildings are required to be licensed for 'public
performance of stage plays'. It is a public performance if the work is
advertised and the public are invited whether there is any admission
charge or not. Most theatres hold a permanent licence which is renewed
annually. In this case a society need not, of course, obtain a licence but
where they are performing in a local hall, institute or school-hall they
should obtain a temporary licence covering the date of performance. Full
information can be obtained from the local County or Borough Council;
such licences cost only a few shillings, but it is absolutely essential that
they are obtained. Fire regulations are very stringent.

Acting Fees. An acting fee (or royalty) is charged for every performance of
a copyright play unless the society has received permission from the
author, or his agent, to perform the play privately. The usual fee for a
full-length play is four to five guineas for the first performance and four
guineas for a consecutive second performance in the same hall. Details of
the acting fee are usually quoted in the front of the acting copy, but if this
is not the case apply to the publishers.

For a private performance no acting fee is charged but it is *essential* to
obtain the consent of the author or his agent. There is no hard and fast
definition of what constitutes a private performance and every case has to
be judged individually. In general, however, the following are regarded as
private:

1. School and College performances, the audience consisting of the
   members of the school and staff together with a maximum of fifty
   relatives or friends. No money may be taken for admission or for the
   programmes.
2. Performances in hospitals or institutes to in-patients, old people and
   resident members of staff.

Licence to use gramophone records (see also page 273). All gramophone
records or tapes used before and during the performance and in the
intervals have to be licensed twice. The two licences should not be con-

fused for one. The Performing Right Society Licence acts on behalf of the composers of the music, while the other (Phonographic Performance Licence) is issued to the dramatic societies concerned and not as in the case of the Performing Right Society licences to the proprietors of the premises where the music is performed. Application should be made at least seven days before the date of the performance. The fees are small. You should apply to Phonographic Performance Ltd., Evelyn House, 62 Oxford Street, London W1.

Proprietors of public hall and theatres are licensed direct by the Performing Right Society and may already hold a comprehensive licence to cover the use of music during performances (see page 275).

Performance rights in musical works. Copyright music used before and during the performance and in the intervals should be licensed. See Chapter 9, Music and Sound.

Entertainments Tax. This does not affect amateur societies, though those who employ a professional conductor or musicians are liable to the tax. The following are exempted:

1. Completely amateur productions (plays and ballets) which are not conducted or established for profits, and when the aims, objects and activities of the society are partly educational.
2. On all entertainments of a wholly educational character or where the entertainment is provided by, or on behalf of, a school or educational establishment not conducted for profit and where all persons taking part are receiving, or have received, instruction in the school or institution.

In these cases (and some others) forms for exemption should be applied for at least fourteen days ahead of the first performance to The Secretary, HM Customs and Excise, King's Beam House, Mark Lane, London EC3.

In the case of application for the first time a copy of the Constitution, Rules and Aims of the Society must be included, together with a copy of the last financial statement (unless it is a new society). Full details of exemption are given in:

Amateur Drama. H. Conway (Hutchinson)
A Handbook of the Amateur Theatre. P. Cotes (Oldbourne)

Playreadings. These are legally on the same footing as performances, therefore the same conditions of copyright apply to them. Messrs. Samuel French however, the largest single publisher of plays, on representations made to them by the BDL, have agreed that for bona fide readings, where neither scenery, make-up, costumes nor properties are used, nor any action portrayed or suggested, and where the reading is made from the published copy, the fee shall be standardised at £1 1s. 0d. for full-length plays and 7s. 6d. for one-act plays. Further concessions are allowed (by Messrs. French) if the reading is undertaken by a society which is only open to members or their guests provided that no money be taken for admission and that the number present, exclusive of the cast of readers, does not exceed fifty persons. In this case the reading can be made without payment but in the event of a proposed reading you should apply to Messrs. Samuel French Ltd, 26 Southampton Street, London WC2, or to the League of Dramatists, 84 Drayton Gardens, London SW10. This arrangement only applies to Messrs. Samuel French Ltd.

Charity Performances. Even if you intend to give a performance in aid of charity the owner of the copyright will not normally consent to reduce, or waive claim, to the usual fee. Playwrights depend on these fees for their living and every performance reduces the potential audience, and therefore the earning capacity of the play.

Insurance. Insurance policies covering damage to borrowed or hired property, loss of expenditure due to abandonment or postponement of the production, or any injury to the cast or audience can be arranged for, on behalf of the society, through the British Drama League or the National Operatic and Dramatic Association. The theatres Mutual Insurance Co. Ltd, have designed an insurance policy for amateur societies affiliated to the British Drama League which covers all the points mentioned above. Full details can be obtained from Rex Thomas (Insurance) Ltd, Copthall House, Copthall Avenue, London EC2. All societies are *very strongly urged* to take out policies for a society may be called upon to bear expensive costs for any of the following:

1. Injury to a member of the public, or to his property or clothing, owing to negligence of the organisers of the performance (e.g. a spotlight falling).

2. Loss of, or damage to, scenery, wardrobe, borrowed furniture and props.
3. Accidents to employees due to the negligence of the society or its members.

Fire Protection. Fire safety regulations vary from County to County and can be obtained from the appropriate Local Authority or County Council. The booklet called *Manual of Safety Requirements in Theatres* issued by the Home Office and published by Her Majesty's Stationery Office, is indispensable and is the basis of most County fire regulations. The Greater London Council regulations are contained in *Places of Public Entertainment* (No. 3651).

If you are using a hired public hall, where the proprietors are responsible for ensuring that safety regulations are carried out, only the scenery draperies or props which you bring on to the stage, and all backstage and stage conditions must conform to safety regulations. A very useful booklet may be obtained from the Fire Protection Association, 84 Queen Street, London EC4. It is called *Fire Precautions in small Halls used for Entertainment Purposes.* Fire-proofing chemicals may be obtained from Brodie and Middleton, 79 Long Acre, London WC2.

If scenery is hired the scenic contractors will have made it fire-proof but if you make your own scenery – which is of course the general case – you must either use canvas which has been fire-proofed or deal with it yourself. All papier-mâché properties should similarly be treated. The following formulas are recommended for this purpose. For coarse fabrics, canvas etc. (one gallon of water to 10 oz. sodium phosphate and 15 oz. boracic acid). Either immerse the object or spray the solution on it. For more delicate fabrics (one gallon of water to 10 oz. borax and 8 oz. boracic acid).

However the most up-to-date fire-proofing liquids of all types, both for delicate fabrics and scenic and exhibition construction are now being produced by Albi-Willesden Ltd, South Victoria Road, London W8.

Theatre Administration. Elizabeth Sweeting (Pitman)

14 Where to look for help

INTRODUCTION

No amateur drama society needs to exist in a vacuum. Not only are there countless other people making drama of all kinds in Junior and Secondary schools, Colleges of Education, Technical Colleges, Drama Schools and Universities; but professional theatres and many individuals and organisations are willing to help and advise if only you know how to contact them. Most counties, for instance, have Drama advisers. The British Drama League is always ready to give assistance. The list that follows is provided so that you will know where to go for such help.

An amateur society's resources are necessarily limited to the talents and experience of those concerned. But organisation on a national scale ensures that many of these limitations can be overcome; equipment can be borrowed, advice sought, courses attended. A group that becomes interested in the idea of film-making can contact the British Film Institute, or their local Drama adviser; a club that intends to purchase lighting equipment might contact the British Drama League. There are many people anxious to help; contact them.

WHERE TO LOOK FOR HELP. Drama Advisers and County Drama Committees

Many Counties have a County Drama Adviser, who will give any advice you may need. A Drama Adviser has many valuable contacts and will know where to obtain almost anything you may want. A list of addresses of Drama Advisers and the officers of County Drama Committees is listed below:

England
Berkshire   Sec.   W. G. A. Brind, Shire Hall, Reading.

	Adviser:	P. Edmunds, Education Offices, Shire Hall, Reading.
Buckinghamshire	Adviser:	A. W. Garrard, County Offices, Aylesbury.
Cambridgeshire and Isle of Ely, Huntingdonshire Peterborough	Sec. Adviser:	M. G. Martingale, 7 Hills Road, Cambridge. F. E. Bacon, Education Offices, Shire Hall, Cambridge.
Cheshire	Sec.:	Miss S. R. Chaplin, 53 Watergate Row South, Chester.
	Adviser:	R. Crawford, 53 Watergate Row South, Chester.
Cornwall	Sec.:	Miss G. A. Lewis, Drama Dept., County Hall, Truro.
	Adviser:	R. Moss, County Hall, Truro.
Cumberland	Sec. and Adviser:	M. G. Payn, 5 Portland Square, Carlisle.
Derbyshire	Sec.:	J. L. Longland, County Offices, Matlock.
	Adviser:	P. Cox, County Offices, Matlock.
Devon	Adviser:	J. Butt, Education Dept., County Hall, Exeter.
Durham	Advisers:	D. Harris, County Hall, Durham. R. C. Hill, County Hall, Durham. D. A. Griffiths, N. Central Division, Education Office, 8 Red Rose Terrace, Chester-le-Street, County Durham.
Essex	Sec.:	Mrs L. Perschky, 8 Beatrice Road, London E11.
	Adviser:	J. Mitchley, 162 Orchard Croft, Mark Hall, Harlow.
Gloucester	Sec.:	Miss F. I. M. Walker, Community House, Gloucester.
	Adviser:	Mrs E. Jupp, Shire Hall, Gloucester.
	Organiser:	C. J. Barker, Community House, Gloucester.
Hampshire	Sec. and Adviser:	Ronald James, The Education Office, The Castle, Winchester.

Herefordshire	Sec.:	Martin's Bank House, 21 Broad Street, Hereford.
Hertfordshire		M. J. Pugh, 113 Wate Road, Hertford.
Holland	Sec.:	Mrs E. Allen, Swineshead, Nr. Boston, Lincs.
Kent	Sec.:	D. G. Prince, Kent Council of Social Service 1 Holmesdale Terrace, Folkestone.
	Adviser:	Miss A. Allchin, County Education Offices, Springfield, Maidstone.
Kesteven	Adviser:	Mrs M. I. Birkett, Westholme, Leicester Street, Westgate, Sleaford, Lincs.
Lancashire	Sec.:	D. Durkley, Selnec House, Wynnstay Grove, Manchester 14
	Adviser:	A. Willett Whittaker, County Hall, Preston.
Leicestershire	Sec.:	S. C. Mason, County Offices, Grey Friars, Leicester.
	Adviser:	P. MacDonnell, County Offices, Grey Friars, Leicester.
Lindsey	Sec.:	G. V. Cooke, County Offices, Lincoln.
	Adviser:	G. Mostyn Lewis, County Offices, Lincoln.
Newham	Sec.:	H. C. B. Rye, Education Offices, Broadway, Stratford, E15.
	Adviser:	T. Jones, Education Offices, Stratford, E15.
Norfolk	Sec.:	C. J. Harper, Education Offices, Stracey Road, Norwich.
	Adviser:	H. L. Mitchell, Education Offices, Norwich.
	Asst. Adviser:	Mrs. S. Doggett.
Northamptonshire	Adviser:	G. J. Gordon, County Hall, Northampton.
Northumberland	Adviser:	S. Harvey, County Hall, Newcastle-on-Tyne.

Nottingham and Nottinghamshire	Sec.:	A. Hunter, 88 Main Road, Burton Joyce, Nottington.
	Adviser:	E. D. Shaw, Education Offices, County Hall, Trent Bridge, Nottingham.
Oxfordshire R.C.C.	Sec.:	L. Wood, 20 Beaumont Street, Oxford.
	Adviser:	G. A. Butterfield, 20 Beaumont Street, Oxford.
Shropshire	Sec.:	G. Raxster, Balihi, Duke Street, St Georges, Oakengates.
	Adviser:	H. T. Amies, Education Offices, County Buildings, Shrewsbury.
Somerset R.C.C.	Sec.:	F. A. Goodliffe, St. Margaret's, Hamilton Road, Taunton.
	Advisers:	Miss R. Ewing, St Margaret's, Hamilton Road, Taunton (Adults)
		Mrs S. Doggett, Education Department, County Hall, Taunton, Somerset (Schools and youth).
Suffolk (West)	Sec.:	B. J. Reid, County Hall, Ipswich.
	Adviser:	Mrs O. Ironside Wood, Clopton Hall, Rattlesden, Bury St Edmunds.
Suffolk (East)	Sec.:	Education Offices, Rope Walk, Ipswich.
	Adviser:	Mrs R. Winter, Education Offices, Rope Walk, Ipswich.
Sussex (East)	Adviser:	J. Nicolson, Barons Down, Brighton Road, Lewes.
	Asst. Adviser:	G. Mealia.
Sussex (West)	Adviser:	George Rawlins, County Hall, Chichester, Sussex.
Warwickshire	Sec.:	Mrs P. D. Cross, 82 Widney Road, Knowle, Solihull.
Westmorland	Sec.:	Mrs W. Mansfield, Mountquharrie, Skelsmergh, Kendal.

Wiltshire	Sec.:	Mrs M. M. Thomas, 93 Frome Road, Trowbridge.
	Adviser:	N. Seiler, 93 Frome Road, Trowbridge.
Yorkshire	Sec.:	G. G. Robinson, Yorks. R. Com. Council, Purey Cust Chambers, York.
	Adviser:	G. Tyler, Education Offices, Bond Street, Wakefield.

Wales

Anglesey	Sec.:	J. D. Williams, 27 High Street, Llangefni.
Brecon	Sec.:	Chief Education Officer, County Offices, Brecon.
	Adviser:	B. Jenkins, 4 Glamorgan Street, Brecon.
Caernarvonshire	Sec.:	A. Jones, 2 Slate Quay, Caernarvon.
Cardiganshire	Sec.:	D. M. Jones, 26 Alban Square, Aberaeron.
	Adviser:	G. Hughes Jones, Co. Education Offices, Swyddfa'r, Aberystwyth.
Carmarthenshire	Sec.:	S. J. E. Samuel, 16a Guildhall Square, Carmarthen.
Denbighshire	Sec.:	G. T. Hughes, 5 Upper Clwyd Street, Ruthin.
Flintshire	Sec.:	G. E. Rowson, 'Solva', Gwernaffield Road, Mold.
Glamorgan	Sec.:	E. L. Williams, 12 Cledwyn Terrace, Aberdare.
	Adviser:	E. Ellis, 32 Garnlwyd Road, Morriston, Swansea.
Merionethshire	Sec.:	J. R. Roberts, Midland Bank Chambers, Dolgellau, Merioneth.
Monmouthshire	Sec.:	D. L. Jones, 8 Pentonville, Newport.
	Adviser:	Melvelle Thomas, County Hall, Newport.
Montgomeryshire	Sec.:	Community House, Newtown, Mont.
Pembrokeshire	Sec.:	D. Miles, 4 Victoria Place, Haverfordwest.

335

Scotland
S.C.D.A. Advisers

National	W. March, 19 Melville Street, Edinburgh 3.
E. Area	B. Onwin, Nesbit Farm Cottages, Pencaitland, East Lothian.
W. Area	E. Horton, 78 Queen Street, Edinburgh.
Highland Area	A. Nelson, 156 Culduthel Road, Inverness.

Other Drama Advisers

Birmingham	P. Slade, Education Department, 154 Gt. Charles Street, Birmingham 3.
Burton-on-Trent	R. H. Whetton, Municipal School of Speech and Drama, Guild Street, Burton-on-Trent.
Cardiff	M. Colborn, Education Offices, Magnet House, Kingsway, Cardiff.
Coventry	R. Prior-Pitt, The Cathedral, Coventry.
Gateshead	Miss J. Wright, Education Offices, Prince Consort Road, Gateshead 8.
Havering	H. Lovegrove, Education Offices, Upminster Court, 133 Hall Lane, Upminster.
London	G. Hodson, Inner London Education Authority, Room 274a, County Hall, London SE1.
Rochdale	D. Morton, Education Offices, Fleece Street, Rochdale.

OTHER USEFUL ADDRESSES OF THEATRE ORGANISATIONS

Standing Conference of Drama Association, 26 Bedford Square, London W.C.1

This body represents all County Drama Committees and other national organisations, runs advisory services, conferences and courses. Very helpful.

The British Drama League, 9 Fitzroy Square, London W.1

The British Drama League is an association of those connected with the theatre, both professional and amateur alike, who desire to support it in any way they can. The League has been active in campaigning for matters of national importance to the theatre, is in the forefront of new ideas and is particularly concerned to protect the interests of its members. It possesses a first-rate library including more than 5,000 sets of plays and a large collection of play programmes, press cuttings and costume designs. It organises many different types of courses annually; there is a full-time course for producers and instructors in amateur drama; there are summer schools in August and September; and weekend courses in London. There are also courses for playwrights and an Annual Conference and Theatre Week in London. The League also publishes a number of dialect records (both British and American). Membership is £2 2s. od. whether for an individual or an organisation and life membership is £12 12s. od. *Drama*, published quarterly by the British Drama League, is sent to all members. The Junior Drama League for young people holds classes during school holidays, and there is a junior summer school annually. There is also a children's branch of the main library. Junior membership is 10s. od.

The Scottish Community Drama Association, 78 Queen Street, Edinburgh 3
This is an organisation in Scotland very similar to the British Drama League.

Drama Association of Wales, 2 Cathedral Road, Cardiff
This is a newly-formed society for amateur drama in Wales. It organises playwriting competitions and a festival of one-act plays. There is a useful library service.

Amateur Drama Council of Ireland, 34 Beech Park, Athlone

The Guild of Drama Adjudicators, 26 Bedford Square, London W.C.1
The Guild supplies qualified adjudicators to any organisation seeking to promote amateur drama.

The National Operatic and Dramatic Association (NODA), 1 Crestfield Street, London W.C.1
This organisation issues a bulletin to members three times a year containing reports on new productions, articles on the amateur theatre etc. There is also a Year Book which gives useful information and guidance on all aspects of amateur theatre; advice on legal matters, special insurance facilities etc. The NODA library has a fine collection of vocal scores, libretti, reference books, periodicals which are available

to members on loan. An Operatic Summer School is held each August, and there is also an Annual Conference held at a different centre each year. NODA gives advice on scores, programme blocks, theatrical make-up, perruquiers, stage properties, sound effects etc. NODA can either supply such wants or give advice where to get whatever is needed.

The Drama Board, 106 Gloucester Place, London W.1

Federation of Repertory Playgoers Societies, Public Library, North Street, Guildford, Surrey

International Amateur Theatre Association, W. E. Lucas, British Drama League, 9 Fitzroy Square, London W.1

Little Theatre Guild of Great Britain, Caxton Players, 120 Cleethorpes Road, Grimsby, Lincs.

London Schools' Drama Association, Mrs R. Conroy, 152 Hamilton Road, London S.E.24

National Association of Drama Advisers, Mrs S. Doggett, Education Department, County Hall, Taunton, Somerset

National Drama Festivals Association, J. Baker, 3 Laird Drive, Sheffield 6

Theatres National Committee, 19 Charing Cross Road, London W.C2

The Educational Drama Association (incorporating The Children's Theatre Players). Headquarters: Nansen Primary School, Birmingham 20
  The Association seeks to promote and carry out the methods and principles of Child Drama as described by its Director, Peter Slade, in his book *Child Drama*. These are mainly but by no means entirely concerned with Drama in Education, and an annual summer school gives training and practice in the work. In addition the Association's lecturers visit Colleges of Education and other groups to conduct one day schools in drama, and from time to time short courses are held at the Birmingham Drama Centre.

There are also a Children's Theatre Group which prepares, for Junior Children, plays based upon improvisation, and an Adult Intimate Theatre Group whose productions are of an experimental nature.

The Association publishes a magazine *Creative Drama* twice annually and its pamphlets include one on *Stage Lighting for Schools and Youth Clubs*.

The British Children's Theatre Association

Headquarters: G. Tyler, Education Office, Bond Street, Wakefield, Yorkshire

The Association, which was formed in 1959, aims to further education for children through drama and to encourage the appreciation of dramatic art in schools, colleges, universities and Theatre Companies. It publishes an excellent bibliography of plays recommended for performance to child audiences, a *Directory of British Children's Theatres*, a Newsletter and it reports and runs various conferences. It is in the forefront of the increasing activity of Theatre for Children and Youth.

The Religious Drama Society of Great Britain, Bell House, Bishops Hall, Ayres Street, London S.E.1

The society was formed in 1929 to promote religious drama, and there is today a world membership of professionals and amateurs. The library will send copies by post to members, and the librarian will readily give advice and help. It contains a large collection of plays and books on drama. Single copies or sets can be borrowed. Besides the organisation of summer schools the society runs the Sesame scheme which brings drama to the handicapped in homes and hospitals.

'Sesame' also acts as agent for the PUMA group of young Cambridge graduates which, together with visiting members of the professional theatre, gives entertainment to the handicapped.

OTHER ADDRESSES

The National Union of Townswomen's Guilds, 2 Cromwell Place, London S.W.7

This organisation encourages dramatic work very actively among its members. A National Drama Conference is held annually; an information leaflet on drama is published containing much useful information on production, festivals, other activities, books, etc. The magazine *The Townswoman* includes regular monthly Drama Notes. The Union has its own Drama Adviser who can visit member federations to help get drama going or give other help.

The National Federation of Women's Institutes, 39 Eccleston Street, Victoria, London S.W.1

Tuition in drama is provided through residential courses at Denham College; some of these are open to members in general, others are solely for students recommended by County Federations. County Federations also arrange tuition, either independently or through the LEA's. WI groups and clubs especially for drama have been set up in a few counties.

Drama Festivals are organised by counties, sometimes annually, sometimes bi-annually.

Recently the NFWI has established a Drama Producer's Training Scheme, to enable members to achieve higher dramatic standards. The courses last for up to ten weeks, with usually one session a week. This scheme has already been taken up by some twenty counties. The NFWI offers assessors for examination on application from County Federations; a certificate for proficiency is available and the first test was held in May 1966.

Arts Council of Great Britain, 105 Piccadilly, London W.1
Arts Council of Northern Ireland, 1 Joy Street, Belfast 2
British Actors' Equity Association, 8 Harley Street, London W.1
Centre 42 Limited, The Round House, Chalk Farm Road, London N.W.1
Educational Puppetry Association, 23 Southampton Place, London W.C.1
National Association of Boys' Clubs, 17 Bedford Square, London W.C.1
National Association of Girls' and Mixed Clubs, 32 Devonshire Street, London W.1
YMCA and YWCA, Great Russell Street, London W.C.1

JOURNALS, MAGAZINES, BOOKS
Drama. The British Drama League's Journal, published quarterly. There are articles on recent productions, details of forthcoming courses, reviews of recent books and a great deal of useful information. 2s. but free to members.

Plays and Players, incorporating *Theatre World* and *Encore*, 16 Buckingham Palace Road, London SW1

Published monthly at 5s. od. this interesting journal contains reviews, articles and comment on current theatre as well as complete texts of plays in production. Early copies of *Encore* (now incorporated in *Plays and Players*) become harder and harder to obtain, but contain amongst the best theatre comment of their period.

The Stage, 19–21 Tavistock Street, London WC2 – published weekly at 10d. This professional theatre newspaper contains very useful information and articles.

Amateur Stage, Stacey Publications, 11 Hawthorndene Road, Hayes, Bromley, Kent

Published monthly at 2s. 6d. Articles on every aspect of the amateur theatre.

Flourish, Royal Shakespeare Club, Aldwych, London WC2

This occasional newspaper contains very lively articles on plays, productions, actors, writers, associated with RSC.

New Theatre Magazine, 99 Woodland Road, Bristol 8

Published by the Drama Department in the University of Bristol, it comes out three times a year at 5s. od. Articles on new movements and current work in the University theatres of Great Britain.

Creative Drama, Westminster Road School, Birmingham

Published twice annually by the Educational Drama Association at 2s. 6d.

Broadsheet, 135 Cricklade Avenue, London SE2

Published by The London Schools Drama Association, *Broadsheet* costs 2s. od.

Tabs, 29 King Street, London WC2. Published three times a year by the Strand Electric and Engineering Company, this magazine is free. It contains a great deal of information on new theatres, lighting etc. Very valuable.

NODA Bulletin, 1 Crestfield Street, London WC1. Published by the National Operatic and Dramatic Association three times a year, 10s. 6d. annually, but free to members.

SCDA Bulletin, 78 Queen Street, Edinburgh 2. Published by The Scottish Community Drama Association every February and September, 1s. od.

World Theatre, 10 Earlham Street, London WC2. Published by the International Theatre Institute this magazine, published quarterly at 8s. 0d., contains articles on the International Theatre scene.

The Drama Review. American quarterly obtainable through Calder and Boyars, 18 Brewer Street, London W1 at £2 10s. 0d. a year. Individual copies 15s. 0d. Special issues are frequently devoted to the work of an author or an aspect of theatre, e.g. Spring '61, theatre of Sartre, Autumn '61, Brecht; Winter '61, modern theatre in Sweden.

Gambit. Calder and Boyars also publish a quarterly theatrical review which contains the text of at least one full-length play as well as articles. Subscription £1 17s. 6d.

OTHER REFERENCE BOOKS AND PUBLICATIONS

Contacts, 43 Cranbourn Street, London WC2 (May and November), 3s. per copy post free.

Spotlight Casting Directory, 43 Cranbourn Street, London WC2 (February and August), £4 0s. 0d. per annum.

Stage Year Book, 19 Tavistock Street, London WC2. Published annually, 31s.

Theatre Notebook, 22 Buckingham Gate, SW1. Published quarterly, 20s. per annum.

REFERENCE BOOKS

Theatre, a Readers Guide. David Cheshire (Clive Bingley)
David Cheshire's guide includes a vast number of books on every aspect of the theatre. It includes significant comments on all the works that are mentioned which include encyclopaedias, dictionaries, catalogues, histories, biographies and autobiographies as well as current periodicals. Most valuable chapter on books on theory.

The Oxford Companion to the Theatre, 3rd edn. Ed. Phyllis Hartnoll (O.U.P.)
The only one-volume encyclopaedia of world theatre. An indispensable reference work.

The Penguin Dictionary of the Theatre. John Russell Taylor (Penguin)
An indispensable guide; containing brief but detailed information about plays, players, playwrights, dramatic theory, stage history etc.

The Development of the Theatre. Allardyce Nicoll (Harrap)
The best general history. Well illustrated.

World Theatre. Bamber Gascoigne (Ebury Press)
   A superbly illustrated history of the theatre which gives life to the theatrical performances of different times through the drawings, paintings and engravings of those times. Every possible kind of stage, performance and drama discussed.

LIBRARIES

Certain libraries hold interesting collections of dramatic material. From time to time they put on exhibitions which are useful. For example the Birmingham Public Libraries have a collection of materials on many varied types of Shakespeare productions including school performances. Birmingham also puts on exhibitions of current Shakespeare productions in its Shakespeare Memorial Library.

If your own library has no such facilities, then at least approach the librarian, you might be able to arrange something together with your group. The work itself would make an interesting project for a group to undertake.

WHERE TO LOOK FOR PLAYS

The British Drama League, 9 Fitzroy Square, London W I
   The Players Library and bibliography of the theatre. This is the BDL Library catalogue published by Faber and Faber. There are Supplements:

   No. 1 – 1951
   No. 2 – 1954
   No. 3 – 1956

   These contain a complete list of plays and books on the theatre, and are by far the best list of plays easily obtainable.
English Theatre Guild Ltd, Ascot House, 52 Dean Street, London W I
   They have a large selection of one-act plays and a free list will be sent on request. Full-length plays are also published. Copies of any play will be sent on approval. Complete details and synopses are published in their catalogue (1s. 0d. post free). In addition the Guild handles a number of American plays for the Dramatists Play Service of New York. Details on application.

H. F. W. Deane & Sons Ltd, 31 Museum Street, London WC1
   They publish a large collection of plays. Details and synopses are given in *Plays and their Plots* and supplements to this list are available free. Many full-length and one-act, all-women's plays are published.

Evans Plays, Montague House, Russell Square, London WC1
   This publisher has catalogues of full-length and one-act plays, both available for 6d. from the above address. Single reading copies can be hired on loan 1s. od. each title. Another catalogue, *New Plays Quarterly*, finished publication in 1965.

Samuel French Ltd, 26 Southampton Street, Strand, London WC2
   The *Guide to Selected Plays* is published free and is available in the following parts:

1. *Full-length Plays for mixed casts*
2. *One-act Plays for mixed casts*
3. *Plays for Women*
4. *Plays for Men*
5. *Plays for Children*
6. *Seasonal Plays*
7. *Revue Sketches*
8. *Books on Acting and the Theatre*
9. *Musical Plays*

   The Supplement to these, *Play Parade*, contains details of the very latest publications.

Heinemann Plays, Educational Books Ltd, 48 Charles Street, London W1
   Quite a number of interesting plays are published in their Drama Library, and their school edition, the *Hereford Plays*. Write for a catalogue.

International One-act Play Theatre, 254 Alexandra Park Road, London N22
   This organisation supplies one-act plays in script. Also supplying duplicated scripts of unpublished plays are:

Leonards Plays, 123 Heythorp Street, Southfields, London SW18

J. Garnet Miller Ltd, 13 Tottenham Street, London W1. Also publish useful catalogues of plays, including plays with all-women casts.

Books and Materials for School and Youth Drama by Joan M. Collins. Theatre in Education Series. Dobson.

This is a very useful collection of lists and addresses but it was published some time ago and needs bringing up to date.

National Book League List 31, Community Drama. Now out of print.
The League Book Information Bureau will, on request, furnish a short list of recent books on drama. Address: 7 Albemarle Street, London w 1

Stacey Publications, 1 Hawthorndene Road, Hayes, Bromley, Kent
Publish theatre booklets, the *Bibliography of Plays for Child Audiences,* also lists of all plays published each year with reviews.

The National Association of Boys' Clubs, 17 Bedford Square, London w c 1
Print their own suggestions.

Plays for Women. Note above:
Deane's *Guide to Selecting Plays* Part III.
J. Garnet Miller publish a similar catalogue listing all-women plays. Also worth consulting:

New Plays Annual for Women (5s. 6d. post free) from Hugh Quekett Ltd, 35 Dover Street, London w 1. This contains several new all-women plays, practical articles and a detailed record of all-women plays issued in the previous year. Write for the half-yearly supplement of plays regularly reviewed in *The Townswoman* to the National Union of Townswomen's Guilds, 2 Cromwell Place, London s w 7

Also write to the National Federation of Women's Institutes, 39 Eccleston Square, London s w 1 for their lists and:

The Girls' Friendly Society, Townsend House, Grey ,at Place, London s w 1

WHERE TO BORROW BOOKS
(a) Local public libraries and County libraries.
(b) A local branch of the Little Theatre Guild.
(c) For those in Scotland: The Scottish Community Drama Association, 19 Melville Street, Edinburgh. This has a lending library and arranges festivals. Club membership is £1 1s. od., individual membership 7s. 6d., and youth club membership 5s. od. per annum.
(d) The British Drama League Library, 9 Fitzroy Square, London w 1. The London library is open from 10.00 a.m. to 5.00 p.m. daily. Wednesdays from 10.00 a.m. to 9.00 p.m. and on Saturdays from 10 a.m. to 12.30 p.m. Sets of books can be borrowed by post. The

Reference Library contains rare books and houses the collections of William Archer, Granville-Barker, Gordon Craig, Nigel Playfair, and Miss A. E. Horniman. Altogether there are over 100,000 volumes of plays and books on drama. The Library is a source of information and should be consulted whenever in need.

(e) Direct from the Publishers, or where unpublished from the Authors' Agents.

PLAY PUBLISHERS

Among publishers specialising in acting editions are:

Allen, 43 Essex Street, London wc2.

Allen and Unwin, 40 Museum Street, London wc1.

Anchor, Trans-Atlantic Book Service, Norfolk House, 28 Norfolk Street, London wc2.

Arnold, 41 Maddox Street, London w1.

Bantam Books, Bashley Road, London nw10.

b.b.c. Publications, p.o. Box 1ar, London w1.

Benn, Bouverie House, Fleet Street, London ec4.

Black, 4–6 Soho Square, London w1.

Bodley Head, 9 Bow Street, London wc2.

Calder and Boyars, 18 Brewer Street, London w1.

Campton, 38 Liberty Road, Glenfield, Leicester.

Cambridge University Press, 200 Euston Road, London nw1.

Cape, 30 Bedford Square, London wc1.

Cassell, 35 Red Lion Square, London wc1.

Chatto and Windus, 40–42 William iv Street, London wc2.

Children's Theatre, Mrs E. Tyler, The Oaks, Huddersfield Road, Brighouse, Yorks.

Combridge, 80 Wrentham Street, Birmingham.

Constable, 10 Orange Street, London wc2.

Curwen, 29 Maiden Lane, London wc2.

Deane, 31 Museum Street, London wc1.

Dent, Aldine House, 10–13 Bedford Street, London wc2.

de Wolfe, 18–20 York Buildings, London wc2.

Dobson, 80 Kensington Church Street, London w8.

Dover Publications (British Agents are Constable)

Duckworth, 3 Henrietta Street, London wc2.

Dutton (New York), Trans-Atlantic Book Service, Norfolk House, 28 Norfolk Street, London WC2.

Elek Books, 2 All Saints Street, London N1.

English Theatre Guild, 52 Dean Street, London W1.

Epworth Press, 25–35 City Road, London EC1.

Evans, Montague House, Russell Square, London WC1.

Faber and Faber, 24 Russell Square, London WC1.

Fortune Press, 15 Belgrave Road, London SW1.

French, 26 Southampton Street, London WC2.

French Inc., 25 West 45th Street, New York 19.

Gollancz, 14 Henrietta Street, London WC2.

Hamilton, 90 Great Russell Street, London WC1.

Harrap, 182 High Holborn, London WC1.

Hart-Davis, 3 Upper James Street, London W1.

Heinemann, 48 Charles Street, London W1.

H.M.S.O., 49 High Holborn, London WC1.

Hutchinson, 178–202 Great Portland Street, London W1.

Indiana University Press: American Univ. Publishers Group Ltd, 27–29 Whitfield Street, London W1.

International One-act Play Theatre, 254 Alexandra Park Road, London N22.

John Lane, The Bodley Head, 10 Earlham Street, London WC2.

League of Dramatists, 84 Drayton Gardens, London SW10.

Leeds University Press, The University, Leeds 2, Yorks.

Lewis, 16 Mythop Road, Marton, Blackpool, Lancs.

Littler Musical Plays, Palace Theatre, Shaftesbury Avenue, London W1.

Longmans, Green, 48 Grosvenor Street, London W1.

MacGibbon and Kee, 3 Upper James Street, Golden Square, London W1.

Macmillan, 4 Little Essex Street, London WC2.

Manchester University Press, 316–324 Oxford Road, Manchester 13.

Methuen, 11 New Fetter Lane, London EC4.

Miller, 13 Tottenham Street, London W1.

Minnesota University Press (British Agents are O.U.P.)

Murray, 50 Albemarle Street, London W1.

Nelson, 36 Park Street, London W1.

Oxford University Press, 37 Dover Street, London W1.

Pan Books, 33 Tothill Street, London SW1.

Penguin Books, Bath Road, Harmondsworth, Middlesex.

Pitman, 39 Parker Street, London WC2.

Princeton University Press (Oxford University Press are British agents)

Putnam, 42 Great Russell Street, London WC1.

Quekett, The Broadway, London W6.

Random House, 457 Madison Avenue, New York 22, New York.

Religious Drama Society, 166 Shaftesbury Avenue, London WC2.

Scribeners, Trans-Atlantic Book Service, Norfolk House, 28 Norfolk Street, London WC2.

Secker and Warburg, 14 Carlisle Street, London W1.

Sheed and Ward, 33 Maiden Lane, London WC2.

Sidgwick and Jackson, 1 Tavistock Chambers, Bloomsbury Way, London WC1.

S.P.C.K., Holy Trinity Church, Marylebone Road, London NW1.

Stacey Publications, 1 Hawthorndene Road, Hayes, Bromley, Kent.

University of London Press, 8 Warwick Lane, London EC4.

Yale University Press, 70 Great Russell Street, London WC1.

Agents

Actac, 16 Cadogan Lane, London SW1.

Associated Plays and Players, Suite 4, 41 Charing Cross Road, London WC2.

Benson and Campbell Thomson, Clifford's Inn, Fleet Street, London EC4.

Clowes, 20 New Cavendish Street, London W1.

Colin, 4 Hereford Square, London SW7.

Curtis Brown, 13 King Street, London WC2.

Glass, 28 Berkeley Square, London W1.

Goodwin Associates, 79 Cromwell Road, London SW7.

Hope, Leresche and Steele, 11 Jubilee Place, London SW3.

Massie, 18 Southampton Place, London WC1.

International Copyright Bureau, 26 Charing Cross Road, London WC2.

League of Dramatists, 84 Drayton Gardens, London SW10.

London Management, 235 Regent Street, London W1.

London Play, 113 Wardour Street, London W1.

M.C.A. (England), 139 Piccadilly, London W1.

N.O.D.A., 1 Crestfield Street, London WC1.

Peters, 10 Buckingham Street, London WC2.

Ramsay, 14a Goodwin's Court, London WC2.

Unna, 14 Beaumont Mews, Marylebone High Street, London W1.

Vosper, 53a Shaftesbury Avenue, London W1.

Watt, 26 Bedford Row, London WC1.

Woodward, 8 Charing Cross Road, London WC2.

THEATRE FOR YOUTH
The National Youth Theatre
Headquarters at 81 Eccleston Square, London SW1, where there is a club-room, also a reading-room and canteen. Youth Theatre is a recognised part of the Youth Service. Its President is Sir Ralph Richardson and its Director Michael Croft. Each year it brings together several hundred young people selected through area auditions to work together during the summer holidays on a major (usually Shakespearean) production, and other productions as well. These have included two new plays by Peter Terson, *Zigger-Zagger* and *The Apprentices*. The main purpose of the National Youth Theatre (or NYT) is to encourage young people to appreciate the arts of the theatre, whether as audience or as participants. Its productions and courses offer its members an exceptional insight into the practical workings of the theatre and it encourages them to respect the basic skills and disciplines of the theatre. It expects them to reach high standards, while gaining a valuable experience of working together in community, and it also helps them to develop a sense of responsibility through their work in the various departments of production.

It does not encourage young people to become professional actors unless they show outstanding promise, but it is able to advise and assist those who do at the start of their careers.

Youth Centres and Theatres in the Provinces
Besides the National Youth Theatre there are approximately 160 youth drama groups undertaking a wide range of activities. Some are attached to repertories as at Nottingham, Coventry, Bolton, Barrow-in-Furness, Sheffield, Exeter, Salisbury etc. Others are part of the local Youth Service, e.g. a number of flourishing groups in Bristol, Gloucestershire, Northumberland etc. A further number come under the wing of a local Education Authority such as the Theatre Workshop at Crediton in Devon. And at least one amateur drama group, the Questors, is concerned with young people; they have eight active training groups serving the under fourteens and up to those aged twenty four or five. These are mainly self-supporting, some groups concentrating on improvisation and studio work, while others are mounting finished productions. To find out more about a

particular area apply to the LEA Drama Adviser or Youth Organiser (see list on pages 331–6).

Of the many exciting Theatre Workshops and Groups now working in the field of youth drama it is possible to mention only a few. Of particular interest are the activities of the Rochdale Youth Workshop (which has produced three young writers, one of whom is now Resident Writer at the Everyman Theatre, Liverpool); Silas Harvey's chain of Theatre Workshops in Northumberland; the work of both Inter-Action (see plate 7) and the Midlands Art Centre for Young People at Cannon Hill Park, Birmingham 12.

The various activities of Inter-Action (156 Malden Road, London NW5) are all concerned with making the arts, particularly drama, more relevant to the community. The Dogg's Troupe, a group who run most of Inter-Action's activities, including street-theatre, drama with and for young people and various workshop activities, is open to new members.

The Midlands Arts Centre at Cannon Hill, Birmingham, has been designed as a place where young people can get to know the arts through personal exploration (there are numerous workshops) and the opportunity of watching performances. Full details are available.

Courses for Young People

The British Drama League provides courses for young people and local education authorities run weekend courses on drama, scene design, etc., and these are usually open to older pupils.

In addition there are a number of short courses and weekend schools organised from time to time by other organisations, particularly by County Drama Associations and Advisers.

Courses and Summer Schools
The British Drama League, 9 Fitzroy Square, London W1

Adult courses for Actors and Producers are held annually in August. The Actors' Section includes classes in characterisation, speech, movement, improvisation, make-up and rehearsal practice. The Producers' Section includes lectures in production, interpretation and technique, improvisation, technical work in stage management and lighting, costume and scenic design.

There is also a Junior Summer School held annually. The programme consists usually of work in groups on different types of scenes, with plenty of opportunity for learning about lighting, stage-management etc. Short courses for Young People are held in London at Christmas and Easter. A series of talks for Young People is held each year in conjunction with the Christmas course.

The Religious Drama Society, Bell House, Snow Hill, London EC1

A summer course in Christian Drama is held annually for a week. Work centres around daily worship; there is coaching in acting, production, music, movement, stage-management, costume, décor. The course is open to anyone of whatever nationality or religious affiliation whether an RDS member or not.

NODA – The National Operatic and Dramatic Association

An operatic summer school is held annually in August.

The Educational Drama Association

Runs an annual summer course giving practice and training in child drama.

The National Federation of Women's Institutes

Residential courses are held at Denham College. Several County Federations organise courses either on their own or in conjunction with the local Education Authority. A drama producers' training scheme has recently been established, while numerous summer schools are organised annually up and down the country. For details consult such magazines as *Drama*, *Plays and Players*, etc.

Appendix

The following account by John Fox traces the development of his thinking and experiments to create a new kind of theatre outside the conventional dramatic forms which he believes have become jaded and outmoded in our present society. We include this not because we want to suggest that amateur groups should necessarily develop in this sort of way but because we believe that it is an interesting demonstration of how one person has attempted to solve certain fundamental questions which are relevant to the amateur theatre. We hope that it will stimulate others into questioning their own values and methods.

In June, 1965 in the tiny moorland village of Hawnby in North Yorkshire we produced an entertainment. It was a mixture of play reading, poetry reading, folk singing, beat and brass band music, organised because we were bored and nothing happened in this remote village, which was even without a bus service. We distributed 3,000 leaflets inviting anyone who could 'sing, shout or play a musical instrument', to come and join in. 300 people turned up. Said the *Northern Echo*, 'When two young people announced their plans for a one-day festival which would include national poets and playwrights like Jon Silkin and John Arden, along with entertainment by village bands and singers, the cynics gloomily prophesied that "art" and "plain folk" would never mix, that hill farmers would have nothing to do with such goings on. But the village entered into the spirit of the event. The burst of enthusiasm has broken down the old barriers between the whist drive group and the cricket and the football group. Suddenly the whole village is united and what could have been a culture-less rural community is within piccolo distance of Aldeburgh. . . . Spontaneous, interesting and relaxing, it was undoubtedly cultural but not really highbrow.' So we learned that you could easily mix different categories of live entertainment and that a play – *Ars Longa, Vita Brevis* produced by Albert Hunt and students from Shrewsbury College of Art – could be performed anywhere and without scenery (it was performed twice; on the school playground and then in the Village Hall and was later done in a Bradford public house). Yet although the play was funny and vigorous in execution it was too far removed from the interests and needs of a small village. Our next event was, therefore, more locally orientated. A 'concert cum social cum dance' as the local press styled it was held in Hawnby Village Hall. It consisted of music hall turns, a film show, a piano recital, a tramp's barn dance and a free supper.

In the interval, echoing from a gale in the night outside, we heard a low mournful chanting coming closer. There was a loud thumping on the barn. The door opened to reveal three blind beggars clad in rags, roped together. Slowly they pushed their way into the hall banging their staffs on the floor, crying out for alms. Then, an unkempt figure garbed in purple sacks leapt on to the stage and shouted. This was the King of the Ditches: we were enacting a Ghelderode play based on Bruegel's painting of the parable of the three blind beggars. It was a valuable failure. The audience were initially surprised by a real dramatic situation (cf. accidents, crimes, falling buildings or rows in public) but we lost their attention because there was no theatrical framework. We had expected silence but the audience joined in and shouted back. Instead of improvising, thankfully accepting their natural reaction and using it, we ploughed on as if we had the artificial props of a proscenium. Our words were too pompous and literary to use in a non-structured context, yet a structured context imposes preconceptions.

The next experiment was another Ghelderode play – *Night of Pity* – for the Beck Isle Museum and Arts Centre, Pickering. The play opens with a melancholy landlord of a depressed pub who is talking to a soldier. He is half talking to himself in a quiet way about his past, when in bursts a crowd of sinister weirdly masked revellers. We got the maximum effect by turning a small room of the museum into a credible recreation of a pub, with advertisements, iron tables, crates of bottles and sawdust on the floor. It looked and smelt like a pub, and we served beer to spectators who sat round the room rubbing shoulders with the cast. When the masked figures burst in, they were inches away from the spectators and the effect was frighteningly claustrophobic. The next step would have to be a real pub with a substitute barman and no warning that a play was about to occur.

So we organised this in a lonely pub on the moors. Three groups of customers arrived at staggered intervals. The first seemed to be a party of hikers. Then two people arrived carrying a life-size papier-mâché female nude, followed five minutes later by two more carrying another female nude. The improvisation continued for half an hour until the customers started to join in. We had no idea of what we were going to say but we invented an elaborate story about them being used to fill up churches to attract customers to a dying industry. As we left, the landlord asked us to return. 'You know what you want to do,' he said. 'You want to go into pubs with them and see what happens.'

In October, 1967, in the streets of Bradford, Albert Hunt and I produced an experiment in public drama to mark the fiftieth anniversary of the Russian Revolution. For the Regional College of Art, Albert Hunt had devised a unique studies programme based on projects, instead of the usual pseudo-University form of liberal studies only done through lectures and seminars where established culture is dutifully handed down like a respectable fig leaf. At Bradford, projects last a fortnight and students from the specialist art departments volunteer for one or two projects a year. In all, about twenty projects are provided and often situations are created which involve students working actively together in a group. A number of these situations are devised as a game. This not only makes learning more enjoyable and gives the project a self-perpetuating internal momentum but it has close affiliations with theatre and drama. The best drama on television in 1967 for instance, was the World Cup and the drama I remember most as a child was playing cops and robbers round an old shelter. The rules of a game provide a similar kind of structured context to that of the concert hall or theatre; they provide a kind of hidden proscenium understood by the players and accepted and observed by the audience who are not usually absorbed as deeply as the participants. For the participants, a game of chess can provide a very tense dramatic situation regardless of the audience. As we will see later, some happenings are largely games of varying degrees of sophistication which recognise the value of giving uninhibited freedom to our basic play instinct.

The Bradford Revolution idea sprang out of a Vietnam War game devised by Albert Hunt in the previous term. In this, each student played out a role in an imaginary future crisis – a threatened American blockade of Haiphong. 'The students got very involved. They learnt not only about Vietnam but about having to work with people whose aims differ from your own, about the need to use words carefully and about the personal as well as the political pressures that affect people who have to make decisions. For a week everyone was talking about Vietnam. Could we extend such an event outside the College? Could we get Bradford thinking for a day about the Russian Revolution?' (Albert Hunt)

Apart from the educational benefit to students and the citizens of Bradford (providing incidentally an interesting variation on the use of drama as social 'therapy' in an educational institution) the Revolution project encouraged us to look at the original recreation of the storming of the Winter Palace, as staged by Meyerhold in St. Petersberg on the first anniversary of the Revolution in November, 1918. This was true street theatre spectacle with stylised antagonism between Reds and Whites, giant puppets of Kerensky and the army itself making a crucial entry at the climax. So we had a feeling for games, an inspired example to follow, and an acceptable framework in which to create subsiduary happenings in the street. The problem was to keep the tension of a game while preserving the dramatic shape; we divided the participants into two teams and gave them four locations to 'capture'. These were Bradford public buildings renamed for the occasion (e.g. the Cartwright Hall Art Gallery became the Winter Palace); and a location would be captured by whichever team had more bodies there – one man one vote – on the stroke of the hour. Extra votes in the shape of red or white discs could be won by carrying out instructions (given in envelopes) with invention and imagination. It was like a giant Treasure or Scavenger Hunt. About 300 students took part, many of them from Art schools in other cities and as they arrived they were divided into groups of twenty, asked to elect a leader and given their first task, such as: 'Find a Communist and take him to the shop'. 'Interview a journalist and ask him what he thinks he is doing'. 'Take six bourgeois heads to an agent in the Technical College canteen'. 'Unite the workers of the world'. 'Put down the red plots'. 'Go off the gold standard'. Student umpires decided how satisfactorily the tasks had been carried out and allotted discs accordingly. Contrary to history, the Whites would have won but for a secret agent cheating and releasing forged discs at the last moment. However, this didn't matter because as in most games, the most interesting things were the ones that happened along the way. And things did happen.

At eleven o'clock on the morning of 2nd November, a dozen students dressed mysteriously in black appeared in the centre of Bradford before a monument of Queen Victoria. They were reading aloud in chorus the thoughts of Chairman Mao; and other students ran up and down the steps of the Co-op reading the Communist Manifesto. At the same time two miles away, a hundred students with wooden rifles and a band marched up to the Art Gallery bearing giant puppets of Capitalists and banners stating 'Support your Government'. 'Down with Red Aggressors'.

A queue of revolutionaries formed outside an expensive cake shop in the centre of town. The slogan said 'Peace and Bread' and each student bought one tea cake and took it across the town to a disused post office in a working class area. This was the moneyless shop. Here a constant flow of trade was sustained for two days with a barter system. Goods were donated and exchanged and at one point, we had more goods than we started with. Twelve yards of Harris tweed appeared, piles of money remained untouched until some school children helped themselves and once customers got over their initial incomprehension, they realised we were challenging a basic assumption of our society. As one woman put it, 'You've made us all feel very uncomfortable refusing to take our money'.

The spectacle almost failed in the streets: events were too scattered to have a total impact, the building of a cardboard tower degenerated into a friendly punch up too reminiscent of a student rag. The rain washed out a propaganda play and we forgot to organise red and white provo bicycles and to release hydrogen filled balloons to signal the capture of a target. And cut-out soldiers to be placed on roof tops didn't appear either.

The papier-mâché figures we took into the pub were accepted as real, although they were really a concrete fantasy and the students in the Revolution were dressed in costume. If it had been our intention to scare the citizens of Bradford into imagining that a real revolution had occurred (which it was not) real uniforms and tanks might have been the answer. It depends on the degree and kind of 'participation' you want from your audience and the value of or need for 'suspension of disbelief'.

Such questions arose in two contrasting treatments of a commemoration of the Dresden air raids in February 1967.

On St Valentine's Eve in February 1945, there occurred the most devastating air attack in the history of war; more devastating than Hiroshima or Nagasaki. It was carried out by 2,000 Allied bombers on the undefended and non-military target of Dresden during the period 13th–14th February, 1945. 3,000 tons of bombs were dropped, including 650,000 incendiaries. 24,866 homes totally destroyed. 1,681 acres of the city totally destroyed. The fire-storm created temperatures of over 1,000 degrees Centigrade and 135,000 people died, more than in the whole of the war during air raids on Great Britain. These facts were taken from David Irving's[1] book and Irving himself came to Bradford Art College to help with the background material for a theatre project on the subject.

Ultimately Albert Hunt presented on the stage of a formal mahogany library theatre a documentary narrative of the events. The audience were briefed as if they were about to take part in the raid. Eye witness accounts were re-enacted with, for instance, amusing impersonations of the circus animals which escaped during the attack into the private gardens. Visual effects included slides of the thousands of mutilated corpses and smashed buildings, cut-out cartoon heads of Churchill and Stalin, and there was a pacifist statement from an airman. Finally a model of Dresden, constructed from piled up white cardboard boxes, was maniacally annihilated. Then pantomime mosquitoes entered, actors dressed as camouflaged angels with roundels on a stick across their shoulders. Robin Page as their leader, armed with a table knife and a small shiny bomb-shaped canister loaded with red powder paint, chanting the original conversation and commands between the bomber leader and the rest of the task force, cut and ripped the boxes to pieces, scattering crimson powder on himself and the heaped fragments of rubbish. The audience left to the echoing strains of Vera Lynn's *We'll meet again* carrying souvenir programmes (cyclostyled sheets containing contradictory statements on bombing from Churchill and other British politicians). The audience had been taught and lectured and shown, through a Brechtian objective style, in a show lasting over an hour.

Before the production we discussed various ways of getting ideas across.

[1] *The Destruction of Dresden*, David Irving.

357

One was to brief a number of professional actors, giving them all the available facts, and allowing them to absorb the feelings and attitudes of Churchill and Bomber Harris, to such a point that they could then be 'prosecuted' in a public law court, with real barristers. They would have to defend themselves as war criminals. If we could have got permission to use an actual court and found actors talented enough, I imagine that this could not only have been a very complex analysis of why the event had occurred, but could have shown the deep reactions and motivations of politicians and soldiers under stress. I think it might have been a lesson for the future.

But this was impossible. Even if we'd had the talent we had not enough time or money, so I decided to solve the problem by a different approach. Unlike Albert Hunt, I aimed to recreate an equivalent of the real terror the civilian population must have felt at the beginning of the Dresden raid. I believed that if I could stretch the imagination of the 'audience' to the point at which it could identify with the original victims, then its members would never perpetrate such a crime. Now I am less sure that an aggressive attack on an audience is not aesthetic fascism, likely in fact, to provoke an equally aggressive reaction. But I am equally sure that the imagination lurks close to the surface and that it can be readily awakened in the right circumstances. The danger is that it can be awakened not only to flights of fancy but also to panic.

I think this nearly happened with our Dresden Happening. Between numbers at a public dance, on the approximate hour when the attack started, 10.00 p.m., we started feeding air raid warnings, explosions and the engine noise of approaching bombers into the amplifiers. At the same time six figures on the dance floor who had been leaping around wearing giant carnival heads, of a clown, a giant, a cross faced woman, a pig, a cow and a cat,[1] started to scream and rush about frantically.

The noise increased violently; the taped explosions were multiplied while real explosions were created through igniting thunder flashes in a bomb tank and fireworks in dustbins on the stage. Stage lights and hall lights were extinguished, searchlight spots swung their beams over the packed floor. A smoke machine blew acrid fumes into their light paths and four orange flares were simultaneously lit in the corners of the hall. In

[1] There was a carnival in Dresden at the time.

between the loud bangs the crackling intercommunication of bomber crews was broadcast intermittently. Thus six sinister airmen were revealed, placed at regular intervals round the whole of the top balcony; they wore leather jackets, helmets, goggles and oxygen masks. A white-faced pierrette on the dance floor rushed hysterically from the room, she was caught on the balcony and thrown over by two bulky airmen. For a second she seemed to be suspended in the air, then hit the floor with a thump.[1] On her impact the airmen threw over 3,000 miniature leaflets. They were heart shaped and contained facts about the original raid. Like leaves, like bleached poppies at the Albert Hall, they floated gently to cover the floor and the dancers.

Suddenly the din stopped, except for a tape of the howling wind, barking dogs and breaking glass, there was complete silence. Then the airmen came down to the dance floor. They dumped the corpses of the carnival children on a crude trolley and trundled it to the side. The papier-mâché heads were thrown into a heap.

Finally the six of them picked up the pierrette, like a limp sack, above their heads and hurriedly marched out with their victim. A man in a white coat appeared and walked round the hall spraying it with mild disinfectant. The final smell was of sweat and fumes damped with a sickly sweet haze. The musicians immediately started a number but the dancers were slow. Some of the audience were very frightened; the attack had been quite unexpected. The panic and the fireworks could have been really dangerous.[2]

This way for a summer Happening on Instow beach in North Devon. July, 1968.
'*The Tide is O.K. for the 30th*'
'A surreal pantomime for beach, sea and the edge of both. An unpredictable unrehearsed conglomeration of music, facts and jokes.'

See: King Canute's integrations of Time and Tide and the appeasement of extraordinary sand creatures.

Receive: Beautiful pea green boats.

Hear: Musical rubbish. Ocharinas and sundry drums.

Experience: Romantic scenes and a few real facts.

[1] She was lowered on a sling and nylon rope.
[2] This event was re-enacted at the Institute of Contemporary Arts, London, in February 1969.

After massive publicity about 1,500 people turned up on the beach. Here, with acknowledgments to Nicholas Cottis,[1] is a description of what occurred.

Candle Power

One warm summery nightfall this week, as the incoming tide lapped across Instow Sands, a line of men, women and children stood at the water's edge. Some had white paper boats which they pushed out on the water. Others stood with lighted candles in their hands, and all had their attention fixed on a fireworks display on the far side of the estuary. There is an Indian religious festival which ends in a similar way, and it is described in a moving chapter of E. M. Forster's novel *A Passage to India*. But this was an English holiday resort, the men, women and children were having an English holiday, and it wasn't a book about India, it was happening. It was the Happening, to be precise, which Happened at the instigation of Bradford College of Art at Instow on Tuesday, with the E.15 Acting School, the Beaford Centre and the Army conniving.

'The first wave – of troops – came in the morning on two DUKW landing craft from the Amphibious Experimental Establishment a mile down the shore. The second wave – of art students – came in with paint pots and brushes and painted flowers and curlicues in bright colours on the battle green hulls of the DUKWs. One student painted a sign which read 'Stores' and planted it in the sand beside their discarded shoes and duffle bags. The next wave brought in a mystifying variety of props. These included a pair of life-size female nude figures made of cardboard and wire netting, which were dumped in deckchairs and left to their own devices. The fourth wave consisted of acting students dressed as pirates, who crewed the DUKWs for children's trips along the sands. The tide was low and the sand stretched for miles. Far away, as the DUKWs swung around each other in gigantic circles, you could hear bursts of cheering as if the passengers were discharging pirate broadsides. 'Be gentle with her, lad', said a salty Yorkshire voice with tenderness as two of the Bradford students manhandled the cardboard figures, 'she's having an orgasm'. 'This whole day is going to be one long orgasm', replied the second student. 'I'll wait and see what happens before I'll say that', said the first

[1] This account appeared in *Dartington Hall News*, Issue 2512.

dourly. It's a view which might be called the Reichian or Student Power theory of happenings. Alternatively, you can take the Jungian theory, which is that people today are starved of ritual and symbol, and that happenings involve them at a level of their imagination which is mostly left untended. Or thirdly, you can take the Artaudian or Theatre of Cruelty theory, which is that happenings shock or provoke people out of the psychological defences which they erect to protect themselves against the challenges of the real world. John Fox, the Bradford lecturer who organised the Instow happening, has been involved in some fairly aggressive happenings in his time, like the dance at Bradford at which thunderflashes and smoke bombs were suddenly let off in a mock re-enactment of the Dresden air raids, and a pilot baled out over the balcony on to the screaming girls beneath. On Tuesday Mr Fox was very concerned not to do anything which would offend or estrange people, and was worried by the complaint of one old lady who objected to a sketch which some of his students were performing for the children on the beach. In this they mimed the pleasures of a runaway monk on a fairground. They turned themselves into one-armed bandits and a try-your-strength machine and a wall of death, and fell about on the sands in T-shirts inscribed 'Jesus Saves' and 'God is Gear' while the children fell about with laughter. But the old lady told Mr Fox that he was taking the Lord's name in vain, and gave him some leaflets.

There were plenty of people who watched for a few minutes, and then drifted sceptically away. But this happening was well-placed and well-planned for getting people to participate. First, it started with an afternoon of children's treats and games, which put everyone but the old lady in a benevolent frame of mind, and secondly the people on the beach were there on holiday and were prepared to take off an inhibition or two with their clothing, and even to be shepherded about the beach from one focus of attention to another. By the evening there was a crowd, willing and waiting to be moulded into a good time.

Back came the acting students in an Army lorry, waving grandly down as civic dignitaries and military persons, with a roadsweeper or two in attendance and a cryptic figure in a sou-wester and oilskins who spent the entire two hours of the happening paddling up and down the shoreline watering the sea from a watering-can. 'We're the officials,' announced a young man in a mayoral chain plummily, 'we've come to Help You to Enjoy Yourselves.' With a mock T.V. team in attendance, a great deal of jostling for the mock microphone, and some well-received parodying of middle-class public mannerisms, the acting students hustled the crowd from one focal point to another. There was a chaotic football game; Sir Francis Chichester arrived, his hair grown curiously long, and was pulled up the beach on a door hauled by a swarm of panting small boys; more boys and a few unwary adults took part in a bingo game in which everyone turned out to have the same card, and all shouted 'House' simultaneously; a Canute Game took place at the water's edge in which two of the official dignitaries and one of the omnipresent small boys were carried into the water on deckchairs at the throw of a gigantic dice; a small boat landed again and again with a black-faced minstrel, who announced that he had set out from England to look for his mammy in Jamaica, and could this really be home? 'Has anyone seen the gentleman's mammy?' enquired one of the lady mayoresses unctuously. 'You, madam?' – this to the dus- kiest face in sight. The acting students improvised resourcefully whenever a cue was missed. At one point an aeroplane flew overhead, and a cluster of tiny leaflets fell over the side. They were poems specially for the occasion by the Bradford students, but the aeroplane was too high and the leaflets fluttered away to sea. 'A diploma for you, madam,' said an imperturbable young man in an officer's cap to a woman in a print dress, and thrust a sealed paper towel into her hand. She looked at it with incomprehension, then exploded into laughter.

Meanwhile John Fox was quietly making cardboard sea-gulls and hanging them on a string stretched between two easels. And down at the water's edge the solitary man in a sou-wester, now a silhouette in the dusk, continued to water the waves from a watering-can. 'I think the theme of everything today is failure – that people could be doing things themselves instead of having things done for them,' John Fox had said earlier. When it was dark the dignitaries lit a bonfire, then shepherded as many people as they could down to the water's edge to watch the firework display at Appledore, on the opposite bank. They handed out candles, lit them – everyone wanted to hold a candle, and there were too few to go round – and then played the last practical joke of the day. Along the beach came the man with the watering-can. Solemnly and with care he extinguished the candles one by one. 'I'm only doing my job,' he explained. 'Gaffer told me it had to be done, so I'm doing it.' The crowd trooped away up the emptying beach, past the two cardboard figures which were now lolling against a board which read 'National Failure Week'. From inside the Lobster Pot Restaurant came the cheerful beginnings of a folksong evening, the planned third stage of the happening. But back in the dark half a dozen subversive people had relit their candles, and were watching the last embers of the bonfire. Not all of them were children. And somewhere out at sea a planeload of poems was drifting away, cast upon the water.

The mood here described is exactly that we hoped for. Other events included the digging up of an enormous mummy-like parcel containing a painted cut-out astronaut. This was thrown on the bonfire at the same moment as the Army let off thunderflashes and the firework display commenced, so that there was a link in the idea of fire, through violence, a funeral pyre, frivolity and the final candle ceremony. Other manifestations of absurdity included a full lecture on UFOs (which nobody listened to), a film on bananas run in reverse so that the bananas sprang back on the trees, a digging and filling in of a trench charade, and a girl who painted a dozen identical pictures of the sea.

Notes on the Plates

Plates 1–7 illustrate approaches to dramatic work which are flexible and inventive. A dramatic experience doesn't necessarily last from 7.30 to 10 o'clock, nor necessarily take place in a 'theatre'.

Plates 8–16 have been chosen to illustrate a variety of venues where dramatic presentations have taken place.

Plate 1 A Naming Ceremony: Rosedale, Yorkshire. Rituals – the celebration of birth, the naming of a child, marriage and death – are occasions when today's artists have a contribution to make. One such event was organised by John and Susan Fox who wished to name their child. It is described by Susan Fox in an article from the *Northern Echo*. 'A Chinese New Year story seemed a good starting-point. It told of a poor man who lived outside a city and earned his living through selling fireworks. At New Year, unlike his neighbours who spent their money on food, he bought a statue of a beautiful girl. He took it home and honoured it with food. In time it came to life, and she began to prepare his food and care for him. They lived together and had a child. But an inescapable longing overcame her to return to her former statue, and he was left with the child who in her turn honoured the statue with flowers. . . . We decided to make the story into a simple mime play, with a narrator, and specially composed music and songs. . . . As the performance was planned for outside the actors and musicians rehearsed and played music all over the dale – particularly in the chosen spot, a sheltered clearing dotted with foxgloves, bracken, wild roses and butterflies. Everything depended on the weather, and the day was perfect. About 60 people arrived, including several other babies to be included in the ceremony. We sat on a grassy slope and waited. Firecrackers went off on the hill facing us and singing was heard from the wood on our left as the band approached. The poor man, in oatmeal robe, white wooden mask and enormous canvas shoes, appeared near the straw bales (indicating his house) and the slow dreamlike play began. The movement was closer to dance, gestures were kept to an absolute minimum and frozen in the pauses; they looked like life-sized puppets. It took over 20 or 30 minutes, during which time the score of children who were watching were enchanted.

'At the end of the play, as he held the child triumphantly, priceless Japanese fireworks were again released on the opposite hill. . . . The poor man began the procession to the top of the hill, and we followed with the musicians. A bonfire blazed, a red banner flapped and coloured smoke billowed up – this was to be the naming. At the sound of a gong the first parent went forward, held aloft his tiny son and shouted his name into the wind.'

Plate 2 A scene from the *Festival of Fools*, an experimental folk play presented by Ewan MacColl and the London Critics Group, a folk club attempting to re-create a basis for popular theatre inside the folk idiom. The photograph shows an operating theatre where Wilson and Brown are extracting the bark from a dog, or power from the workers. This was part of a sequence of episodes dealing with the events of 1965, as a living Newspaper (see page 58).
Photograph: Jim Tierney.

Plate 3 A scene, taken during rehearsals, from a modern version of a Cornish Mystery play *The Making of the World* directed by Roland Miller at Hoxton Hall, London in 1965. The photograph shows Adam and Eve expelled from Eden, watched by the animals and birds and trees in the Garden. The production took place in the whole space of the theatre – an old Victorian Music Hall – with the audience inside the setting, either in Hell (in the stalls) or with the angels in Heaven (in the balconies). The majority of parts were played by students from a U.N. work camp at the Hall, by local children and teenagers; only two professional actors took part (see page 78).
Photograph: Christopher Mantell.

Plate 4 Photograph of the music 'cage', and of Luke, the soldier, from John and Margaretta Arden's comedy-pantomime *The Royal Pardon*, performed by the Ardens themselves, a few professional actors and a company of students from L.A.M.D.A. in a converted billiard room measuring 30 feet by 20 feet at the Beaford Centre in North Devon. Music and sound are an integral part of the production. For a fuller description see page 269.

Production: John and Margaretta Arden.
Photograph: John Lane.

Plate 5. A jousting match, on hobby-horses, which formed the climax of *The Tournament of Ancient Sports* staged by members of the estate, students and children at Dartington Hall, near Totnes in Devon on Foundation Day, 1957. This event is a good example of what a contemporary pageant can become when developed with imagination.
Photograph: Nicholas Horne.

Plate 6 A scene from a simple glove-puppet production staged, written, and acted by 12-year-old children without adult help at Scarsborough College (see page 25).
Photograph: Peter Burton.

Plate 7 This 52-foot reconstruction of Moby Dick in a Notting Hill playground involved children and a few adults who worked together on this community project in the summer of 1968. The adults belonged to the Dogg's Troupe, a street-theatre group, one of maybe a dozen around the country. Dogg's Troupe is a hard core of seven actors and writers who involve children in their street theatre by getting them to participate. Ed Berman who runs Inter-Action (of which the Dogg's Troupe is a part) says, 'Right now the streets are just a vehicle for commerce and advertising – they've made busking illegal. We'd like to make the streets into a vehicle for joy and relaxation and understanding. You see people smiling down at us out of windows as we pass – we'd even like to sing outside their doors, like carollers at Christmas. Right now that's only acceptable at one time of the year, but why not do it all the time?

'Our purpose is not quite to get kids to have fun. Any clown can get kids

to enjoy themselves – that's a very adult standard of evaluation. Participation is what counts. You're not feeding kids lollipops, then saying, "Right, you've had a suck, now we're taking it away". You want them to carry on.'
Photograph: Paul Morrison

Plate 8 The Booth Stage: A simple booth-stage on the sands is all you need to make a theatre, but the audience gathering round is making a bigger contribution than it realises. The date around 1910 – Catlin's Favourite Pierrots on Scarborough beach. By permission of Scarborough Public Library (see page 207).

Plate 9 The Elizabethan Theatre: A scene from *The Knight of the Burning Pestle* freely adapted and largely improvised by secondary school boys and students at Bretton Hall, a College of Education near Wakefield. The students worked and acted with the boys on the production, which was given in a modern reconstruction of an Elizabethan theatre.
Production: John Hodgson.
Photograph: Peter Burton.

Plate 10 Open Air in the Round: The Noah play, showing Noah's Ark (foreground) Heaven (booth on left) and the Torturer's scaffold and gaol (to left) from the Bristol University Drama Department's production of the *Cornish Cycle* at Piran Round, Perranporth. The earthwork amphitheatre dates from the Middle Ages – perhaps converted into a theatre from an Iron Age fortification. It is about 130 feet in diameter and is surrounded by a round or rampart 10 feet high, on which, at regular intervals along lines indicated by Richard Southern's *Mediaeval Theatre in the Round*, seven booths or stations and a hell-mouth were situated. Entries and exits were made in and out of the Hell-mouth and the Entrance gate opposite and up and down from the booths or 'scaffolds'.
Production: Neville Denny.
Photograph: Shirley Denny.

Plate 11 Theatre in the round: A scene from Clifford Williams' *The Disguises of Arlecchino* produced for Stephen Joseph's Studio Theatre, Scarborough, in 1956 by its author. This one-act play is based on the Com-

media dell'Arte character of Arlecchino, here seen putting on one of his numerous disguises, that of a chef. The photograph is an interesting record of the intimate involvement of a theatre in the round production, the 'theatre' used being a large square room in the Library converted for use with raked seating and lighting.
Photograph: Ken Boden.

Plate 12 Street Theatre: Theatre from a Cart: A scene from *Noah* from the *York Cycle of Mystery Plays* now performed every three years in the city of York as part of the York Festival. This photograph, taken immediately outside the west front of the Minster, shows a performance in progress on a cart, which is driven to several 'stations' in the city. The actors are all amateurs (see page 207).
Photograph: Harland Walshaw.

Plate 13 Street Theatre: Carnival: Carnival Procession in Nice on the French Riviera where lavish carnival celebrations are still held. The highlight is a procession through the main streets of revellers in all sorts of gay disguises – masks and dominoes, huge grotesque heads, and fancy dress. Elaborate tableaux are organised and wheeled along on carts (see left).

Plate 14 Traverse staging: A scene with masked figures from the Orchard Theatre Company's production of George Dibdin Pitt's Victorian melodrama *Sweeney Todd*. This production, which was toured to village and town halls throughout North Devon, was performed on portable rostra of varying heights arranged like a sort of cricket pitch across the middle of the hall, with the audience on both sides of the stage facing each other. The masks were improvised by the actors for one particular scene.
Production: Charles Lewsen.
Photograph: Terry Warboys.

Plate 15 Music Hall: An illustration of a Music Hall scene (by Alfred Concanen) from *The Wilds of London* by James Greenwood, published in 1874. Though the text refers to an imaginary Music Hall called the *Grampion*, the lithograph is obviously based on fact. It gives an excellent

idea of the easy and spontaneous informality of this kind of popular entertainment where refreshments are being served and drunk during the performance – an idea developed by Stephen Joseph in his fish and chip
theatre.

Plate 16 Street Theatre: A scene from the six-hundred-year-old play of the
Mummers at Marshfield in Gloucestershire, one of the best preserved of
the Mummers' plays. It is performed every Boxing Day by the villagers
who dress up in strips of paper and parade around the little streets led by
the village crier. In this scene, two of the characters indulge (with sticks)
in mimic fight and one of them (who is lying on the ground in the photograph) is awaiting the 'Doctor' who heals him with his magic ointment.
Other characters include Old Father Christmas, King William, Little
John and Beelzebub, the Devil.
Photograph: Reece Winstone.

Index

Playwrights whose names are listed in Chapter 5 *Choosing the Play* are not indicated in this index.

Addresses: of costume hire firms 255–6; courses 350–1; Drama advisers 331–5; effects records 273; fabric stockists 248–9; Film and T.V. organisations 50–1; lighting specialists 294–5; periodicals 340–2; property hire firms 265–7; publishers 346–9; scenic materials and contractors 231–3; theatre for youth 349–50; theatre organisations 336–9, 343–5, 346, and other organisations 339–40; wig-hire firms 287.

370